The rise of bilateralism

The United Nations University Programme on Comparative Regional Integration Studies, UNU-CRIS, is a research and training programme of the UNU located in Bruges (Belgium) that focuses on the role of regions and regional integration in global governance. The aim of UNU-CRIS is to build policy-relevant knowledge about new forms of governance and cooperation, and to contribute to capacity-building on issues of integration and cooperation, particularly in developing countries. Among the areas studied at UNU-CRIS are the global/regional governance of peace and security, the socio-economic dimensions of regional integration and the development of indicators for monitoring integration processes.

www.cris.unu.edu

UNITED NATIONS UNIVERSITY

UNU-CRIS

Programme on Comparative
Regional Integration Studies

The rise of bilateralism: Comparing American, European and Asian approaches to preferential trade agreements

Kenneth Heydon and Stephen Woolcock

United Nations
University Press

TOKYO · NEW YORK · PARIS

United Nations University Press
United Nations University, 53-70, Jingumae 5-chome,
Shibuya-ku, Tokyo 150-8925, Japan
Tel: +81-3-5467-1212   Fax: +81-3-3406-7345
E-mail: sales@hq.unu.edu   general enquiries: press@hq.unu.edu
http://www.unu.edu

United Nations University Office at the United Nations, New York
2 United Nations Plaza, Room DC2-2062, New York, NY 10017, USA
Tel: +1-212-963-6387   Fax: +1-212-371-9454
E-mail: unuona@ony.unu.edu

United Nations University Press is the publishing division of the United Nations University.

Cover design by Joyce C. Weston

Printed in Hong Kong

ISBN 978-92-808-1162-9

Library of Congress Cataloging-in-Publication Data

Heydon, Kenneth.
The rise of bilateralism : comparing American, European, and Asian approaches to preferential trade agreements / Kenneth Heydon and Stephen Woolcock.
    p.   cm.
 Includes bibliographical references and index.
 ISBN 978-9280811629 (pbk.)
 1. Tariff preferences—United States. 2. Tariff preferences—Europe. 3. Tariff preferences—Asia. I. Woolcock, Stephen. II. Title.
HF1731.H49   2009
382'.753—dc22   2009000015

Contents

Figures

Tables

Boxes

Abbreviations

ACP	African, Caribbean and Pacific Group of States
AFL-CIO	American Federation of Labor and Congress of Industrial Organizations
AFTA	ASEAN Free Trade Area
ANSZCEP	Agreement between New Zealand and Singapore on a Closer Economic Partnership
APEC	Asia-Pacific Economic Cooperation
ASEAN	Association of Southeast Asian Nations
ASEAN+3	Association of Southeast Asian Nations, plus China, Japan and Korea
ASEAN+6	Association of Southeast Asian Nations, plus Australia, China, India, Japan, Korea and New Zealand
BIT	bilateral investment treaty
BSE	bovine spongiform encephalopathy
CA	conformance assessment
CAFTA	Central American Free Trade Agreement [with the United States]
CAN	Andean Community
CARICOM	Caribbean Community
CARIFORUM	Caribbean Forum of ACP States
CEECs	Central and Eastern European countries
CEPT	Common Effective Preferential Tariff
CGE	computable general equilibrium model
cif	cost, insurance, freight valuation
CRTA	Committee on Regional Trade Agreements [WTO]
CT	change of tariff classification

CTC	change of tariff chapter at HS 2 level
CTH	change of tariff heading at HS 4 level
CTI	change of tariff item at HS 6 level
CTS	change of tariff sub-heading at HS 8 level
DDA	Doha Development Agenda
ECJ	European Court of Justice
ECT	exception attached to a particular change of tariff heading
EEA	European Economic Area
EEC	European Economic Community
EFTA	European Free Trade Association
ENP	European Neighbourhood Policy
EPA	Economic Partnership Agreement
ESFTA	Europe-Singapore Free Trade Agreement
EU	European Union
Euro-Med	Euro-Mediterranean Partnership
FAO	Food and Agriculture Organization
FDI	foreign direct investment
fob	free on board valuation
FTA	free trade agreement/area
GATS	General Agreement on Trade in Services
GATT	General Agreement on Tariffs and Trade
GCC	Gulf Cooperation Council
GDP	gross domestic product
GIs	geographical indicators
GPA	Agreement on Government Procurement [WTO]
GSP	Generalised System of Preferences
HS	harmonized system of tariffs
ICSID	International Centre for the Settlement of Investment Disputes
ILO	International Labour Organization
IPPC	International Plant Protection Convention
IPRs	intellectual property rights
JSEPA	Japan–Singapore Economic Partnership Agreement
JSFTA	Jordan-Singapore Free Trade Agreement
KORUS	Korea–United States Free Trade Agreement
KSFTA	Korea-Singapore Free Trade Agreement
LDC	least developed country
MAI	Multilateral Agreement on Investment
MC	import content
MEA	multilateral environmental agreement
Mercosur	Common Market of the Southern Cone
METI	Ministry of Economy, Trade and Industry [Japan]
MFN	most favoured nation treatment
MRA	mutual recognition agreement
NAALC	North American Agreement on Labor Cooperation
NAFTA	North American Free Trade Agreement
NAMA	non-agricultural market access negotiations [DDA]
NT	national treatment

NTB	non-tariff barrier
OECD	Organisation for Economic Co-operation and Development
OIE	World Organisation for Animal Heath
PTA	preferential trade agreement
QR	quantitative restriction
RoO	rules of origin
RVC	regional value content
SAA	Stabilisation and Association Agreement [EU]
SACU	Southern African Customs Union
SAFTA	South Asia Free Trade Agreement
SAT	substantially all trade [WTO]
SCM	Agreement on Subsidies and Countervailing Measures [WTO]
SDR	Special Drawing Rights
SGM	safeguard measure
SPS	sanitary and phytosanitary measures
TBT	technical barriers to trade
TDCA	Trade, Development and Cooperation Agreement [EU]
TIFA	Trade and Investment Framework Agreement [United States]
TPA	Trade Promotion Authority [United States]
TPL	tariff preference level
TPSEPA	Trans-Pacific Strategic Economic Partnership Agreement
TR	technical requirement
TREATI	Trans-Regional EU–ASEAN Trade Initiative
TRIMs	Agreement on Trade-Related Investment Measures
TRIPS	Agreement on Trade-Related Aspects of Intellectual Property Rights
TRQ	tariff rate quota
USFTA	US-Singapore Free Trade Agreement
USITC	United States International Trade Commission
USTR	United States Trade Representative
VC	value content [for rules of origin]
VS	voluntary standard
WTO	World Trade Organization

Acknowledgements

This study is based, in part, on work undertaken by us on behalf of the Swiss Secretary of State for Economic Affairs (SECO). We appreciate the understanding of SECO in allowing material from that project to be used in the present publication and, in particular, thank Peter Balaster and Chantal Moser of SECO for their support and insights in the course of the earlier project.

Special thanks go to a team of graduate students from the London School of Economics (LSE) who made an invaluable contribution to this book by their careful analysis of the fine print of a range of preferential trade agreements. They are Adam Dean (who focused on PTA treatment of intellectual property rights, labour and environment); Marina Henke (public procurement and commercial instruments); Lior Herman (services and investment); Thor Jonsson (rules of origin, TBT/SPS and EFTA); and John Polley (tariffs).

We have also benefited from our close association with colleagues, past and present, at, respectively, the Organisation for Economic Co-operation and Development and the LSE. OECD research has been particularly useful in the preparation of this study and special appreciation goes to Massimo Geloso Grosso, Przemyslaw Kowalski, Molly Lesher, Caroline Lesser, Douglas Lippoldt and Sébastien Miroudot.

Thanks are also due to Luk van Langenhove of UNU-CRIS (United Nations University – Comparative Regional Integration Studies). UNU-CRIS provided support for the publication of the research and the results should be seen as a UNU-CRIS product.

Finally, we would like to thank Robert Davis and all those at the United Nations University Press involved with bringing this book to its published state, as well as two external referees and all our students at the LSE who have provided a critical testing ground for our consideration of trends in trade diplomacy.

Kenneth Heydon
London School of Economics

Stephen Woolcock
London School of Economics and UNU-CRIS, Brugge

August 2008

Part I
Introduction

1

Overview

The contribution of this volume

Preferential trade agreements (PTAs)[1] conducted on a bilateral basis have become the centrepiece of trade diplomacy. With multilateral negotiations becoming increasingly complex and protracted, trade deals among selected partners are seen, rightly or wrongly, to hold the promise of quick and comprehensive improvements in market access and rules for trade and investment.

As discussed fully in Chapter 11, there is already a substantial literature on PTAs. Much of this dates from earlier phases of intense activity in the field of regional preferential agreements. The literature on the economic effects of PTAs has been rather limited, however, by its continued focus on tariff preferences, which, although still important, are not the main thrust of the PTAs negotiated by the major industrialized countries. The recent increase in PTA negotiations has stimulated analysis of the motivations and effects of PTAs and their implications for the multilateral trading system. This large and valuable literature, however, largely eschews detailed analysis of the content of the agreements themselves.[2] This is the gap the current volume seeks to fill and thus to add flesh to the bare bones discussion of the growth of preferential agreements.

By looking in detail at the substance of PTAs concluded by a number of key players this study examines whether PTAs should be seen as an alternative to multilateralism, as interim measures to keep the wheels of international trade and investment moving during the difficulties faced at

The rise of bilateralism: Comparing American, European and Asian approaches to preferential trade agreements, Heydon and Woolcock, United Nations University Press, 2009, ISBN 978-92-808-1162-9

the multilateral level, or indeed as an impediment to multilateral efforts. In other words, are PTAs building blocks or stumbling blocks for multilateralism? Are the main promoters of comprehensive PTAs pursuing their own distinctive agendas, using their market power to coerce smaller countries into accepting their rules of the game? If they are, they risk creating divergent norms and rules that will make a future multilateralization difficult. Or are the approaches adopted broadly similar, so that they could be seen as constituting an emerging international norm?

In order to address these questions, the volume considers the PTAs negotiated by the United States, the European Union, the European Free Trade Association (EFTA), Japan and Singapore – the "core entities". These are some of the leading proponents of preferential agreements and the ones that have promoted the idea of comprehensive agreements or agreements that include a range of deeper integration issues as well as tariffs and non-tariff barriers to trade. They are thus more likely to shape the nature of the international trade and investment system.

Reflecting the main focus of research for this book, the chapters that follow look at: tariffs and rules of origin; a number of established non-tariff barrier issues – commercial instruments, technical barriers to trade (TBT), sanitary and phytosanitary measures (SPS) and government procurement; the pursuit of deep integration through trade in services and foreign direct investment; and a group of issues sharing a concern about market failure – intellectual property rights and labour and environmental standards. This focus on the actual content of agreements facilitates an assessment of the revealed policy preferences of the parties concerned. The volume also compares the substance of agreements with the declared policies of the "core entities". All the "core entities" covered affirm that their PTA policies are compatible with multilateralism. The detailed consideration of what has been negotiated enables an assessment to be made of whether this is likely to be the case in practice.

The volume also seeks to shed light on a number of specific questions. First, to what extent do the PTAs really go beyond the World Trade Organization (are WTO-plus) in terms of the detail of each policy area? Second, how do the approaches of the "core entities" compare? Third, what trends in the use of PTAs by the core entities exist? Fourth, how do the core entities accommodate developing countries through the use of asymmetric provisions in PTAs? Finally, how does the substance of PTA policy relate to domestic policies in the United States, the European Union, EFTA, Japan and Singapore (the core entities)?

The world of preferential trade agreements is rapidly evolving and some of its popular characterizations are no longer valid. The picture that emerges from a comparison of the agreements concluded by the European Union, EFTA, the United States, Japan and Singapore is rather more complex than the image of the "spaghetti bowl" used in many depictions of the network of PTAs that has developed. Preferential agreements do add complexity to trade, especially given the fact that the various agreements use different rules of origin. But, in some policy areas, agreements concluded between trading partners do not constitute a preference as such and can facilitate trade. This is the case when agreements promote transparency or regulatory best practice, such as in government procurement or the service sector. PTAs that promote the use of agreed, common international standards can reduce technical barriers to trade. Agreements that provide for enhanced cooperation or consultation can help to remove barriers caused by sanitary and phytosanitary measures. Even in the case of rules of origin, the picture is rather more nuanced than the "spaghetti bowl" characterization suggests. Rather than innumerable different rules of origin, there are in fact a number of dominant frameworks derived from the United States and European Union that find application in other PTAs. The existence of a limited number of framework rules for rules of origin does not, however, make the task of developing agreed international norms for preferential rules of origin any less intractable.

The notion of "regionalism" has become much less relevant, and much less useful. There has been a clear trend towards the use of bilateral trade agreements in recent years. These agreements also cut across many existing regional initiatives as individual members of regional groupings conclude bilateral PTAs with third parties outside the region.

The presumption that preferential deals amongst the willing can somehow compensate for slow progress multilaterally is as inappropriate as the idea that PTAs inevitably undermine wider multilateral efforts. Preferential arrangements, though they may break new ground and offer lessons for wider application, can never be a substitute for multilateral action. There is clearly a need for a strong and vigorous multilateral system. This volume will suggest that the reconciliation of the apparent conundrum whereby PTAs can be both building block and stumbling block comes from the realization that PTAs will complement the multilateral trading system only if that system is itself strong, reducing the distortions of preferential arrangements by bringing down MFN (most favoured nation treatment) tariff barriers and strengthening the rules of the game. The key question in international trade and investment policy today is not about choosing between preferential agreements or multilateralism, but about understanding how the various, interacting negotiating forums are used by the leading countries or regions.

There is a shared objective, whether in the Americas, Europe or Asia, of using preferential agreements to improve market access and to

strengthen trade rule-making. This goal is driven by a number of considerations: dissatisfaction with progress multilaterally in the WTO's Doha
Development Agenda (DDA); a desire to pursue deeper integration, including in areas such as investment, government procurement and competition, which have been excluded from the DDA; a desire to avoid
perceived unfair competition associated with poor labour and environmental standards; a wish to use PTAs as a spur to domestic reform; and,
not least, a concern not to be left behind as others proceed with preferential, and hence discriminatory, arrangements. Together, these market-
driven objectives have contributed to the complexity and geographical
diversity of the web of preferential agreements and shifted the focus of
PTAs from regional to bilateral agreements.

An overview of the policies of the core entities

In pursuit of its "gold standard" PTAs, the United States goes beyond
the WTO, or is WTO-plus, in many respects. On the central issue of
tariffs, this means almost 100 per cent tariff elimination on the US part,
at least in the case of industrial products. This is important because welfare gains to parties to PTAs will be higher the more comprehensive is
the product coverage of the agreements. In services, the United States
has pioneered the prohibition of local presence requirements, consistently supported greater transparency through negative listing, and gone
beyond the General Agreement on Trade in Services (GATS) in rule-
making in critical sectors such as financial services and telecommunications. The United States has been able to obtain the comprehensive
investment provisions of the North American Free Trade Agreement
(NAFTA) in almost all its agreements. And it has been a driving force
behind provisions in PTAs that go beyond the Agreement on Trade-
Related Aspects of Intellectual Property Rights (TRIPS-plus), introducing tougher protection for both copyrights and trademarks. In the area
of government procurement, the United States has used PTAs to extend
the number of its trading partners that effectively comply with plurilateral rules of the Government Procurement Agreement (GPA) type. In
the case of commercial instruments, US PTAs have consistently applied
time limitations that are tighter than those found in the WTO.

Though this is a solid performance, whether it constitutes a "gold standard" is open to debate. A characteristic of the US approach to PTAs is
the uniformity of provisions across agreements, regardless of the level of
development of the PTA partner. Product coverage, particularly in agriculture, seems to slip in the preferential agreements with Australia and
Korea. And the use of complex NAFTA rules of origin takes some of

the shine off the standard, even when coverage is comprehensive. In services too, sectors that are difficult multilaterally, such as air transport or governmental services, tend to be excluded and there is a pronounced tendency for the United States to use negative-list reservations to exclude services measures maintained at the sub-national level. In government procurement, the coverage of US purchasing entities is shaped by the rigorous application of reciprocity, with the result that US commitments in some PTAs are significantly below the level of commitments in the GPA. In areas of lower policy priority, such as TBT, the United States is content to rely on existing WTO provisions. Finally, where US PTAs seek to address a perceived race-to-the-bottom in labour and environmental standards and, ultimately, to impose penalties for non-compliance with internationally agreed norms, it needs to be acknowledged that, although undoubtedly WTO-plus, these provisions are not necessarily "better" or without risk of protectionist capture.

In contrast to the United States, the European Union's approach to PTAs has been characterized by flexibility and, to date (2008), relatively modest results in terms of the liberalization achieved by existing agreements. This finds expression in the European Union's coverage of tariffs in PTAs, which excludes relatively more agricultural tariff lines, and in services, where the European Union uses a positive-list approach and therefore leaves greater flexibility for the exclusion of sensitive sectors for both itself and its trading partners. The European Union's domestic experience with non-tariff barriers and the need for comprehensive provisions on SPS and TBT means that it takes efforts in this field, including the promotion of agreed international standards, more seriously than does the United States, though again there is flexibility. The European Union favours SPS-minus rules in the sense that it wants an interpretation of precaution that allows for social as well as science-based risk assessment. Competition and procurement have found their way into the European Union's PTAs, though the proposals for a minimum platform for investment provisions in EU PTAs have to date fallen short of the comprehensive US rules on investment. Foreign direct investment remains a topic of mixed competence in the European Union, with the EU member states retaining national policies and negotiating their own bilateral investment treaties (BITs).

A positive side of EU flexibility has been that there is more scope for asymmetric provisions favouring the European Union's developing country partners. But on some occasions it is the European Union that is benefiting from the asymmetry, such as in the agricultural tariff elimination provisions in the EU–Chile agreement.

As with the United States, Japanese PTA motivations, based on a fear of being left out, dissatisfaction with progress in the WTO and the pursuit of deeper integration, all have an important market access dimension. A primary aim of the PTA under negotiation with Switzerland has been an increase in Japanese exports of electronic goods, while also strengthening the protection of intellectual property rights. However, Japan, like the European Union, has been relatively less aggressive and thus less successful than the United States in implementing ambitious market-opening PTAs. Both of the agreements examined in detail here (with Singapore and Chile) exclude over half the agricultural schedule, and Japan's industrial schedules are more restrictive than for any of the other countries examined. Moreover, Japan, unlike both the United States and the European Union, has a measure of inconsistency in its approach to PTAs that goes beyond flexibility, in that from one agreement to another it alternates positive and negative listing, lacks a consistent treatment of domestic tariff schedules and switches between hard and soft rules of origin.

Japan is a relative newcomer to PTAs, with only a handful agreements in force at the time of writing, so firm judgements are difficult. It seems clear, however, that the lack of a strong domestic mechanism for PTA policy coordination, combined with the power of agricultural and labour lobbies, has so far served to compromise the quality of Japan's agreements.

Although the focus of this study is the detailed substance of PTAs, these must still be seen in the context of broader commercial and political objectives. For all countries, and not least the five core entities that are the focus of this study, the pursuit of preferential trade agreements reflects underlying strategic objectives that are particular to the countries concerned.

The United States' agreement with Peru is at least in part about the exercise of US influence in its immediate neighbourhood. The Korea–US agreement (KORUS) was presented to Congress by President George W. Bush as "further enhancing the strong US–Korea partnership, which has served as a force for stability and prosperity in Asia". As such, KORUS can also be seen as consolidating the US presence in the region in the face of growing Chinese influence as reflected in the idea of an East Asian preferential bloc, now characterized as ASEAN+3 (Association of Southeast Asian Nations, plus China, Japan and Korea).

The way in which the European Union differentiates among its PTA partners is a reflection of the strategic goals that the European Union wishes to pursue with them. Near neighbours and potential accession states are expected to sign up to the full *acquis communautaire* (the total body of EU law). PTAs with its partners in the Euro-Mediterranean Partnership (Euro-Med), seeking stability in a volatile region on the European Union's doorstep, offer free trade in industrial products but exclusions for sensitive agricultural products. PTAs with African, Caribbean and Pacific (ACP) states have been driven by development objectives, which presume flexibility to accommodate the needs of the countries concerned, notwithstanding an increased focus on reciprocity. And the recent PTAs with Asian partners such as Korea, ASEAN and India are clearly driven by a desire to strengthen the European Union's presence in the Asian region.

EFTA's approach to PTAs shares many of the features of EU policy. However, not having the political clout of the European Union, EFTA's approach has been not so much to seek to emulate the strategic objectives of the European Union's agreements, but rather to seek to match their provisions. Thus, in the formative stages of EFTA's PTA policy, the agreements with Central and East European states after 1991 and the Euro-Med agreements after 1995 were designed to ensure that EFTA's interests were not undermined by the EU agreements.

Japan is drawn in opposing directions: the pursuit of closer Asian integration, in recognition of regional vulnerability exposed by the 1997–1998 Asian financial crisis; and a widening of formal links beyond East Asia in order to pursue broader economic, foreign policy and strategic interests. The latter, perhaps stronger, tendency is seen in Japan's support for a free trade area of the Asia Pacific, a US proposal that, if ever realized, would see Asia-Pacific Economic Cooperation (APEC) converted into a preferential arrangement and would serve both to draw in key raw material suppliers and to contain the influence of China.

Singapore, like Japan, has drawn lessons from the Asian financial crisis. Unlike Japan, however, whose political and strategic influence it does not share, Singapore has deliberately pursued a single, overriding objective in its PTA strategy: to use its preferential agreements with all continents as a way of extending Singapore's role as a hub for investment and trading in Asia.

Recent trends in PTAs

It is not an exaggeration to describe recent growth in preferential trade agreements as a proliferation.[3] The annual average number of notifications since the WTO was established has been 20, compared with an annual average of less than 3 during the four and a half decades of the General Agreement on Tariffs and Trade (GATT).[4] As of June 2008, 394 PTAs had been notified to the WTO.

Two clarifications are in order. First, the number of notifications does not correspond to the number of PTAs actually in force. There were 205 PTAs notified and in force as at May 2008. However, if all agreements currently in the pipeline come to fruition then, by 2010, it is estimated that there will be close to 400 PTAs in force in the global trading system. Second, the number of agreements in force does not in itself indicate their impact on world trade – many of them may be quite small. But here again the trend is clear; within the past five years, the share of world trade accounted for by PTAs has risen from some 40 per cent to over half.[5]

Behind these numbers, some clear trends are apparent. For most countries, PTAs have become the centrepiece of their trade policy and the principal focus of their trade officials' attention. In recognition of this increased importance, attempts are being made to improve the monitoring of PTAs within the WTO (WTO, 2006). A new Transparency Mechanism has been introduced, under which the Committee on Regional Trade Agreements (CRTA) produced 10 "Factual Presentations" in the 12 months to May 2008.[6] The aim of the WTO is to complete the "Factual Presentations" including consideration by the CRTA, for notifications under Article XXIV, in 35 weeks and by the Committee on Trade and Development, for notifications under the Enabling Clause, in 45 weeks.

PTAs are showing an increased degree of sophistication in the range of issues they address. Many of the newer agreements cover trade in services and include provisions dealing with investment, competition policy, government procurement and intellectual property rights.

There is also a clear preference for free trade agreements (where members retain their own tariff regime against third parties), as opposed to customs unions (where members form a common external tariff). Among projected agreements, 92 per cent are planned as free trade areas, 7 per cent as partial scope agreements, and only 1 per cent as customs unions.

There is a pronounced increase in the number of North–South PTAs, which now represent the bulk of agreements. And the trend towards North–South agreements is being accompanied by a commitment to the principle of reciprocity by all parties, developing as well as developed. Where asymmetric liberalization commitments are present, these seem to be more common in South–South than in North–South agreements (Heydon, 2008).

In parallel with the increase in North–South agreements is a trend towards cross-regional PTAs. Whereas only 12 per cent of PTAs notified to the WTO and in force are cross-regional, the number rises to 43 per cent for agreements signed or under negotiation, and to 52 per cent for those at the proposal stage.

Finally, an increasing number of PTAs are being concluded on a bilateral basis. Bilateral agreements account for 80 per cent of all PTAs notified and in force; 94 per cent of those signed or under negotiation; and 100 per cent of those at the proposal stage.

Together, these trends point to some broad observations about the underlying motivations for entering into preferential arrangements. First, there is clearly a pursuit of speed and flexibility. The predominance of free trade areas rather than customs unions and of bilaterals rather than plurilaterals is testimony to this.[7] Second, there is nevertheless a concern to conclude agreements that are ambitious both in the scope of issues (if not always products) covered and in the sharing of liberalization commitments among the parties. Third, there appears to be a relative decline in the goal of *regional* integration. Indeed, the proliferation of cross-regional agreements may even be weakening regional integration and diluting intra-regional trade patterns (Fiorentino et al., 2007).[8] The experience of ASEAN is a case in point (see Box 1.1). The result is a consolidation of a hub-and-spokes system, whereby a small, though growing, number of hubs (including those centred in Washington and Brussels) exchange preferential treatment with a diverse range of countries, which are likely to discriminate against one another. The conclusion of interim Economic Partnership Agreements (EPAs) between the European Union and the African ACP states at the end of 2007 points to a similar trend. One of the main declared aims of the EPAs was to promote regional integration and thus development in sub-Saharan Africa but, for a number of reasons, individual interim EPAs were negotiated with ACP states in southern and West Africa. If the final EPAs do not resolve the issue, these bilateral EPAs may therefore complicate regional integration in Africa rather than promote it.

Drawing together all of these elements, there seems to be an overarching concern to use PTAs to enhance market access, both more speedily and more comprehensively: by range of issue, by geographical coverage and by the sharing of commitments.

Overview of the volume

The volume proceeds as follows. In Part II we consider how the parties concerned use PTAs in a range of key policy areas, specifically: tariffs, rules of origin, commercial instruments, technical barriers to trade and sanitary and phytosanitary measures, government procurement, services, investment, intellectual property rights, the environment and labour standards. The following questions are addressed: what are the differences in the substance of the PTAs between core entities; in which areas do the PTAs go beyond existing WTO coverage of commitments; to what extent

Box 1.1 Bilateralism and ASEAN

From its inception in 1967, the Association of Southeast Asian Nations (ASEAN) embodied the goal of strength through regional coherence. Founded on a shared perception of the threat posed by
China, ASEAN in 1992 agreed to form a free trade area (AFTA) to
promote trade amongst the members, to compensate for the lack of
progress then evident in the Uruguay Round and to create negotiating
leverage in APEC. In the course of the 1990s, the six ASEAN members (Brunei, Indonesia, Malaysia, Philippines, Singapore and Thailand) were joined progressively by the Mekong 4: Cambodia, Laos,
Myanmar and Vietnam. In what might appear to be a dynamic progression towards ever more comprehensive regional cooperation, links
are being fostered between ASEAN and its large northern neighbours, China, Japan and Korea (ASEAN+3).

In reality, however, the trade relationship amongst these Asian
countries is highly fragmented.

- AFTA itself is a permutation of separate bilateral preferential
  agreements amongst the members, with complex rules of origin
  such that only some 10 per cent of intra-ASEAN trade receives
  preferential access (Robertson, 2008). In this respect, AFTA differs
  from EFTA, which is not a matrix of bilateral deals but rather a
  duty-free pool, and which has to date been a successful "anti-spoke"
  strategy of European nations that would otherwise have become
  spokes to the European Union's hub (Baldwin, 2008).
- The China–AFTA PTA follows the AFTA model, with each
  ASEAN government signing a bilateral trade agreement with
  China. And, although the Japanese government has expressed the
  hope that the Japan–AFTA agreement, signed in March 2008, will
  be more than just a compendium of the individual bilateral agreements between the ASEAN states and Japan, this is by no means
  guaranteed. China and Japan are emerging as "hubs" to the
  ASEAN "spokes". Moreover, given the rivalries between China,
  Japan and Korea, the political impediments to more cohesive trade
  diplomacy in Asia are formidable (Drysdale, 2005).
- Lack of Asian cohesion is compounded by the fact that many of the
  players in ASEAN have concluded, or are negotiating, important bilateral agreements with third-country "hubs" beyond Asia, such as
  the planned or operational bilateral agreements between the United
  States and Malaysia, Singapore and Thailand. At the same time,
  some ASEAN members, such as Singapore, have become global
  hubs themselves as a result of their own complex web of bilateral
  agreements.

Box 1.1 (cont.)

> In short, ASEAN, which might be regarded as the embodiment of strong regional cooperation based on shared economic and strategic interests, is in fact highly fractured, both within itself and in its trade relations with the rest of the world.
>
> The opportunities presented by bilateral deals with third parties cannot be denied but they are nevertheless weakening the fabric of regional cooperation. And because of the discrimination inherent in these preferential bilateral arrangements as well as the opportunities for welfare-reducing carve-outs of sensitive sectors – amply demonstrated by the exclusions of agriculture in the Japan–ASEAN bilaterals (Sally and Sen, 2005) – they are a clear second best to broader liberalization conducted on a multilateral basis.

do PTAs have asymmetric provisions; what are the links, if any, between domestic policies (of the core entities) and the content of the PTAs; and what, if any, has been the evolution over time of the specific provisions in PTAs? In other words, does the content of PTAs show how the core entities' revealed preferences in PTA policy are evolving over time?

Following the issue focus of Part II, Part III examines the differing motivations of the core entities in pursuing preferential agreements and the extent to which they succeed in meeting their objectives. Among the questions addressed are: how close does the United States get to its self-imposed "gold standard" for bilateral and regional agreements; how do the development aspirations of EU agreements match up with the EPAs being negotiated with the African, Caribbean and Pacific states; and how far do domestic political constraints explain the relatively modest achievements of Japan's preferential agreements?

In Part IV we consider how different preferential agreements have impacted upon patterns of trade and investment. We draw on our own analysis, a review of the literature and a discussion of some of the theoretical underpinnings of trade preferences. We focus in particular on the pattern of trade and investment between the United States, the European Union, EFTA, Japan and Singapore, on the one hand, and their existing and envisaged PTA partners in Asia, North Africa, the Gulf States and Latin America, on the other. This section confirms that the pioneering works of Jacob Viner, augmented by the likes of Meade, Lipsey and Corden, are still valuable pointers to the trade- and investment-diverting effects that are inherent in preferential trade agreements and that are particularly apparent in disaggregated analysis.

The concluding section draws out the principal findings of the study and suggests how bilateral trade diplomacy is likely to evolve and how it will affect the multilateral trading system.

Notes

1. The term PTA is preferred here to regional trade agreement (because most agreements are now bilateral and cross-regional) or to free trade agreement (which is used here to differentiate between FTAs and customs unions, which have a common external tariff). Moreover, as stressed in Bhagwati and Panagariya (1996), all the agreements offer preferential market access (and are rarely "free").
2. The Organisation for Economic Co-operation and Development (OECD) has examined the substance of PTAs though, given member sensitivities, generally not gone beyond descriptive analysis. This valuable work has been drawn on in the present study; see, in particular, OECD (2003), Houde et al. (2007), Lesser (2007), Miroudot and Lesher (2006), Solano and Sennekamp (2006), Tebar Less and Kim (2006) and Tsai (2006).
3. See Fiorentino et al. (2007).
4. Of the total of PTAs notified, 307 were notified under Article XXIV of the GATT, 62 under Article V of the GATS and 25 under the Enabling Clause. A total of 189 PTAs were classified by the WTO as inactive. See regional trade agreements notified to the GATT/WTO and in force, ⟨http://www.wto.org/english/tratop_e/region_e/region_e.htm⟩ (accessed 11 September 2008).
5. This is not the same as saying that over half of trade is preferential trade. It has been argued that only some 15 per cent of trade is actually preferential, if one accounts for tariff lines already at zero or less than 5 per cent "covered" by preferential agreements (World Bank, 2005a).
6. These are US–Morocco (Goods and Services): WT/REG208/3, 26 November 2007; EC–Albania (Goods): WT/REG226/1/Rev.1, 29 April 2008; Panama–Singapore (Goods and Services): WT/REG227/1, 16 January 2008; India–Singapore (Goods and Services): WT/REG228/1, 27 February 2008; Chile–China (Goods): WT/REG230/1, 23 April 2008; Panama–El Salvador (Goods and Services): WT/REG196/3, 8 May 2008; Mercosur (Services): WT/REG238/1, 9 May 2008; Trans-Pacific Strategic Economic Partnership (Goods and Services): WT/REG229/1, 9 May 2008; EC–Chile (Services): WT/REG164/7, 28 September 2007; Turkey–Morocco (Goods): WT/REG209/3, 27 September 2007.
7. Negotiations on non-agricultural market access (NAMA) in the DDA have demonstrated how customs unions complicate the process. The Southern African Customs Union has asked for additional flexibilities under NAMA since ordinarily none of South Africa's (least developed) neighbours would have to apply the eventually agreed NAMA formula and would stand to be disproportionately affected by a WTO-driven cut to the bloc's common external tariff.
8. Although the European Union, with its successful process of widening and deepening, can be seen as an exception to this proposition, EU experience is unique and, with its high degree of supranational authority, unlikely to be replicated elsewhere (see Baldwin, 2008). This is certainly the lesson that tends to be drawn in Asia.

Part II

The issues: The nature and scope of PTA policy provisions

2

Tariffs and rules of origin

Successive Rounds of multilateral trade negotiations under the General Agreement on Tariffs and Trade (GATT) have seen average industrial tariff rates fall impressively, from close to 40 per cent at the establishment of the GATT in 1947 to less than 5 per cent following the Uruguay Round some 50 years later. But tariff barriers are still an issue. Among the most difficult challenges in the course of negotiations under the Doha Development Agenda has been the treatment of tariff barriers in agriculture, while the debate on non-agricultural market access (NAMA) has been focused almost entirely on the modalities for the "Swiss" formula of tariff reduction, providing for bigger cuts to higher tariff rates.

Remaining tariff barriers are a particular concern for developing countries, as a result of the persistence of tariff peaks in sensitive areas such as textiles and clothing or motor vehicles, and tariff escalation, whereby tariffs rise with successive degrees of processing. The result, compounded by the perverse effects of special and differential treatment in the GATT under which developing countries in effect opted out of the tariff-cutting process, is that tariffs on products of interest to developing countries are generally higher than those of interest to the advanced industrialized countries. The average tariff on industrialized countries' imports from developing countries, at 4.8 per cent, is higher than that on products from other industrialized countries, at 3.0 per cent. Moreover, average tariff rates maintained by developing countries are themselves higher than those applied by more advanced economies: 13.2 per cent in the least developed countries and 11.1 per cent in the low- and middle-income

The rise of bilateralism: Comparing American, European and Asian approaches to preferential trade agreements, Heydon and Woolcock, *United Nations University Press, 2009, ISBN 978-92 808 1162-9*

developing countries, as compared with 3.8 per cent in the industrialized countries.

The persistence of relatively high developing country tariff barriers means that in multilateral trade negotiations there are disproportionately high welfare gains to be made by developing countries from further tariff reductions. It also means that in the framework of preferential trade agreements (PTAs), as long as product coverage is comprehensive, there are correspondingly large opportunities for trade creation associated with developing countries' trade, as local production is replaced with that of preferred partners, which benefits from reduced tariff barriers. But it also means that there are higher risks of trade diversion, as cheaper-sourced goods from third-country suppliers – still subject to relatively high most favoured nation (MFN) tariffs – are displaced by those of preferred partners from within the PTA. These effects, based in particular on the work of Jacob Viner and James Meade, will be discussed in more detail in Chapter 11 on the economic effects of PTAs.

The protective, and distorting, effects of tariff barriers are often accentuated by the rules of origin needed to ensure that third-country goods cannot enter a free trade area via the member with the lowest barriers and hence gain access to the whole protected market. As will be explored below, generally speaking, the greater the gap between MFN and preferential tariffs the tougher are the rules of origin applied by the PTA in question.

Tariffs and rules of origin also have two important systemic effects. First, they contribute to the proliferation of different rules amongst preferential groupings and hence hinder trade and complicate the process of any eventual harmonization. And, second, they create a disincentive on the part of those who benefit from preferential treatment to engage in multilateral tariff reduction that would see the value of those preferences eroded, even though – as we shall see – for all but a handful of countries the benefits of across-the-board MFN tariff reduction more than offset any negative effects from the erosion of preferences.

Tariff preferences

Introduction

Tariffs are the first issue to be considered when assessing the scope and depth of any PTA and thus the degree of preference. Tariff preferences are of course WTO-plus in the sense that they reduce tariffs to below the level of the MFN bound rate in the World Trade Organization (WTO).

Article XXIV of the GATT requires PTAs to cover "substantially all trade (SAT)". This is based on the view, which was articulated as early as the League of Nations discussions on the topic in the 1930s, that complete coverage is better because it means that the parties to a PTA do not exclude sensitive or difficult sectors from tariff liberalization and thus help to maximize gains. There remains no agreement in the WTO's Committee on Regional Trade Agreements (CRTA) on the definition of SAT. Suggestions range between 80 per cent and 100 per cent of all trade, with developing countries seeking more flexibility. The first question to address is therefore what the coverage of tariff liberalization is for the "core entities" (the United States, the European Union, EFTA, Japan and Singapore).

A second question is what trends, if any, can be identified in the coverage of tariff preferences? For example, are recent PTAs extending the sector coverage of the preferential agreements? Is the structure of tariff liberalization pursued by the core entities the same for all the PTAs they negotiate, or does it vary from case to case? A trend towards greater coverage could be interpreted as PTAs being building blocks for future liberalization. Varying structures of liberalization and overlapping PTAs would make for greater complexity of preferences.

As there are more and more North–South PTAs and developing countries are pressing for greater flexibility in the application of GATT Article XXIV, how do the PTAs negotiated accommodate countries at different levels of development? Is there asymmetric tariff liberalization favouring the less developed partners in agreements? Finally, how do the approaches to tariff preference of the core entities compare?

Although tariff barriers are generally seen as being the more transparent form of protection compared with non-tariff or regulatory barriers, providing an answer to the questions above is far from straightforward. Assessing the degree of preference requires a detailed comparison of applied or multilaterally bound tariffs on a line-by-line basis with the preferential tariff. Even though the aim of this volume is to look at the detail, this degree of detail for anything but a few agreements was beyond the scope of the research. The approach adopted was to consider the preferential tariffs of the core entities as set out in the various texts of the PTA agreements. This involves identifying which tariff lines are liberalized by any agreement, which are excluded and which are subject to partial liberalization or tariff rate quotas (TRQs). Unfortunately, the information provided by the various parties is not standardized, making the scope and sector coverage of agreements often opaque.[1] There is also no consensus on the measure for coverage and depth of tariff preferences in PTAs. For example, should coverage be determined by the number of tariff lines for which tariffs are reduced to zero as a result of a PTA, or should the measure be the percentage of trade at zero tariffs (WTO, 2002a: 2)? The different methods produce different results.

The approach adopted in this study has been to measure the percentage of tariff lines covered on the basis of the texts of the agreements at the HS 8-digit level. This approach is broadly in line with previous WTO work (WTO, 2002a) and thus facilitates some comparison. This approach does not take account of the trade between the parties in each sector, so that removal of tariffs has equal weight regardless of the volume of trade in the product concerned. Methods of measurement that take account of trade will, on the other hand, tend to overstate the importance of lines where tariffs are not in place or not restrictive and understate the absence of trade where tariffs are prohibitively high.

The study assessed 13 selected PTAs, with the position for each party being studied; in other words, the coverage by the European Union of imports from Chile and Chile's coverage for imports from the European Union. In each case, tariff lines (at the HS 8 level) for fully liberalized products, for excluded products and for partially liberalized products were identified. In order to give a somewhat wider picture, in addition to the new research carried out for this study a comparison was made with other available data, such as that carried out by the WTO in 2002, which adopted a similar approach.

Comparison of approaches

The United States

The United States maintains a relatively low level of MFN tariffs; in 2005, the average US bound and applied tariff rate was 3.5 per cent,[2] and approximately 31 per cent of American tariff lines receive duty-free treatment.[3] According to a 2006 WTO estimate, 2 per cent of American tariff lines are covered by tariff rate quotas.[4] Industries with the highest level of tariff protection include dairy (10.5 per cent), canned tuna (11.6 per cent), apparel (11.1 per cent), and footwear and leather products (10.7 per cent). Tobacco, sugar, beef, peanuts and cotton have also traditionally been protected.[5] See Figure 2.1 for an overview of the bound and applied tariffs for the countries covered by the research.

American PTAs are characterized by fairly consistently comprehensive liberalization of tariff lines by both parties. In the four agreements closely analysed in this study, 100 per cent of tariff lines in the American schedule were liberalized entirely by the end of the transition period. Whereas 2–3 per cent of American lines were subject to tariff rate

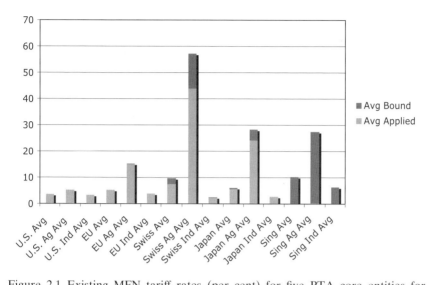

Figure 2.1 Existing MFN tariff rates (per cent) for five PTA core entities for agricultural and industrial products.
Source: compiled by the authors from WTO data.
Notes: Swiss tariffs are used as a proxy for EFTA. Avg = average; Ag = agriculture; Ind = industrial tariffs; Sing = Singapore.

quotas, all such quotas were eliminated by the end of the transition period. These American agreements are thus highly WTO-plus with regard to US tariff elimination, albeit from a low initial level of tariff protection.

In the PTA with Chile, the United States also made use of reference prices and quantities for a small number of US tariff lines (0.5 per cent of the American schedule) as a trigger for safeguard measures. All such measures were forbidden after a transition period.

The US "gold standard" thus brings the United States well within the current range of definitions of SAT and explains why the United States is pressing for 100 per cent or near full coverage in the WTO discussions on SAT. However, not all US PTAs have been strictly liberalizing. Agreements with countries at higher levels of development have notably included carve-outs on both sides of the agreements. The US–Israel agreement of 1985, for example, allowed both sides to retain import bans, quotas and fees to protect sensitive agricultural sub-sectors. The agreement also explicitly allowed for infant industry protection within a transition period, and balance of payments related protection for limited periods. But this is now an old agreement.

Table 2.1 The coverage of HS 8 tariff lines for imports into the United States from various PTA partners (per cent)

PTA partner	All products					Agriculture					Industrial products				
	Ex	Part	Full	TRQs		Ex	Part	Full	TRQs		Ex	Part	Full	TRQs
Israel (1985)[a]	n.a.	n.a.	100.0	n.a.		n.a.	n.a.	98.0	n.a.		0.0	0.0	100.0	n.a.
Canada (1988)[a]	n.a.	n.a.	100.0	n.a.		n.a.	n.a.	98.0	n.a.		n.a.	n.a.	100.0	n.a.
Mexico (NAFTA 1993)[a]	n.a.	n.a.	90.0	n.a.		n.a.	n.a.	87.0	n.a.		n.a.	n.a.	91.0	n.a.
Chile	0.0	0.0	100.0	1.8		0.0	0.0	100.0	10.0		0.0	0.0	100.0	0.05
Morocco	0.0	0.0	100.0	3.0		0.0	0.0	100.0	11.0		0.0	0.0	100.0	1.60
Singapore	0.0	0.0	100.0	1.8		0.0	0.0	100.0	10.0		0.0	0.0	100.0	0.10
Bahrain	0.0	0.0	100.0	1.8		0.0	0.0	100.0	10.0		0.0	0.0	100.0	0.10

Source: compiled by the authors from data taken from each of the PTAs.
Notes: Ex = number of tariff lines excluded from liberalization; Part = number of tariff lines partially excluded; Full = number of tariff lines fully included (i.e. liberalized); TRQs = tariff lines subject to tariff rate quotas or other quotas.
[a]Figures from WTO (2002a: Annex 2).

More recently, the US–Australia PTA (2004) allowed the United States to maintain duties after the transition period on sensitive American agricultural tariff lines. Duties will remain on some US beef, dairy, cotton, peanut and horticultural product tariff lines. The United States also placed tariff rate quotas on some dairy products, which will increase indefinitely by a fixed percentage but will not be removed completely. Australian agricultural tariffs, on the other hand, were fully liberalized.

On ratification, the US–Korea PTA will also include important exclusions. The Korean side has excluded some lines completely – including rice and rice-related lines – and will maintain quotas on dairy, honey, potatoes, oranges and soybeans. In contrast to the US–Australia agreement, the United States appears to be more consistently liberal on both industrial and agricultural goods in the US–Korea PTA negotiations. However, the US motor vehicle industry has called for a guaranteed market share as part of the agreement, together with an incremental reduction of Korean tariffs on imports of US vehicles, tied to the number of vehicles sold.

The United States affords protection for its sensitive domestic sectors by providing relatively long transition periods for tariff and quota elimination, sometimes as long as 12 years (Chile PTA) or 18 years (Morocco PTA). Sectors consistently receiving the longest transition periods are predominantly agricultural, including beef, various dairy lines, sugar, tobacco, peanuts, wine and cotton, but may also include industrial lines (as with quotas for tyres, copper and some chinaware in the Morocco agreement). The percentage of lines in the agreements with long transition times was relatively small in the PTAs included in the comprehensive assessment: at least 79 per cent of American tariff lines were liberalized immediately in each of the agreements, and at least 92 per cent of lines were liberalized within six years.

The US PTAs closely scrutinized in the study are also characterized by comprehensive tariff elimination by trade partners; asymmetry in tariff reductions favouring the United States' PTA partners is either zero or very nearly so. American PTA partners generally did not make more extensive use of long transition times than the United States, and partners introduced fewer tariff rate quotas as a percentage of tariff lines in all of the studied agreements.

The exception was Morocco, where a modest 0.4 per cent of Moroccan tariff lines either maintained quotas at the end of the transition period or did not completely liberalize tariffs. Approximately 34 per cent of Moroccan lines had transition times of over 8 years – a significantly greater figure than for the American schedule – and transition times of 18, 19 and 25 years were allowed in a limited number of cases.

The United States' PTA tariff schedules are presented as comprehensive lists, specifying line-by-line tariff treatment in both countries' schedules. The United States used the same format for all of the studied agreements and designated tariff rate quotas for similar sectors. Southern trade partners conformed to the American style of tariff schedules in all of the agreements analysed. This uniformity in the US tariff schedules enhances transparency and reduces the complexity that results from the use of partial or different tariff schedules in PTAs.

The European Union

The European Union binds 100 per cent of tariff lines in the WTO at an average bound (and applied) MFN tariff of 5.4 per cent. The European Union maintains a high level of tariff protection on agricultural goods, for which the average MFN applied tariff is 15.4 per cent.[6] Among the most supported and protected sectors are beef, sheep, goats, poultry, dairy, rice, barley, various fruits and vegetables, sugar, wine and tobacco.[7]

Preferential agreements of the European Union are liberal with respect to industrial goods and defensive on agricultural goods. The agreements typically use a short negative list (of tariff lines excluded from liberalization) for industrial goods in the EU schedule, excluding less than 1 per cent of all tariff lines. By contrast, large parts of the EU agricultural schedule are excluded from tariff reductions or liberalization, allowing for the protection of key Common Agricultural Policy products such as beef, poultry, dairy, olive oil, rice, barley, wheat, rye, sugar and wine.

The trend in Table 2.2 appears to be towards greater coverage of both industrial products and agricultural tariff lines. In the case of industrial products, there is a trend towards 100 per cent coverage and a significant shift towards more coverage of agricultural tariff lines, albeit at a much lower level. The EU–Chile agreement is seen by the European Union as a model for its current phase of PTAs. Indeed, in the negotiations with South Korea the European Union has offered almost complete coverage of all tariff lines including agriculture. It would be premature to view this as a clear trend towards near complete coverage as Korea does not constitute a competitive threat for EU agriculture. Other PTAs, such as with some ASEAN countries with greater agricultural exporting capabilities, are likely to revert to more restrictive measures.

Asymmetry in EU agreements differs for the industrial and agricultural sections of the partners' tariff schedules. Although tariff line coverage is symmetrical for industrial goods, partner countries are typically allowed a long transition period; Morocco, Chile, Tunisia and Egypt were allowed maximum transitions of between 12 and 15 years. EU agreements also

Table 2.2 The coverage of HS 8 tariff lines for imports into the European Union from various PTA partners (per cent)

PTA partner	All products			Agriculture			Industrial products		
	Ex	Part	Full	Ex	Part	Full	Ex	Part	Full
South Africa (1995)[a]			55.0			27.0			61.0
Morocco (2000)	15.0	4.0	81.0	63.0	16.0	21.0	0.1	0.2	99.6
Chile (2003)	6.0	4.0	90.0	25.0	17.0	58.0	0.3	0.0	99.7

Source: compiled by the authors from data taken from the text of each PTA covered.
Notes: Ex = number of tariff lines excluded from liberalization; Part = number of tariff lines partially excluded; Full = number of tariff lines fully included (i.e. liberalized).
[a] Figures from WTO (2002a: Annex 2).

allow developing country partners to take safeguard measures on industrial goods in the form of increased tariffs to protect "infant industries" and industries facing "difficulties [that] produce major social problems", though all such measures are time limited and may not continue after the transition period. Neither long transition periods nor explicit safeguard clauses are extended to the European Union on industrial goods.

On agriculture, by contrast, the European Union's developing country partner does not typically receive more lenient treatment. The right to convene discussions of sensitive agricultural sectors is extended to both parties, as are agricultural transition periods. Whereas the agreement with Morocco was largely symmetrical, the agreement with Chile appears generally favourable to the European Union: Chile liberalized a far greater proportion of its schedule in its PTA and the European Union enjoyed longer transition periods for its fishery products. The picture on agricultural asymmetry is thus mixed, but shows no clear tendency for lenience for developing country trade partners.

In terms of tariff structure, EU Association Agreements are largely consistent. Industrial goods are treated in a simple, straightforward manner for the EU schedule. Agricultural lines, for both the European Union and its partners, have more extensive and varied treatment in the annexes, including tariff rate quotas, exclusions and stipulations for future negotiations. There is, however, a variation between the EU PTA agreements in their differing use of positive, negative and comprehensive lists. The agreements with Chile, Egypt, Morocco and Tunisia varied on this point without a clear trend. In the investigated agreements, negative and comprehensive treatment resulted in more liberal regimes than positive lists.

EFTA

With average applied MFN tariffs ranging between 7.6 and 8.6 per cent, the European Free Trade Association (EFTA) countries individually maintain higher average tariffs than any of the other core entities covered in the research. The countries also bind their tariffs at relatively high rates, introducing greater uncertainty into their tariff regimes; Norway and Iceland bind their rates at averages that are respectively 12.3 and 15.8 per cent higher than the applied average.[8] The average bound and applied agricultural rates of the EFTA countries are far greater than any of the other core entities. All EFTA members maintain average applied rates of over 40 per cent, and Norway and Iceland each bind their agricultural lines at an average of greater than 109 per cent.[9] See Table 2.3 for Swiss data.

The EFTA countries enter into trade agreements as a group, but negotiate agricultural schedules independently, and do so for primary agricultural products on a bilateral basis. As a result, whereas industrial treatment is shared by all of the EFTA countries and their partners, the agricultural tariff coverage varies by EFTA member. This study has analysed the agreements from the perspective of Switzerland.

Like the PTAs of the European Union and Japan, EFTA agreements are liberal on industrial goods and defensive on agricultural goods. Industrial tariffs are eliminated with a short negative list of excluded goods; in the investigated agreements, those lists included dairy-related products and animal feeds. With large portions of the agricultural schedules excluded entirely (see Table 2.3), EFTA agreements afford extensive protection for sensitive agricultural products, including beef, dairy, cereals, milling products, animal and vegetable fats and oils, sugar products, cocoa products, and others, and do so in all its PTAs. There does not appear to be a trend towards greater liberalization.

As in EU agreements, partner countries are allowed the extensive use of longer transition periods for the elimination of industrial goods, a consistent source of asymmetry favouring developing country partners. That said, tariff line coverage for both industrial and agricultural goods was highly symmetrical. The extensive treatment of agricultural lines by both parties in EFTA agreements means that the agricultural agreements do not afford significantly greater lenience for developing country partners.

Because EFTA executes preferential agreements as a group but does not present a common tariff schedule to its partners, EFTA agreements take on a fragmented character. The treatment of industrial lines in EFTA agreements is similar to that for other core entities, but even here the excluded lines for EFTA are broken out by member country.

Within the common preferential agreement, all partners to the agreement provide a Protocol detailing positive-list treatment of processed

Table 2.3 The coverage of HS 8 tariff lines for imports into EFTA (per cent)

PTA partner	All sectors				Agricultural products				Industrial products			
	Ex	Part	Full	TRQs	Ex	Part	Full	TRQs	Ex	Part	Full	TRQs
Israel[a]	n.a.	n.a.	79.0	n.a.	n.a.	n.a.	23.0	0.0	0.0	0.0	100.0	0.0
Morocco (1999)	18.0	4.0	78.0	0.0	62.0	15.0	23.0	0.0	0.0	0.2	99.8	0.0
Chile (2004)	17.0	5.0	78.0	0.0	48.0	18.0	34.0	0.0	5.0	0.0	95.0	0.0

Source: compiled by the authors from data taken from the text of each PTA covered.
Notes: Switzerland was taken as a proxy for EFTA. Ex = number of tariff lines excluded from liberalization; Part = number of tariff lines partially excluded; Full = number of tariff lines fully included (i.e. liberalized); TRQs = tariff lines subject to tariff rate quotas or other quotas.
[a]Figures from WTO (2002a: Annex 2).

agricultural goods. In parallel to the main agreement, each of the EFTA member countries then executes a bilateral agreement with the partner country on primary agricultural goods. Treatment of tariff lines varies between and within the agricultural annexes, and includes *ad valorem* tariff elimination, specific duty elimination, explicit reference to EU-compatible treatment, currency-denominated tariff reductions, and deductions from the existing MFN level. This all adds to the complexity of the tariff schedules, reduces transparency and facilitates special treatment for defensive sectors.

Beyond the pattern of tariff coverage that EFTA agreements share with EU agreements (a comparison of the EFTA and EU agreements with Morocco shows a remarkable similarity in the percentage of tariff lines covered and excluded), there are also some explicit ways in which EFTA has linked its agreements to those of the European Union. In the Morocco agreement, both EFTA and Morocco agreed to designate a positive list of processed agricultural lines for which treatment would be no less favourable than that afforded to the European Union. EFTA adopted the same approach in the EFTA–Chile agreement, specifying that the same processed agricultural products would be covered as were covered by the EU–Chile agreement.

Japan

Japan binds 99.6 per cent of tariff lines in the WTO at an average rate of 6.1 per cent and has an applied MFN average tariff of 5.6 per cent (see Figure 2.1),[10] a higher applied average than the United States, European Union or Singapore. Although agriculture accounts for only 1.1 per cent of Japanese GDP,[11] Japan has been defensive in its approach to agricultural tariff liberalization. The average applied rate for agricultural products of 24.3 per cent contrasts sharply with an average rate of 2.8 per cent for industrial goods.[12]

Japan provides high tariff protection for dairy, vegetables, milling industry products, sugar products and footwear, and often uses large non-*ad valorem* tariffs to do so. Japan also maintains tariff rate quotas on dairy, rice, barley, wheat, silk-related products, and edible fats and starches, often with peak duties on out-of-quota rates.[13]

In contrast to the consistent treatment of the domestic tariff schedule by the United States and Singapore, the Japanese treatment of the domestic schedules has varied. The two PTAs closely analysed in this study (with, respectively, Singapore and Chile) illustrate a significant contrast (see Table 2.4). In the 2002 Japan–Singapore PTA – Japan's first – Japan took a highly defensive, positive-list approach. Japan excluded 81.5 per cent of its agricultural schedule (over 1,600 lines), and excluded 7.2 per

Table 2.4 The coverage of HS 8 tariff lines for imports into Japan from selected PTA partners (per cent)

PTA partner	All products				Agriculture and fishery				Industrial products			
	Ex	Part	Full	TRQs	Ex	Part	Full	TRQs	Ex	Part	Full	TRQs
Singapore (2002)	23.6	0.0	74.0	0.0	81.5	0.0	18.0	0.0	7.2	0.0	93.0	0.0
Chile (2007)	11.9	0.5	88.0	0.5	47.9	2.0	50.0	2.0	2.0	0.0	98.3	0.0

Source: compiled by the authors from data taken from the text of each PTA covered.
Notes: Ex = number of tariff lines excluded from liberalization; Part = number of tariff lines partially excluded; Full = number of tariff lines fully included (i.e. liberalized); TRQs = tariff lines subject to tariff rate quotas or other quotas.

29

cent of industrial lines; only India could claim to be more defensive on either agricultural or industrial goods in any of the studied agreements.

Moreover, of the relatively few Japanese agricultural lines that were included in the agreement for duty-free treatment, 97.5 per cent had already been bound at zero in the Uruguay Round, rendering the agricultural schedule in the Japan–Singapore PTA largely meaningless. Where Japan maintained its most significant tariff protection, the PTA did not go beyond Japan's WTO commitments.

The Japan–Chile PTA, for which information was released in March 2007, presents a somewhat different picture. Japan agreed to a comprehensive list with Chile that liberalized 32.0 per cent more of the total Japanese agricultural schedule than the Singapore agreement, and went beyond Japan's duty-free commitments in the WTO. Moreover, with 98.3 per cent of industrial lines liberalized, it provided significantly more duty-free treatment than in Japan's agreement with Singapore. In fact, Japan's agreements show a clear pattern of progressively greater coverage of preferential liberalization over time. The number of excluded chapters in agriculture has fallen steadily through the agreements with Singapore (81.5 per cent of tariff lines excluded), Mexico (54.3), Chile (47.9), Thailand (43.4) and the Philippines (39.8). A similar pattern is observed for the percentage of tariff lines of "all products" excluded: Singapore (23.6), Mexico (13.3), Chile (11.9), Thailand (10.8) and the Philippines (9.6).[14]

Despite this dynamic shift following the agreement with Singapore, Japanese agreements as a whole remain relatively defensive. Both of the agreements covered by detailed analysis exclude over half of the agricultural schedule, and the industrial schedules are more restrictive than for any of the other core entities. The excluded agricultural lines cover beef, dairy, fish, rice, wheat, barley, sugar products and numerous other sensitive industries. Japan has also made increasing use of longer transition times for sensitive sectors, as noted in greater detail below.

Owing to Japan's defensiveness, Japan's PTA partners have tended to be relatively more liberal in agricultural and industrial goods and have used fewer quotas (where quotas were used) than Japan. Singapore and Chile respectively liberalized 26 per cent and 7 per cent more of their domestic tariff lines. Although the longer transition periods used in more recent Japanese agreements have often been extended to both parties, the asymmetry in the agreement with Thailand allowed Japan the longer maximum transition period (16 years, versus 11 years for Thailand). The existing asymmetry in Japanese agreements thus provides more protection for Japan than for its partners.

There have also been changes in the structure of agreements used by Japan. The 2002 Japan–Singapore agreement used an all-or-nothing approach, where lines were either liberalized immediately or excluded entirely (only 10 lines in the entire Japanese schedule were liberalized over a transition period, and that period was capped at six years). There were no tariff rate quotas.

With the 2005 agreement with Mexico, Japan shifted to a comprehensive list approach and extended transition times to as long as 11 years; more recent agreements with Malaysia, Chile and Thailand include transitions of 16 years. The Mexico PTA also introduced tariff rate quotas for the first time. The former extensive and cumbersome list of varied quota and tariff treatments in the Mexico agreement was consolidated into a shorter, clearer and more uniform list of tariff rate quotas by the 2007 agreements with Chile and Thailand.

Beginning with the 2006 PTA with Malaysia, Japan also excluded a portion of tariff lines for future negotiations (often with a time limit for negotiation), a feature that has now become standard in Japanese PTAs.

Singapore

While the simple average of Singapore's bound WTO tariff is 10.4 per cent,[15] Singapore's applied tariff schedule is almost entirely duty free (see Table 2.5). Singapore maintains tariffs on only 6 tariff lines (covering beer and samsu) out of over 10,000 total lines. Despite its liberal applied tariff regime, Singapore has bound only 69.2 per cent of tariff lines in the WTO, a practice that Singapore's authorities have indicated has been maintained in part for negotiating purposes.[16]

Singapore's PTAs are characterized by complete and immediate liberalization of all of Singapore's tariff lines, usually executed in a single sentence. In the sense that the agreements bind Singapore's tariffs at the applied rate of zero, and in the sense that they bind *all* of Singapore's tariff lines (i.e. the remaining 30.8 per cent), the agreements are WTO-plus. In practice, however, they have little or no effect on the customs rates being applied at Singapore's ports, which continue to be duty free.

Perhaps as a result of the fact that Singapore has little to offer in the way of tariff elimination, Singapore's PTA partners do not appear to deviate from their usual tariff elimination preferences. The United States pursued complete elimination of tariffs, Japan liberalized industrial lines (7 per cent of tariff lines excluded), but remained defensive on agriculture (81 per cent excluded from liberalization), and India remained highly defensive in both agriculture and industrial goods. India agreed to fully liberalize only 12 per cent of agricultural and fishery tariff lines and only 25 per cent of industrial tariff lines. The level of asymmetry in the Singaporean tariff negotiations therefore varied widely depending on the PTA partner.

Table 2.5 The coverage of HS 8 tariff lines for imports into Singapore (per cent)

PTA partner	All products				Agriculture and fishery				Industrial products			
	Ex	Part	Full	TRQs	Ex	Part	Full	TRQs	Ex	Part	Full	TRQs
India (2005)	0	0	100	0	0	0	100	0	0	0	100	0
Japan (2002)	0	0	100	0	0	0	100	0	0	0	100	0
USA (2004)	0	0	100	0	0	0	100	0	0	0	100	0

Source: compiled by the authors from data taken from the text of each PTA covered.
Notes: Ex = number of tariff lines excluded from liberalization; Part = number of tariff lines partially excluded; Full = number of tariff lines fully included (i.e. liberalized); TRQs = tariff lines subject to tariff rate quotas or other quotas.

In the agreements analysed in detail, Singapore allowed partners to pursue their preferred style of tariff elimination schedules. As a result, there is little continuity in the structure of agreements, with some comprehensive, some negative-list and some positive-list treatment by PTA partners. Treatment of transition periods was similarly varied.

Conclusions on tariffs

Comparing the core entities' PTA policies on tariff preferences, the US "gold standard" liberalization covers more tariff lines and in many cases is close to 100 per cent, but uses longer transition periods (up to 18 years) when it wants to provide some degree of continued protection. At the same time, the United States expects its PTA partners to do the same, which by and large they have. As a result, there is little asymmetry favouring the United States' PTA partners. This general finding is based on the agreements covered by the detailed analysis for this volume. If one looks at the more recent PTAs with Australia and Korea, the US schedules appear to include rather more exclusions.

The European Union and EFTA have similar approaches in that they have close to 100 per cent coverage of industrial tariffs, but exclude large parts of agriculture, EFTA somewhat more so than the European Union.[17] In the case of the European Union, there appears to be a trend towards greater coverage of tariff liberalization in PTAs, but it remains to be seen whether this will be continued in the PTAs the European Union is negotiating with South Korea, ASEAN and India. On the other hand, the European Union and EFTA have accepted more asymmetry in industrial tariff liberalization, allowing developing countries a good deal of flexibility in their sensitive sectors. But there is also asymmetry favouring the European Union, such as through longer transition periods for some agricultural sectors.

Japan, has tended to exclude rather more industrial tariff lines than the other core entities, along with many agricultural products, but its recent PTAs appear to suggest a move towards greater coverage.

Singapore combines the US and European approaches in that it offers 100 per cent liberalization but tolerates the exclusion of sensitive sectors on the part of its PTA partners, in part owing to a lack of negotiating leverage, an absence of offensive interest on the part of Singapore, and a desire to press ahead with the PTA for other reasons. This is illustrated in the case of the Singapore–India agreement, in which Singapore accepted the exclusion of nearly 75 per cent of India's tariff lines.

There is a clear trend towards the elimination of all industrial tariffs, either immediately or after a fairly short transition (i.e. six years) by all the core entities. There remain some exceptions however, and in some cases protection is provided in the form of longer transition periods. Many of the core entities' PTA partners have also agreed to full coverage of industrial products. In other words, a move towards free trade in industrial goods appears to be accepted as the norm among the major players in PTAs.

The position in agriculture is, however, different. There is no clear trend here. Some core entities (the United States, with exceptions, and Singapore) are moving towards nearly complete coverage of agriculture as well as industrial products, but others (the European Union, EFTA and Japan) exclude large parts of agriculture from tariff and other liberalization.

There is some asymmetry favouring developing country PTA partners of the core entities. This takes the form of accepting the exclusion of more tariff lines, longer transition periods and in some cases scope to reintroduce tariffs in certain circumstances.

Generally speaking, trends in the scope and depth of tariff liberalization are not easy to identify because the coverage varies according to the potential of the PTA partner as a competitor. There are, however, some indications of greater coverage of tariff lines in PTAs, but this remains to be confirmed in future PTAs.

Rules of origin

Introduction

Preferential rules of origin (RoO) are used to determine which suppliers or producers should benefit from any preference granted by a PTA. They therefore constitute an integral part of all preferential agreements. With no agreed international rules of origin, at least for preferential RoO, each country has more or less a free hand to determine the rules it wishes to apply. As a result, different approaches have evolved. In order to facilitate a comparison between the various approaches of the core entities it is helpful to distinguish between what might be called framework provisions on RoO and the detailed sector-by-sector or even product-by-product "rules" for determining origin. Table 2.6 sets out a typology of framework provisions on rules of origin.

The broad principles for determining rules of origin are that products are either wholly obtained (in other words, originate entirely from the exporting country) or undergo substantial transformation in the exporting country in order to benefit from a preference. Over the years, "substantial transformation" is a principle that has been defined in different ways and there are competing claims as to the best criteria. A change of

Table 2.6 Typology of rules of origin (Kyoto Convention)

Coverage	Primary criterion	Secondary criterion	Tertiary criterion	Prohibitive	Liberalizing
Product-specific	Wholly obtained/produced			x	
	Substantial transformation	Change of tariff classification (CT)	Chapter (HS 2) (CTC)	2	
			Heading (HS 4) (CTH)	1	
			Sub-heading (HS 8) (CTS)		1
			Item (HS 6) (CTI)		2
		Exception attached to particular CT (ECT)		x	
		Value content (VC)	Domestic/regional value content (RVC) (min %)		
			Import content (MC) (max %)		
			Value of parts (max %)		
		Technical requirements (TR)		x	
Regime-wide	De minimis rule (max %)				x
	Roll-up/absorption principle				x
	Cumulation	Bilateral			1
		Diagonal			2
		Full			3
	Drawback provision			x	
Administration	Certification	Private self-certification			x
		Public (government sponsored)		x	

Source: Garay and De Lombaerde (2004).

tariff heading (CTH) is argued as being simple and clear cut, but this is not necessarily the case. Detailed annexes to PTAs can define rules of origin on the basis of 6-digit tariff headings or even higher, thus adding to complexity. Using the lower-digit tariff changes, i.e. at HS 2 or 4, can require significant transformation, resulting in the rules being relatively more restrictive. It is also argued that value content (VC) is the most straightforward approach. This means that a set percentage of value content must originate in the exporting country. The level can be set at anything from 25 to 70 per cent. Although simple on paper, this method requires an audit trail in order to calculate the value content resulting from work in the country claiming the preference, and as a result can be costly to apply and thus equally represent a restriction to trade. Less costly to apply is perhaps the technical requirement (TR) criterion, which requires a specific production process to be carried out in the exporting country. Although it is easier to show origin, such a criterion requires investment in specific productive capacity in the exporting country and can lead to the preferential agreement having a more distorting effect on investment and trade. With no consensus on the best approach, there has been a variation across PTAs and even across different sectors and products within PTAs, thus creating considerable complexity.

Compliance with any of the various RoO can constitute an important cost and can approach the cost of the MFN tariff producers would have to pay in the absence of a preference, so that utilization of the preference is reduced. For example, it has been estimated that, for firms wishing to take advantage of preferences under the EFTA–EU PTAs, the administrative and technical work needed to achieve compliance with the rules of origin added around 5 per cent to production costs. Where there are tariff peaks, such as in textiles and clothing, however, the option of paying the tariff can be prohibitive, so rules of origin can have a considerable effect. Textiles and clothing are also characterized by more complex RoO than normal (such as sequential changes of tariff headings from yarn to thread, thread to cloth, and cloth to clothing), which have been used to provide strong incentives for preferential suppliers to use yarns and fibres from the hub country – even if sourcing from this location is more expensive and less efficient.

Framework provisions also include *de minimis* rules and cumulation. *De minimis* excludes a set percentage of the value of a product from the calculation of origin and thus eases the restrictiveness of origin rules. Cumulation allows products originating in a third country (C) to be further processed or combined with products in a preferential country (B) so that the combined product then qualifies for a (tariff) preference in the importing country (A). Bilateral or diagonal cumulation can facilitate intra-regional trade. Bilateral cumulation operates between two countries where a PTA contains a provision allowing them to cumulate origin. This is the basic type of cumulation and is common to all origin arrangements. Only originating products or materials can benefit from it. Diagonal cumulation (as in the Euro-Mediterranean Partnership agreements or the African, Caribbean and Pacific Group of States) operates between more than two countries, provided they have PTAs containing identical origin rules and provision for cumulation between them. As with bilateral cumulation, only originating products or materials can benefit from diagonal cumulation. Full cumulation dispenses with this requirement so that all goods, including those that originate outside of any preferential agreement, can be included in a product, provided all working or processing required to confer origin status is carried out in the exporting country (B).

One final framework issue is that of the method for certification of rules of origin. Here the options are private self-certification or public/government sponsored. It is generally assumed that public/government-sponsored certification is more time consuming than private self-certification.

Comparison of approaches

As there are no agreed detailed RoO for preferential agreements, the focus of this section will be on a comparison of the various approaches. Rather than a "spaghetti bowl" of different rules, there are in fact three dominant models for rules of origin; the NAFTA model, the Pan-Euro model and what has been called the Asian/Indian Ocean model. The NAFTA model is used by the United States in its PTAs and has also found fairly wide general application in the western hemisphere. The Pan-Euro approach has emerged from the standardization of the various rules of origin used by the European Union in its preferential agreements and is used by the European Union and EFTA in their PTAs. Both the NAFTA and Pan-Euro approaches are complex, making use of a range of different criteria (see Table 2.7). As a result, they are seen to be more "restrictive" of trade than simpler systems. The Asian/Indian Ocean model is used by Japan and Singapore, as well as by most developing countries in its more simple formats. This approach makes extensive use of value content.

NAFTA

The North American Free Trade Agreement (NAFTA) contains some of the most complex RoO. As Table 2.7 shows, the agreement uses the full range of criteria. Some 70 per cent of products use multiple criteria (families) for defining origin. Change of tariff heading at HS 4 level is used for 45 per cent of all products, but in only 17 per cent of products is CTH the

Table 2.7 Comprehensive comparison of rules of origin frameworks

Regimes	Selectivity	CTC	CTH	CTS	CTI	ECT	VC	TR	Application	Administration	Cumulation
Pan-Euro	SS		x				X+	x	EU and EFTA agreements	Public or Private	Bilateral Diagonal
NAFTA	SS	x	x	x	x	x	X++	x	US PTAs and those in western hemisphere	Private	Bilateral
US–Bahrain/ Jordan/Morocco	AB	v	v			v	X+++	x		Private	Bilateral
ASEAN	AB		v				X+++			Public	Bilateral
Japan–Mexico	SS	x	x			x	X++	v		Public	Bilateral
Japan–Malaysia	SS	x	x			x	X++++	v		Public	Bilateral
Singapore–Korea	SS	x	x			x	X+++++	v		Public	Bilateral
Singapore–Jordan	AB						X++++++	x		Public	Bilateral

Source: Garay and De Lombaerde (2004), based on Estevadeordal and Suominen (2003).

Notes: CTC = change of tariff heading at HS 2 level; CTH = change at HS 4 level; CTI = change at HS 6 level; CTS = change at HS 8 level; ECT = exceptions for particular products; VC = value content; TR = technical requirement.

SS = sector specific
AB = across the board
x = used extensively
v = less used
X+ = import content (MC) 30–50%, ex works
X++ = RVC 50–60% (60 fob, 50 cost prod.)

X+++ = MC 30–70%; RVC 25–35%
X+++++ = RVC 45–55%
X+++++++ = RVC 45–55%
X+++++++++ = RVC 35%
Public = certification predominantly by customs/public bodies
Private = certification by private agents including exporter

only criterion. In 17 per cent there is one other criterion and in 7 per cent even two other criteria. The more restrictive change of tariff heading at the 2-digit level (CTC) criterion is used in 42 per cent of cases (for 25 per cent of products by itself). The HS 8 level is used for change of tariff rules in just 6 per cent of cases. Value content (of 50 or 60 per cent) is used in 30 per cent of cases and technical requirements in 43 per cent of cases. There are also specific RoO for sensitive products such as textiles and clothing. Here NAFTA uses the infamous yarn forward rule alluded to above, which in effect provides a captive market in any PTA partner for US producers of textiles (Cadot, 2004).

The NAFTA approach as used by the United States provides for a 7 per cent *de minimis* rule and bilateral cumulation. Roll-up and duty drawback are precluded five years after the agreement. Duty drawback exclusion is considered trade restrictive because exporters are prevented from recouping tariffs paid for foreign materials that are subsequently used in products being exported to the partner country. Rules of origin are issued through self-certification by producers or exporters so the administration is private.

The US approach to RoO with Bahrain is simpler in that it makes use of a 35 per cent VC rule for most products. For developing countries the costs of complying with such a rule may still be significant, but the RoO are not based on complex combinations of rules. The exception is again sensitive products, such as textiles and clothing where the yarn forward rule is applied as it is in NAFTA. Since Bahrain has little domestic production of yarn or cloth, this means that almost all the cloth is purchased in the United States. In the case of Bahrain there is a tariff preference level (TPL), which in effect excludes a specified volume of cloth from the yarn forward RoO, thus providing some limited flexibility.

The approach to RoO in the US–Jordan and US–Morocco agreements is essentially the same as for US–Bahrain, with a 35 per cent value content, but specific rules for sensitive sectors such as textiles and clothing. In the case of Morocco, the TPL has to be phased out after 10 years so that it appears to be even more restrictive than US–Bahrain. The scale of the TPL is in any case limited and is equivalent to only about 1 per cent of the US exports of cloth and yarn to Morocco.

As noted, the NAFTA administrative approach uses self-certification by exporting countries. Certificates of Origin are issued directly by producers or exporters (private law). If there are questions as to the validity of the certificate then partner officials (private sector) can make inspections in the host country. The NAFTA Certificate of Origin for a product is valid for a whole year, which facilitates trade and reduces transaction costs and is considered to be a much simpler and more efficient approach than other models.

The European Union and EFTA

The Pan-Euro approach dates from 1997 when the European Union standardized the rules used for its various preferential agreements with the European Economic Area (EEA), Switzerland and the accession states in Central and Eastern Europe. In 2003, it was agreed to apply the Pan-Euro approach to the whole of the Euro-Med region in an attempt to promote intra-regional trade. The Pan-Euro approach has formed the basis of the European Union's RoO in its subsequent PTAs.

Although harmonized across the various EU (and EFTA) agreements, the Pan-Euro system is still complex. In 60 per cent of cases it uses CTH (HS 4 level change of tariff heading), but in 25 per cent of cases there is also a value content criterion. Some 20 per cent of products are subject to technical requirements. As in NAFTA, the restrictiveness of certain rules of origin criteria is mitigated by an either/or option. This means that exporters can choose between two different criteria to confer origin status.

The Pan-Euro framework provides for a 10 per cent *de minimis* rule, but there are exclusions to this, in particular for textiles and clothing. Full cumulation applies to the EEA. Bilateral cumulation and diagonal cumulation are also applied. With diagonal cumulation, Morocco, for example, can count products originating in Algeria or Tunisia when origin rules are applied. This is intended to assist in promoting intra-regional trade between the European Union's Euro-Med partners, but still requires all the countries to prove originating status using the Pan-Euro rules.

There are two options for administration of RoO under the Pan-Euro system. Certificates of Origin can be issued by a competent agency (e.g. chamber of commerce) or by an invoice declaration for approved exporters with a recognized record of good administration. But the importer is liable for any false declaration or incorrect certification and must pay the full tariff unless any irregularity is corrected within 30 days.

The specific agreements considered in the study all illustrate the progressive application of the Pan-Euro model to EU PTAs. This holds for the EU–Mexico agreement as for the Euro-Med agreements. There are, however, exceptions to this pattern in the sensitive sectors such as textiles in trade with Mexico, where two alternative approaches to rules of origin are applicable.

In terms of future agreements, the European Commission is in the middle of a reform of preferential rules of origin with the aim of simplifying them for developing countries. The proposals envisage a move to a value content (VC) approach based on ex-factory prices rather than the more costly to administer net production cost basis and supported only by a list of working or processing operations that are insufficient as means of defining origin (European Commission, 2005). The level of value content is still to be set, but the European Commission has proposed 45 per cent for the Generalized System of Preferences and 35 per cent for the Everything But Arms programme for least developed countries. Estimates by the Commission put the existing rules at the equivalent of 60 per cent of value content. The Economic Partnership Agreements will continue to use the RoO as defined in Cotonou, owing to the lack of time, but the Commission paper envisages that these will also convert to a pure value content system. If these reforms are introduced, it will mean the European Union maintaining two regimes, the Pan-Euro regime and the simpler regime for developing countries.

The EFTA PTAs largely follow the Pan-Euro model in RoO. This is the case for the European region and for the Euro-Med. The framework provisions for EFTA–Mexico and EFTA–Korea are also more or less the same as the Pan-Euro approach, but with a number of specific changes. First, the EFTA states negotiate agriculture (HS Chapters 1–24) separately and thus determine their own rules of origin for these sectors. For the most part, the restrictive wholly obtained rule is applied. For Chapters 82–92, which were negotiated by EFTA as a group, there are also complex rules of origin, suggesting a restrictive use of such rules. For the other chapters the EFTA offers a choice between CTH and VC (at 50 per cent) for the EFTA–Mexico and EFTA–Korea PTAs. One area in which the EFTA PTAs are simpler than the Pan-Euro model is that, outside of the Euro-Med region, EFTA importing authorities accept exporter declarations rather than using the EUR.1 procedure.

Japan

Japan's Economic Partnership Agreements usually combine a CTH and a value content test in RoO for processed and manufactured goods. Regional value content (RVC) differs according to the partner (RVC 50 per cent for Mexico and RVC 60 per cent for Singapore in most chapters). The nature and thus restrictiveness of the RoO appear to depend on the economic capabilities of the partner. For example, Chapter 24 (tobacco) of the Japan–Mexico PTA specifies a 70 per cent RVC and does not allow cumulation – a result of pressure from domestic lobbying interests – compared with 60 per cent RVC and cumulation with Singapore. Chapter 86 (transport equipment) specifies CTH plus a 65 per cent RVC for road vehicles in the Japan–Mexico PTA, but only a CTH rule for Singapore. Clothing (Chapters 61–62), however, is more restrictive in the Singapore agreement as it requires a CTH plus 60 per cent RVC, as opposed to only CTH with Mexico. Japan does not provide for alternative (either/or) methods for proving origin so in this respect is more restrictive than NAFTA or the Pan-Euro.

Japan also tends to use official administrative procedures, meaning that an exporter can validate a consignment only once it has been approved by the relevant governmental authority, which tends to add to costs. In the Japan–Mexico PTA, Certificates of Origin have to be issued by the competent governmental authority or its designees in the exporting country. If there is doubt as to the accuracy of the origin claim, the importing authority may request a verification visit to the exporting country. This is similar to the NAFTA model (verification visits – although they are conducted privately), whereas the Pan-Euro model does not provide for such verification visits.

Singapore

The Singapore RoO regimes differ dramatically across Singaporean PTAs, with very comprehensive (almost 300 pages) product-specific rules with the United States (NAFTA rules), more simple and flexible RoO with Asian partners (making greater use of VC) and Pan-Euro type rules with the EFTA states (mainly specifying maximum non-originating content rules and TR rules with CTH). VC rules also vary across agreements: 45 per cent or 35 per cent for the United States, 35 per cent for Jordan, 45 per cent in general for Asian partners, and 50 per cent VC maximum with EFTA.

Singapore is an example of a country that has very diffuse RoO with virtually no harmonization, even with Australia and New Zealand. This clearly increases costs of compliance for exporters/importers. For example, the Singapore–Korea PTA uses RVC of approximately 45–55 per cent for selected sectors (55 per cent for Chapters 38, 60–62, 84–87). The TR rule is used only under Chapters 60–62. And there is a special consideration for outward processing, important in the case of Singapore, provided that the import content (MC) of the good does not exceed 40 per cent.

Administratively, Certificates of Origin are public. This means that, when claiming preferential tariff treatment, an importer of a product has to produce a Certificate of Origin issued by the exporting customs authority to prove origin.

The Asian approach initially used by Japan and Singapore was characterized by a relatively simple across-the-board criterion, usually a value content criterion, although the VC criterion has tended to be rather higher than the NAFTA and Pan-Euro levels (see Table 2.7). This is the approach that also tends to be applied by most developing countries. However, recent PTAs concluded by Japan and Singapore suggest that, as trade agreements become more complex, so do the rules of origin.

In terms of framework rules, the Asian model tends not to provide for *de minimis*, and the customs authorities of the exporting country are required to certify origin. This is less flexible than the approach used by the Pan-Euro and especially the NAFTA models.

Conclusions on rules of origin

There are three main models for rules of origin: the NAFTA model, the Pan-Euro model and a more diffuse Asian (and developing country) model. The NAFTA and Pan-Euro models are both complex regimes that make use of all the main criteria for determining rules, so that rules vary from product to product. With the harmonization of the EU rules there is at least now a large measure of uniformity across the various PTAs, but the rules still vary from product to product. The European Union is, however, moving towards a simplified system for developing countries. Singapore and, to a lesser degree, Japan still have different rules of origin for different PTAs, even if the basis for the Asian model for RoO is on paper more straightforward in that it is based on value content.

In addition to the "simplified" RoO applied to developing countries by the European Union, there are a few innovative ways in which PTAs have introduced an element of special and differential treatment. A number of regional agreements provide lesser developed members with advantageous rules of origin. They do so by lowering the threshold for the local value added requirement in order for goods to qualify for originating status (Heydon, 2008). There is no parallel for this in WTO rules.

- Mercosur provides Paraguay with more flexible rules of origin (50 instead of the normal 60 per cent of regional value added requirement).
- The Andean Community (CAN) provides that, in adopting and establishing the special provisions or specific requirements of origin, the Commission and the General Secretariat will seek to ensure that they do not hinder Bolivia and Ecuador from deriving the benefits of the Agreement (Art. 102). In this connection, CAN Decision 416 approved on 30 July 1997 provides that, for manufactured goods to be considered originating, the cif (cost, insurance, freight) value of non-native materials should not exceed 50 per cent of the value of the final product in the cases of Colombia, Venezuela and Peru, but this threshold is increased to 60 per cent in the cases of Bolivia and Ecuador (Decision 416).
- The general rule for qualifying products for originating status within the Caribbean Community (CARICOM) is that the value of materials from outside the community cannot exceed 65 per cent of the cost of repair, renovation or improvement in cases where goods have undergone processing in more developed countries. Lesser developed

CARICOM members benefit from a lifting of the corresponding figure to 80 per cent (Art. 84.2).

- The South Asian Free Trade Agreement provides that the threshold for determining originating status is raised by 10 per cent for products from least developed member states in the case of both rules concerning the determination of origin as well as the rules governing cumulation (Ann. III, 10).

Rules of origin have clearly been shaped by protectionist interests that have sought to ensure that increased import competition owing to tariff liberalization in PTAs has been qualified by complex rules of origin. In some cases one could argue that rules of origin are even used as a means of creating artificial benefits for producers by establishing what are in effect captive markets for producers from the "hub" country. Textiles is probably the best example of this.

Each of the main "core entities" has, however, varied its approach to rules of origin in order to address criticism from developing countries concerning the complexity of the rules. Thus the United States uses a simple value content approach to RoO in its PTAs with Morocco and other developing countries, but still retains the protection afforded to sensitive sectors, such as textiles, by requiring more detailed rules. The European Union is also introducing simplified value content rules for its preferential agreements with developing countries.

The expectation must therefore be that there will be a form of two-tier system in which PTAs involving relatively developed economies will make use of the NAFTA, Pan-Euro or Asian models whereas PTAs involving developing countries will use a simplified system of rules of origin based on value content.

Notes

1. As noted in Chapter 1, the WTO has recently started producing Factual Presentations of the PTAs notified to the CRTA. These follow the agreement on a Transparency Mechanism for Regional Trade Agreements (WT/L/671) adopted in December 2006. These should prove helpful as a source of comparable data as more and more studies are made available.
2. WTO, *Statistics Database*, 2007, ⟨http://www.wto.org/english/res_e/statis_e/statis_e.htm⟩ (accessed 11 September 2008).
3. Based on lines identified as already receiving duty-free treatment in the US–Chile PTA.
4. WTO, *Trade Policy Review Body – Trade Policy Review – Report by the Secretariat – United States*, 2006, WT/TPR/S/160, p. viii.
5. Rates are *ad valorem* equivalents as calculated by the International Trade Commission, from *The Economic Effects of Significant U.S. Import Restraints: Fourth Update*, USITC Publication 3701, 2004, p. xvii.
6. WTO, *Statistics Database*.

7. WTO, *Trade Policy Review Body – Trade Policy Review – Report by the Secretariat – European Communities*, 2007, WT/TPR/S/177, pp. 88–92.
8. The somewhat higher figure for EFTA than for the European Union or the United States is owing to the higher tariffs for sensitive agricultural products.
9. All EFTA figures from WTO, *Statistics Database*.
10. WTO, *Statistics Database*.
11. WTO, *Trade Policy Review Body – Trade Policy Review – Japan – Report by the Secretariat*, 2002, WT/TPR/S/107, p. 55.
12. WTO, *Statistics Database*.
13. WTO, *Trade Policy Review – Japan*, pp. 55–56.
14. Data obtained from an unpublished MSc dissertation at the London School of Economics by John Polley.
15. WTO, *Statistics Database*.
16. WTO, *Trade Policy Review Body – Trade Policy Review – Singapore – Report by the Secretariat*, 2004, WT/TPR/S/130, p. 30.
17. This study has used Swiss tariff schedules as a proxy for EFTA as a whole.

3

Non-tariff barriers: Commercial instruments, TBT/SPS and public procurement

Notwithstanding the continued importance of tariff barriers to trade, the steady reduction of tariffs through a succession of Rounds of negotiation of the General Agreement on Tariffs and Trade (GATT) has increased the relative importance of non-tariff barriers (NTBs). This chapter deals with some of the most important: commercial instruments, also referred to as trade remedies, in the form of safeguards, anti-dumping measures, state aids, and subsidies and countervailing measures; technical barriers to trade (TBT) and sanitary and phytosanitary measures (SPS); and public or government procurement. Simply listing these measures gives an idea of their range and complexity.

Thanks to the notification process established under the Doha Round negotiations on non-agricultural market access (NAMA), we have quite a good idea of the non-tariff barriers that countries regard as being the most troublesome. The NAMA inventory of NTBs shows TBTs as having the highest incidence of notifications, with 530 entries, almost half of the total, followed by customs and administrative procedures (380 entries) and SPS measures (137 entries). Perhaps surprisingly, quantitative restrictions (QRs), commercial instruments or trade remedies (such as anti-dumping and safeguard measures), government participation in trade, charges on imports and other barriers amount to less than 5 per cent of total NTB entries (Fliess and Lejarraga, 2005).

It should be noted, however, that observations about the incidence of NTBs depend very much on the source. An analysis of NTBs arising in the course of World Trade Organization (WTO) dispute settlement gives

The rise of bilateralism: Comparing American, European and Asian approaches to preferential trade agreements, Heydon and Woolcock,
United Nations University Press, 2009, ISBN 978-92-808-1162-9

quite different results from those in the NAMA inventory, with the largest number of disputes arising in the areas of trade remedies, QRs, customs and administrative barriers, and government participation in trade.

Within manufactures, the product groups reported as being most affected by NTBs are machinery and electronics (with barriers being mostly in the form of technical regulations and standards), chemical and allied industry products, and textile and clothing articles. As with tariffs, the incidence of non-tariff barriers is likely to fall with disproportionate severity on sectors or products of particular importance to developing countries. Distortions related to government procurement, for example, are especially prevalent in the construction sector, an area where many developing countries have competitive strengths.

As we will see in this chapter, preferential trade agreements (PTAs) deal extensively with non-tariff barriers. A fear arising is that, because PTAs reduce border barriers among members, there will be increased resort, by way of compensation, to non-tariff barriers. Against this, however, is the possibility that the pursuit of deeper integration among PTA members will lead them also to reduce reliance on NTBs among themselves. The evidence goes both ways, but with perhaps a greater tendency towards stronger NTB disciplines.[1]

Frequently, PTAs deal with NTBs in a way that goes beyond and is tighter (more liberal) than the provisions of the WTO; for example, by replacing anti-dumping action amongst PTA parties with resort to members' provisions dealing with competition policy; by introducing stronger disciplines on the use of safeguard action; by holding out the promise of more effective implementation of the WTO's TBT and SPS principles; or by extending to non-signatories the principles embodied in the WTO Agreement on Government Procurement (GPA) – an agreement that remains a plurilateral arrangement mainly among developed economies, covering a topic that has now been excluded from the scope of the Doha Development Agenda (DDA), but which covers some 14–20 per cent of countries' gross national product (OECD, 2003).

As we shall see, there is also evidence, however, of PTA tariff liberalization being accompanied by greater resort to non-tariff protection. This is the case, for example, with the progressive lengthening of the permissible duration of safeguard measures in Japan's PTAs.

The evidence on the effects on third parties of PTA provisions on non-tariff barriers also goes in both directions. With PTA action on non-tariff barriers there may be opportunities for third parties to benefit in a way that does not happen with preferential tariff treatment. For example, where PTAs succeed in increasing the transparency of measures, such as those dealing with standards conformity or transparency in government procurement contracts, all countries gain, not just those that belong to the preferential grouping. Disciplines on domestic subsidies are difficult if not impossible to implement in a discriminatory way. Nevertheless, it cannot be denied that there is also ample scope for PTA treatment of non-tariff barriers to have a discriminatory effect on non-members. For example, continued use of anti-dumping action against third parties when it has been proscribed among PTA signatories is discriminatory. Mutual recognition agreements in the area of standards are by their very nature discriminatory against those excluded. And the application of non-discriminatory national treatment of foreign suppliers under PTA provisions on government procurement – in other words, the liberalization aspect of government procurement agreements – generally applies only among members of the respective agreements.

Commercial instruments

Introduction

This section examines the treatment in PTAs of commercial instruments, also referred to as trade remedies, namely: safeguards, anti-dumping measures, state aids, and subsidies and countervailing measures. In the trading system more broadly, the tightening in the Uruguay Round of discipline relating to the use of safeguards has led to fears that anti-dumping would become the trade remedy of choice. This makes the treatment of anti-dumping in PTAs of particular interest.

Competition policy is closely associated with trade remedies insofar as some parties to preferential agreements have agreed to forgo anti-dumping action against each other and rather rely on competition policy to monitor and discipline dumping. Similarly, there is scope for agreement on anti-subsidy rules in the framework of competition policy as an alternative to countervailing duties. It is appropriate to recall, therefore, that there are broadly two approaches to competition policy in preferential trade agreements: those that contain general obligations to take action against anti-competitive business conduct (for example, a requirement to adopt a domestic competition law without setting out the specific provisions the law should contain) and those that call for more explicit coordination of specific competition standards and rules. As a general rule, most of the agreements containing substantive provisions addressing anti-competitive behaviour have been concluded by the European Union. On the other hand, agreements that focus more on general obligations have been concluded in the Americas, or involve a North or South American party (Solano and Sennekamp, 2006).

Comparison of approaches

United States

US agreements tend to have tighter disciplines on the use of safeguard measures (SGMs) than are found in the WTO. Whereas the WTO limits the use of SGMs to 4 years (8–10 years for developing countries), in US agreements the limit ranges from 2 years (US–Singapore, 2003; US–Peru, 2005; US–Oman, 2006) to 3 years (North American Free Trade Agreement, 1994; US–Chile, 2003; US–Morocco, 2006; US–Bahrain, 2006), with no reapplication possible on the same product. The US–Chile agreement also provides that, on the termination of the safeguard, the rate of duty shall not be higher than the rate that would have been in effect one year after the initiation of the measure according to the agreed tariff schedule. US–Peru provides that tariff rate quotas or quantitative restrictions are not considered as permissible safeguard measures.

A number of US agreements also include provisions relating to competition policy (US–Singapore, US–Chile, US–Peru), although it cannot be assumed that this is a precursor to the elimination of anti-dumping action between the signatories. The more recent agreements with Morocco, Bahrain and Oman do not include competition provisions.

In NAFTA, each party reserves the right to apply its anti-dumping law and countervailing duty law to goods imported from the territory of any other party. Article 1904 provides each party with the right to replace judicial review of final anti-dumping or countervailing duty determinations by a bi-national panel review. As to global safeguard action, Article 802 establishes that, when a country that is a party to NAFTA takes a safeguard action, its NAFTA partners shall be excluded from the action, except where their exports of the good in question (a) account for "a substantial share" of imports (among the top five suppliers) and (b) contribute importantly to a serious injury or threat thereof. Articles 1501, 1502 and 1503 state only the importance of cooperation and coordination among competent authorities to further effective competition law enforcement.

NAFTA's subsidies disciplines correspond to those of the WTO, with the exception of export subsidies in the agricultural sector. Members may adopt or maintain an export subsidy for an agricultural product exported to another member where there is an express agreement with the importing country.

European Union

In EU–Mexico, SGMs are limited to one and a maximum of three years, no reapplication is possible on the same product and compensation for

SGMs needs to be offered prior to its adoption. The agreement with Chile states that the WTO Agreement on Safeguards is applicable between the parties but that the provisions apply only when a party has a substantial interest as an exporter of the product concerned (the party must be among the five largest suppliers of the imported product during the most recent three-year period). In EU–Egypt, tariff rate quotas and quantitative restrictions are excluded as permissible safeguard measures.

All the EU agreements examined contain provisions on competition policy, though again without any presumption that this will facilitate the elimination of anti-dumping action among the parties. In the case of the EU–Morocco agreement, a proxy for all the Euro-Mediterranean Partnership (Euro-Med) agreements, explicit reference is made to core EU legislation dealing with competition and state aid. The direct reference to EU law signifies that Morocco will import EU law where it concerns competition or state aid that could touch upon trade with the European Union, in a time-frame of five years after the agreement entered into force.

EFTA

All of the European Free Trade Association (EFTA) agreements examined provide for a limited period for the application of SGMs of one year, with a maximum of three. EFTA–Morocco excludes tariff rate quotas and quantitative restrictions as permissible safeguards. In EFTA–Mexico and EFTA–Singapore, compensation for SGMs needs to be offered prior to its adoption. In EFTA–Korea, no reapplication of SGMs on the same product is possible, and, in EFTA–Chile and EFTA–Singapore, reapplication is not possible for five years. In EFTA–Korea (2006), the parties are to review the bilateral safeguard mechanism to determine whether it is still needed.

All the EFTA agreements examined contain provisions dealing with competition policy, and the three more recent agreements (with Singapore, Chile and Korea) all foresee the abolition of anti-dumping measures between the parties.

Japan

In the Japanese agreements examined, SGMs have a limited duration: one and a maximum of three years in Japan–Singapore; three and a maximum of four years in Japan–Mexico; and four and a maximum of five years in Japan–Malaysia. In the agreements with Malaysia and Singapore, tariff rate quotas and quantitative restrictions are not considered permissible safeguard measures. Japan–Mexico and Japan–Malaysia provide for the phasing-out of SGMs within 10 years, and the parties are allowed 60 days of consultation before the adoption of SGMs, compared with 30 days in the WTO. All three agreements include provisions on competition policy.

Singapore

In Singapore–Korea, SGMs are limited to two years and a maximum of four. In Singapore–Jordan, tariff rate quotas and quantitative restrictions are not permissible safeguards, SGMs may not be reapplied on the same product and the phasing-out of SGMs is envisaged within 15 years.

Both agreements contain provisions on competition policy and more precise criteria for the application of anti-dumping action than are found in the WTO; when anti-dumping margins are established on the weighted average basis, all individual margins, whether positive or negative, should be counted towards the average (Art. 6.2.3(a)). This contrasts with the practice of many countries in the WTO, including the United States, of "zeroing" (i.e. excluding cases where the domestic price is lower than the export price), a practice that has recently been the subject of dispute settlement. On 9 January 2007, the WTO Appellate Body ruled that the US methodology of zeroing for calculating anti-dumping duties, which had been challenged by Japan, was incompatible with multilateral trade rules.

Conclusions on commercial instruments

There are no major differences in the approach of the "core entities" towards the treatment of commercial instruments in PTAs. On the contrary, there is a considerable degree of similarity in approach and a tendency for countries to copy from each other – notably, Japan and Singapore from the United States and EFTA from the European Union. US PTAs show a clear tendency to a blueprint application. The agreements with Oman, Bahrain and Morocco are very similar in their provisions. The same is true of US–Peru and US–Chile. EU–Morocco demonstrates the European Union's ambition to spread its "normative" influence by the way in which competition is treated. This, however, is not a constant tendency in EU agreements. EFTA is distinguished from the other "core entities" by providing for the replacement of anti-dumping action with competition policy. Although Singapore is differentiated by the approach to anti-dumping reform, this is again not a constant tendency.

In this section, the provision that foresees the substitution of anti-dumping action with the application of competition policy has been characterized as WTO-plus, because the generalized application of competition criteria to domestic and import competition is considered to be more consistent and to reduce the scope for the abuse of anti-dumping measures as a form of contingent protection. As such, if PTAs provide a model for the replacement of anti-dumping by general competition rules, they could be seen as building blocks for more objective rules in this field. Here as elsewhere, however, "WTO-plus" does not necessarily mean "better". The practice of partners to a preferential agreement undertaking not to anti-dump one another when they continue to take anti-dumping action against third parties is arguably discriminatory, even though, within the preferential agreement, resort to trade remedies has been disciplined.

The core entities tend to have tighter disciplines on safeguard measures than those found in the WTO, although in the case of Japan the permitted duration of safeguard action appears to be increasing with successive PTAs.

In the case of the EU agreements, the inclusion of an obligation to apply European competition policy has the potential to go beyond existing WTO disciplines on state subsidies. The EU rules on subsidies are similar to those in the WTO Agreement on Subsidies and Countervailing Measures. For example, the criteria for allowing state subsidies in the WTO agreement are more or less the same as the EU provisions, with subsidies permitted when the gross domestic product (GDP) of a particular region is a specified level below the GDP for the country as a whole, or for the promotion of research and environmental policies. But the use of the full EU *acquis communautaire*, including decisions and rulings of the European Court of Justice interpreting these rules, implies a potential for much more effective implementation.

EU agreements provide two examples of asymmetric treatment in favour of the less advanced party. In EU–Egypt, the competition provisions are less stringent for Egypt, with a longer transition period. In EU–Morocco, it is provided that, in the transition period during which state aid is phased out, Morocco will be treated in the same way as those areas of the Community identified as suffering economic hardship. Hence the agreement allows for aid, during the transition period, to promote the economic development of areas where the standard of living is abnormally low. De facto, most state aid in Morocco is therefore deemed compatible with the agreement. There are similar provisions in all the Euro-Med agreements. Notwithstanding these provisions, it cannot be concluded that asymmetric treatment is an unvarying feature of EU agreements; as noted, provisions limiting the use of SGMs are tougher than in the WTO, and, in the agreement with Morocco, that country is required to adopt EU competition policy.

In EFTA–Morocco, under Article 21, Morocco may apply increased customs duties to protect its infant industries or certain sectors undergoing restructuring or facing serious difficulties, particularly where these difficulties produce important social problems. This is similar to the EU agreement and appears to be general for the Euro-Med partners of the European Union and EFTA.

No significant asymmetric provisions relating to trade remedies have been identified in the agreements of the United States, Japan or Singapore.

Provisions in PTAs dealing with trade remedies reflect two potential tendencies (OECD, 2003). On the one hand, border barriers between parties have been reduced below most favoured nation levels, which could give rise to fears of an increased resort to contingency measures. At the same time, the objective of deeper integration may obviate the need for, or lead members to forgo or limit the scope of, contingency measures. On the basis of the present study, the latter trend seems to have prevailed. The agreements examined commonly provide for stricter provisions (limiting the use of contingency measures) than those provided for under the WTO rules.

On the basis of our observations here, two trends might be expected to develop: first, greater resort to competition policy provisions, assuming this remains outside the ambit of the DDA, including, in some cases, to address concerns about dumping; and, second, adoption of an approach to "averaging out" in anti-dumping actions similar to that of Singapore, in light of the Dispute Settlement Mechanism finding in the WTO.

One pointer to possible future trends may come from negotiations between the European Union and Korea. Seoul has asked the European Union, in the framework of the PTA, to ease anti-dumping rules and to reduce countervailing duties (*Bridges*, 11(17), 17 May 2007). This of course will be a pointer only if the European Union responds. A major aim of Canada in NAFTA was to ease administrative protection measures on the part of the United States, but that did not lead anywhere.

Technical barriers to trade and sanitary and phytosanitary measures

The general trend is for all PTAs to include provisions on TBT and SPS and for these to become more comprehensive and sophisticated,[2] although these are WTO-plus only in terms of pushing forward faster with the application of the approach envisaged in the WTO. The TBT and SPS agreements do, however, leave a good deal of scope for divergent approaches. For example, the SPS Agreement is being interpreted by the United States and the European Union rather differently on issues such as the use of precaution. Thus the PTAs, although reaffirming the rights and obligations of parties under the WTO agreements, do reflect rather different views on how these should be interpreted and applied.

This is good in the sense that the WTO rules are broad enough to encompass these variations, but the down-side is that differences in application can, over time, result in divergence. Having said this, the PTAs negotiated by the core entities are complementary to the aims of the WTO in facilitating trade by containing or removing TBTs and by seeking to ensure that SPS measures are not unjustified restrictions to trade.

Technical barriers to trade

Introduction

The WTO TBT Agreement envisages the use of international standards, mutual recognition and equivalence. This reflects a lack of fundamental consensus on how to address TBTs, as is shown in the divergence between, for example, the North American and the European approaches.

This section discusses the various policies of the core entities in some detail.

Comparison of approaches

The United States

The US PTAs include provisions that reaffirm the parties' rights under the TBT agreement (e.g. Art. 903 NAFTA), including therefore the national treatment provisions for technical regulations and conformance assessment. In terms of coverage, US PTAs tend to focus on mandatory regulations at the level of the (federal) government. Voluntary standards-making is seen as something for the market and compliance with TBT rules at sub-central/federal government level is based on best endeavours.

In terms of transparency, US PTAs require the parties to provide prior notification of any new regulatory measure.[3] Because the United States has only a weak central standards-making system in the American National Standards Institute, the range of private standards-making bodies are not bound to such transparency rules (unless they have signed the Code of Conduct of the WTO TBT Agreement). US PTAs provide that (legal) persons should be treated no less favourably than nationals when it comes to consultation in regulatory and standards-making processes. This goes beyond the WTO's TBT requirements and was included in NAFTA and confirmed in the US–Chile and US–Morocco agreements.

In terms of "substantive measures", the US PTAs oblige parties to use international standards (Art. 905 of NAFTA) – again this is unlikely to

Table 3.1 Comparison of TBT provisions

Rule-making elements	WTO TBT	EU	EU–CHILE	NAFTA
Coverage	Central government for technical regulations and conformance assessment Code of conduct only for standards bodies	Central and local government as well as standards organizations	Confirms rights under WTO TBT	WTO compatible
Principles	National treatment and MFN for TRs and CA	Common rules		National treatment
Transparency	Notification to WTO and scope for comments from other parties Information clearing houses Central and first sub-national levels only	Prior notification of TRs and VSs Freezing of national rules while EU rules considered	Reference to transparency but details to be developed	Prior notification Access to national regulatory processes for interested parties
Substantive rules				
• approximation	Use of performance standards "whenever possible"	Harmonization	Menu of options, including promotion of regional and international standards	Harmonization in some sectors; otherwise "compatibility" sought
• recognition	Mutual recognition encouraged	Full mutual recognition	Mutual recognition or "equivalence"	Equivalence; parties to give reasons for not accepting equivalence
Cooperation and technical assistance	TBT Committee and a Standards and Trade Development Facility	Common institutions for TRs, VSs and CA	Special Committee on Technical Regulations, Standards and Conformity Assessment Intensification of bilateral cooperation with details to be determined	Joint Committee promoting technical cooperation
"Regulatory safeguard"	General exemption under Art. XX subject to proportionality test	General exemption under Art. 28 subject to proportionality test	"Necessity and proportionality" tests "Legitimate policy objectives"	"Less trade distorting measures" may be below WTO standard Explicit right to adopt higher standards

Box 3.1 Elements of TBT provisions explained

Coverage

TBT rules at the regional and multilateral levels typically cover all sectors with regard to principles such as non-discrimination or the application of transparency rules. But sector-specific measures are often found when it comes to substantive rule-making such as harmonization or mutual recognition. For example, there are sector-specific harmonization provisions in NAFTA, and the European Union and mutual recognition agreements are nearly all limited to specific sectors (with the exception of internal EU mutual recognition). GATT rules apply only to central government, with "best endeavours" provisions for sub-central government. PTAs that reach down beyond the level of central government to require binding rules at the sub-central government level will therefore go beyond the WTO. The GATT 1994 Agreement on Technical Barriers to Trade includes only a voluntary code of conduct for standards-making bodies. PTAs therefore go beyond the WTO if they include binding rules for standards-making bodies and/or more comprehensive rules for conformance assessment.

Principles

Rules requiring non-discrimination in the application of technical regulations (TRs) or conformance assessment (CA) have existed in the GATT for many years and feature in all PTAs. PTAs that require *national treatment* in TRs and CA are therefore unlikely to go beyond the WTO rules. But facially non-discriminatory TRs can still constitute a de facto barrier to market access. Rule-making may attempt to address this problem by requiring the use of other principles such as *"least (or less) trade distorting provisions"*. Some rules may offer a definition of least trade distorting, for example the TBT Agreement in the Uruguay Round defines "least trade distorting" as equivalent to measures that satisfy "legitimate objectives" (which tends to shift the debate onto what is a legitimate objective).

Transparency

TBT provisions typically require *notification* of technical regulations, conformance assessment procedures and/or voluntary standards (VSs). One test of the stringency of transparency rules is whether they require *prior notification* and whether potential suppliers have an opportunity to make *submissions or comment on the rules*. Some agreements may also contain obligations on the regulator or standards-making

Box 3.1 (cont.)

body to give a *reasoned response* to such submissions. For example, a regulator may be required to explain why it has not made use of existing international standards when it specified a national standard. Rules may give foreign suppliers *equal right of access* to regulatory procedures. Finally, notification of proposed rules may provide for cessation of work on national rules until regional or international initiatives have been explored, such as in the European Union and the Trans-Tasman Mutual Recognition Agreement.

Substantive provisions

Most OECD countries have adopted the view that *national treatment* is insufficient in addressing TBTs, because of the scope for de facto discrimination in TR, VS and CA (OECD, 1997: Chapter 6). TBT rules involving developed economies therefore tend to include substantive rules such as *approximation* of TRs, CA or VSs as a *general aim*, *selective harmonization* (for key sectors), *harmonization of essential requirements* (as in the European Union) or *full harmonization*. Because of the difficulties and potential costs of harmonization, there has been a move to include *recognition* or *equivalence* as a means of facilitating market access while leaving national regulatory entities with some regulatory autonomy. Recognition generally takes the form of mutual recognition of test results. Only in exceptional cases do rules provide for full mutual recognition, which means that the countries concerned in effect recognize each other's regulatory regimes as equivalent. The use of equivalence in TBT rules is rather different. Equivalence, for example in the context of NAFTA, is a generalized aspiration. In the NAFTA application there are no implementing provisions, so national regulatory bodies in effect retain regulatory autonomy. The principle is the same as for mutual recognition, but implementation is entirely up to the political will of the parties, subject to any reviews or remedies available under the relevant dispute settlement provisions.

Cooperation

Agreements on TBTs typically include provisions on cooperation, such as *committees on TBTs* to promote the development of common technical regulations, standards and conformance assessment and may provide for *financial and technical cooperation*. For example, the WTO has established the Standards and Trade Development Facility for this purpose. Agreements may also provide for *exchanges* or

Box 3.1 (cont.)

twinning of regulators, standards bodies or conformance assessment agencies, to promote common norms or mutual recognition.

Regulatory safeguards

Just as there are safeguards in the field of tariff reductions, so there are with respect to regulatory measures. In the area of TBTs, the regulatory safeguard takes the form of exceptions to protect *human, animal or plant life*. At the multilateral level, Article XX (b) of the GATT 1994 provides for such an exception, and equivalent provisions exist in all regional agreements. The danger with such exceptions is that they may be abused to provide covert protectionism. Rules are therefore also likely to include some form of *proportionality principle* to ensure this discretion is not abused. As for all "regulatory safeguard" measures, how these provisions are interpreted will be important. TBT rules may also provide a right to maintain *higher standards* (than the internationally or regionally agreed standard). This is the case in both the European Union and NAFTA and can be considered to be a regulatory safeguard. An important issue here is whether the rules leave the *burden of proof* of the need for higher standards with the exporter or the importing regulator.

Interpretation and enforcement

The interpretation will shape the scope of rules. The GATT rules are relatively loose and as a result fewer TBT cases have been brought under dispute settlement than, for example, in the European Union, which has very strict and expansive rules. The European Court of Justice's interpretation of Article 28 of the Treaty on European Union (formerly Art. 30, EEC) goes well beyond the GATT in arguing that *all* national regulatory measures may be potential barriers to trade (Case 8/74, *Procureur du Roi* v *Dassonville*, European Court Reports 837, 11 July 1974). Access to dispute settlement, reviews and remedies is crucial, because new regulations and standards are being generated all the time. Agreements may therefore provide for *review* of the regulatory decisions and *remedies* in cases of non-compliance. To enhance implementation and enforcement, agreements may include *specific dispute settlement* or *central enforcement* through official bodies or facilitate the use of private actions through the courts through *product liability laws*.

apply to private standards bodies – but, like the WTO TBT text, NAFTA provides considerable scope not to adopt such standards if these are seen to be ineffective or inappropriate. Given the general antipathy towards agreed international standards on the part of the United States, such measures cannot be expected to result in much pressure for more effective international standards.

The United States emphasizes what might be called an "organic" approach to TBTs. The aim is for exports from one party to be treated as *equivalent* by the competent bodies in the importing country (Art. 906.4 of NAFTA for example). The competent body in the importing country retains discretion to reject equivalence, but must then explain why. The approach to conformance assessment (Art. 906.6 of NAFTA) also applies the same approach. This approach is organic in that the expectation is that equivalence will be achieved through the general application of best practice and dialogue without significant institutional provisions. The United States expects its PTA partners to follow a similar approach, as illustrated by the US–Chile and US–Singapore agreements. As a result, Chile and Singapore have included the option of equivalence in their other agreements, such as the Trans-Pacific Strategic Economic Partnership Agreement (TPSEPA) of November 2006.[4]

Taking a broader view, the United States does not preclude mutual recognition or regional harmonization of standards. It has been supportive of the mutual recognition framework in Asia-Pacific Economic Cooperation (APEC), which has resulted in a number of sector agreements, and NAFTA set up a number of sector standardization committees. Equally, the United States, or the relevant professional bodies in the United States, has signed a range of mutual recognition agreements (MRAs) in specific sectors, including six with the European Union (although only three were implemented) and MRAs on wine with Chile, Australia and New Zealand (Agreement on Mutual Acceptance of Oenological Practices, 2003).

The US PTAs include provision for cooperation, technical assistance and information exchange on TBT issues. As with the other core entities, this benefits the less developed partner, but also provides a means of promoting one's own standards. The United States generally spends less on such support than the European Union or Japan (only US$3.4 million between 2001 and 2005 compared with US$29.0 million for the European Union and US$9.6 million for Japan).[5] Generally speaking, the US PTAs have weaker bilateral institutional machinery for cooperation than the European Union or other core entities. In recent PTAs there has been a shift towards establishing "TBT coordinators" (e.g. US–Morocco, Art. 7.7 and Annex 7a, and the same articles in US–Bahrain) in each of the parties to deal with disputes, rather than establishing Joint Committees.

This reflects a preference for a lighter institutional framework compared with the European Union for example, which generally establishes a specific Joint Committee for TBT (and SPS) in addition to any general Association Council.

The European Union

Whereas the internal EU regime for TBT covers all levels of government, its PTAs tend to be equivalent with WTO coverage and thus limited to central government. The EU PTAs also reaffirm rights and obligations under the TBT Agreement. In terms of transparency, the EU PTAs are consistent with the TBT Agreement.

On substantive measures, the European Union has been rather unambitious in its PTAs compared with the comprehensive approach to TBTs adopted within the European Union itself. In PTAs with its near neighbours in North Africa the European Union has been content with a general objective of harmonization to the European standards and practice. This is set out in a short statement of aims that will require considerable time and effort to achieve (Art. 40 of EU–Morocco, 1996). When the circumstances are right this would lead to mutual recognition agreements (Art. 40(2), EU–Morocco). The European Union is seeking to negotiate a recognition agreement with Morocco for industrial products (in the first instance electrical goods, machinery and construction equipment). Given the level of development of such countries, it will be some time before circumstances are right for extensive MRAs.

More surprising perhaps is the relative weakness of the TBT provisions in the EU–Chile agreement, which is in other respects seen to be a "model" for future EU PTAs. This agreement offers little more than a menu of various possible approaches, including the promotion of regional and international standards, mutual recognition and equivalence (Art. 87, EU–Chile). The general lack of provisions in the PTA did not, however, stop the European Union negotiating a mutual recognition agreement with Chile on wines in 2003.

The European Union promotes technical cooperation in the field of TBT issues. Indeed, the impact of PTAs in the field of TBTs will largely depend on how the various special Joint Committees that are established work. For example, the Special Committee on Technical Regulations, Standards and Conformity Assessment set up with Chile (Art. 88) has the task of developing a work programme for the TBT field. With the Association of Southeast Asian Nations (ASEAN) the European Union has negotiated the Trans-Regional EU–ASEAN Trade Initiative (TREATI), which has as one of its central features cooperation in the development of TBT and SPS measures.

In more recent PTAs, including those under negotiation with ASEAN and India, the European Union appears to be moving away from any attempt to "export" the EU approach to TBTs in the form of mutual recognition. A general disenchantment with mutual recognition agreements has set in owing to the complexity and difficulty of negotiating with partners that do not share the same institutional structure as the European Union. The European Union therefore appears to be moving more towards the promotion of international standards as a means of facilitating the reduction of TBTs, especially in PTAs with developing countries.

The Economic Partnership Agreement (EPA) negotiated with the Caribbean Forum of African, Caribbean and Pacific States (CARIFORUM) in December 2007, the only comprehensive EPA negotiated by the European Union at that time, focuses on transparency and cooperation. Article 49 of the agreement sets out how the parties are to inform the other party of new technical regulations, standards or conformance assessment measures. Article 50 provides fairly detailed measures for technical cooperation and exchange of expertise. There is no reference to mutual recognition.

Finally, the EU approach to enforcement has been to use the Joint Committees for TBT measures for consultation and conciliation.

EFTA

The EFTA approach to TBTs has been very similar to that of the European Union. This is not surprising because the EFTA parties are also members of CEN (the European Committee for Standardization) and CENELEC (the European Committee for Electrotechnical Standardization), and have to a very large extent adopted the EU *acquis* in this field, through either the European Economic Area or bilateral agreements in the case of Switzerland. Like the European Union, the EFTA agreements reaffirm the rights and obligations under the TBT Agreement (e.g. Art. 2.8 of EFTA–Korea). The more developed status of Korea provided scope for the specific aims of promoting mutual recognition of products tested by conformance assessment bodies that have been accredited in accordance with the relevant guidelines of the International Organization for Standardization and the International Electrotechnical Commission.

Japan

The Japan–Malaysia PTA illustrates the Japanese approach to TBT provisions in its preferential agreements. Again this reaffirms the rights and obligations of the parties under the existing WTO TBT Agreement (Articles 59–67). There then follow a number of options for dealing with TBTs, including the use of equivalence, harmonization and/or mutual recognition. Equivalence as applied here is very similar to the US usage, with importing regulators obliged to explain when they do not accept equivalence. Mutual recognition is a general aim, with either party able to initiate negotiation of specific (sector by sector) mutual recognition agreements. A subcommittee is established to promote the application of the TBT provisions and the various forms of cooperation envisaged, which include exchanges of experts, promotion of strengthened capacity in certification and testing. The Japan–Malaysia agreement, like other Japanese PTAs, excludes TBT provisions from the bilateral dispute settlement provisions.

Singapore

All the PTAs concluded by Singapore include provisions on TBT, with the exception of Singapore–Jordan. Singapore is also actively engaged in TBT work in ASEAN, APEC and TREATI. In almost all respects the Singaporean domestic institutional capacity in terms of standards-making, certification, accreditation and the ability to negotiate TBT provisions matches that of the countries of the Organisation for Economic Co-operation and Development (OECD). As with the other core entities, Singapore's PTAs reaffirm TBT rules and generally provide transparency measures that contribute to the effective application of the WTO rules on transparency.

On substance, Singaporean PTAs, as well as Singapore's engagement in ASEAN, cover the whole range of policy options. For example, ASEAN and the bilateral agreements with New Zealand and Korea all stress the need for the use of harmonized international standards. Within the ASEAN Free Trade Area, Singapore is involved in an approach that focuses on harmonization of essential safety requirements. It is initially covering electrical equipment, cosmetics, pharmaceutical products and foods and essentially emulates the EU approach. Within APEC, Singapore is involved in negotiating MRAs, and has even negotiated one MRA with India. In its PTA with Korea, Singapore has negotiated provisions on regulations, verification and monitoring of conformance assessment that represent a fairly centralized approach, which is again similar to the European approach. On the other hand, the PTA with the United States adopts the more organic approach based on equivalence.

In terms of cooperation, Singapore, with its strong domestic capacity, provides technical assistance to the more developing members of ASEAN through the ASEAN Consultative Committee on Standards and Quality and is active in APEC. Enforcement of the TBT provisions tends to be through dedicated bilateral committees. In the case of ASEAN these exist at a sector level. In the PTA with the United States there is no separate committee for TBT but a "coordinator" in each party to resolve disputes, following the US approach. In short, Singapore appears to be able and willing to gear the structure of its TBT provisions to the desires and requirements of its PTA partners.

Sanitary and phytosanitary measures

Introduction

The approach to sanitary and phytosanitary measures in PTAs is broadly similar to that adopted in the TBT provisions of such agreements. For the most part, the PTAs refer to the existing WTO SPS Agreement of 1994 and reaffirm the rights and obligations of the parties under this agreement. The 1994 SPS Agreement constitutes an attempt to strike a balance between the right to protect human, animal and plant health on the one hand, and a desire to facilitate trade in food and animal and plant products on the other. Thus the SPS Agreement grants rights to take action to protect health and food safety but only when these are necessary and when the measures are supported by scientific evidence (Art. 5.7). Precautionary measures are possible when the scientific evidence is not available, but only on a temporary basis until the parties can gather the requisite scientific evidence. Under the SPS Agreement there is a presumption that risk assessment and risk management should be science based.

In recent years, public opinion in some regions, and in particular within Europe, has shifted against a purely science-based approach following the failures of science-based regulation in the BSE (mad cow) case and various other cases. This has led to pressure for the use of the precautionary principle in the application of SPS measures and other regulation.

Comparison of approaches

The United States

NAFTA was finalized one year before the SPS Agreement and does not therefore refer to it. In fact, the WTO SPS Agreement is said to be more stringent than Chapter 7 of NAFTA. However, the SPS provisions in both the WTO and NAFTA are generally similar. In all SPS (and TBT) provisions, NAFTA transparency measures require the parties to notify any new or revised regulation 60 days in advance and to provide an opportunity for the parties to comment on such regulations (Arts 718 and 719). To facilitate trade, countries are encouraged to use relevant international standards and work towards harmonization – that is, the adoption of common SPS measures. To promote harmonization, the agreements cite, as sources of scientific expertise and globally recognized standards, international bodies such as the Codex Alimentarius Commission, which deals with food safety issues; the World Organisation for Animal Health (OIE), for animal health and diseases; and the International Plant Protection Convention (IPPC), for plant health. However, Article 713(2) states that a measure that "results in a level of SPS protection different from that which would be achieved by a measure based on a relevant international standard, guideline or recommendation shall not for that reason alone be presumed to be inconsistent with this section."

The requirement to use agreed international standards is further weakened by provisions that allow each country to decide its own "appropriate level of protection" of human, animal, or plant life or health. Such measures – which can be more stringent than other countries' and differ from international benchmarks – are acceptable as long as they are based on scientific principles and risk assessment, applied consistently to all countries, and not used as disguised trade barriers. This provides for considerable national policy autonomy, but is firmly based on scientific risk assessment.

To reconcile these two potentially divergent aspects, NAFTA, like the SPS Agreement, stresses the benefit of equivalence (Art. 714). In other words, parties are to recognize the other's products as equivalent to their standards. NAFTA therefore set a precedent for the SPS Agreement in its use of equivalence, but there is not much detail on how this should work in practice. Nor does SPS appear to be a priority issue included in the US "gold standard" for PTAs (see Table 3.2).

NAFTA supports the principle of regionalization; in other words, the differentiation between regions in the exporting country so that any restrictions on exports from the country can be limited to the affected region, thus mitigating the effects of any health controls on trade.

Finally, NAFTA established a specific Committee on Sanitary and Phytosanitary Measures to oversee the implementation of the agreement and subsequent cooperation.

The US agreements with developing countries such as Morocco and Bahrain do not have extensive SPS rules. The US–Morocco Agreement provides for a Joint Committee on SPS measures, but apart from this is content to reiterate the parties' rights and obligations under the WTO SPS Agreement.

European Union

The European Union's provisions on SPS fall into three broad categories. There are the agreements with near neighbours and potential accession states, which take over the entire *acquis communautaire* and thus in

Table 3.2 Provisions concerning SPS measures within PTAs

Agreement	Harmonization	Equivalence	Mutual recognition	Technical cooperation/ assistance
APEC	N/A	N/A	Yes	Yes
ASEAN–China	NP	NP	NP	Further negotiations
Canada–Chile	NP	NP	NP	NP
EU–SA	Yes	NP	NP	Yes
EU–Tunisia	Yes	NP	Yes	Yes
EFTA–Turkey	NP	NP	NP	NP
NAFTA	No	Yes	No	Yes
EU	Yes	Yes	NP	Yes
Japan–Singapore	NP	NP	NP	NP
US–Chile	No	NP	NP	Institutional
US–Australia	No	NP	NP	Institutional
EU–Mexico	NP	Yes	NP	Yes
US–Morocco	NP	NP	NP	Yes (non-committal and mild)
US–Bahrain	NP	NP	NP	NP
Japan–Mexico	NP	NP	NP	Yes
Japan–Malaysia	NP	NP	NP	Yes
Singapore–Korea	NP	NP	NP	NP
Singapore–Jordan	NP	NP	NP	NP

Source: authors based on the texts of the agreements.
Notes: Institutional – signifies the establishment of a committee or institution dedicated to SPS matters; NP – no provision found.

effect assume the same rules as the European Union. For countries such as Turkey or potential accession states in the Balkans, the agreements with the European Union assume the progressive adoption of EU rules and standards for all issues, including SPS.

A second group of countries includes the Euro-Med partners, with which the PTAs tend simply to restate the parties' obligations under the WTO SPS Agreement and set out a general objective of promoting the approximation or harmonization of SPS standards, but without any specific binding obligations or details of how this should be achieved. The aim of harmonization of SPS standards is included in Article 46 of the EU–Israel agreement; Article 51f of EU–Lebanon; Article 58 of EU–Algeria; and Article 40 of EU–Morocco. All the EU bilateral agreements include provisions on cooperation in a wide range of policy areas and generally include SPS policy and standards as an area for cooperation and technical assistance (for example, Article 71 of the EU–Jordan agreement). In the case of EU–Israel, the more developed national procedures in Israel mean there has been scope for rather more cooperation. PTAs with developing countries, such as the African, Caribbean and Pacific (ACP) Group of States, are likely to take a similar form. Here there has been an evolution of EU policy over time. The Trade, Development and Cooperation Agreement (TDCA) with South Africa simply included general references to the desire to cooperate in the SPS field to promote a harmonization of SPS standards and rules in conformance with existing WTO obligations (Art. 61, TDCA). The Economic Partnership Agreement (EPA) negotiated with CARIFORUM in December 2007 includes somewhat more developed provisions. This restates the commitment to existing WTO rules as well as to the relevant international standards emanating from the Codex Alimentarius, OIE and IPPC. There are cooperation provisions, including exchange of expertise, as in the TBT section of the EPA (Art. 59), and the European Union undertakes to help the CARIFORUM parties comply with EU SPS rules. But on policy approximation or harmonization the agreement simply refers to an agreement to "consult with the aim of achieving bilateral arrangements on recognition of equivalence" (Art. 56).

The third category of PTAs is with major emerging markets or developed markets outside of Europe, such as the agreements with Mexico and Chile and the potential agreements with ASEAN, India and Korea. The agreements negotiated with Mexico and especially Chile include some WTO-plus provisions in the SPS field, especially with regard to process. Table 3.3 sets out these in a simple tabular form.

The most important SPS provisions in the EU–Mexico agreement can be found in Article 20 of the supplement to the agreement, resulting from a decision of the EU/Mexico Joint Council 2/2000 of March 2000. This reaffirms the SPS Agreement but establishes a WTO-plus Special Committee on SPS matters to progressively develop cooperation in the SPS field. The pace with which more developed procedural measures are introduced in Mexico will therefore be dependent on the work of this Special Committee. It is possible that more advanced provisions for Chile (see below) will provide a precedent for the European Union's approach to this work.

In general terms, the EU–Chile PTA is seen as a model for future EU agreements. The SPS provisions in the agreement are also the most developed and are therefore likely to provide a precedent for future PTAs. The *aims* of the EU–Chile SPS agreement are set out in Article 89 (2) of the PTA. Details are, however, included in Annex IV to the agreement. A special Joint Management Committee is established to develop work on SPS measures. There are also 12 appendices detailing specific procedures and definitions with a view to:

Table 3.3 SPS provisions in existing EU PTAs

	Euro-Med	TDCA	EPA	EU–Mexico	EU–Chile
WTO-consistent rules					
Reaffirmation of WTO SPS obligations	Yes	Yes	Yes	Yes	Yes
General cooperation in SPS	Yes	Yes	Yes	Yes	Yes
Harmonization of SPS standards as an objective	Yes	Yes	Yes	Yes	Yes
General exception possible similar to GATT Art. XX	Yes	Yes	Yes	Yes	Yes
Provision for specific technical assistance in the SPS field			Yes		Yes
Procedural WTO-plus measures					
Establishment of a Joint Committee on SPS				Yes	Yes
Detailed rules for determining equivalence					Yes
Guidelines for conducting verifications, checking imports and certification of testing					Yes
Schedules for reporting and consultation					Yes
Specific rules on import administration					Yes
Requirement to exchange information			Yes		Yes
Provisional approval of certain establishments					Yes

Source: compiled by the authors on the basis of texts of the various agreements.

- ensuring full transparency of SPS provisions (to enable each party to comply with the detailed SPS rules and procedures);
- establishing the mechanism for recognizing equivalence (Arts 6 and 7 of Annex IV) (which would enable the importing party to recognize animal and plant products as satisfying the importing party's rules);
- applying the principle of regionalization (Art. 6b of Annex IV) (which allows exporting parties to show that specified regions are free of pests and thus facilitate trade);
- promoting the application of the WTO SPS Agreement;
- facilitating trade (such as through building confidence on verification and control applying FAO standards) (Art. 10 of Annex IV) and;
- improving cooperation and consultation.

The EU–Chile agreement does not appear to cover genetically modified crops (owing to the sensitivity of this issue). On the other hand, there is no specific reference to science-based approaches. One innovation, however, is the inclusion of a specific reference to animal welfare standards in Article 1 of Annex IV, with the aim of "developing common approaches to the treatment of animals and compliance with OIE standards falling within the scope of this Agreement".

EFTA

EFTA has relied on reiterating the rights and obligations of the parties under the WTO SPS Agreement. This is done through a single article (EFTA–Mexico FTA Art. 9; EFTA–Korea FTA, Art. 2.7). However, each agreement goes nominally beyond the WTO by stipulating that the parties shall exchange names and addresses of contact points with SPS expertise in order to facilitate technical consultations and the exchange of information.

Japan

The SPS measures in Japan–Mexico reflect those typically incorporated within Japanese PTAs (Section 2, Arts 12–15). These include explicit reference to the reaffirmation of rights and obligations under the WTO SPS Agreement, enquiry points, institutional cooperation via a subcommittee, and *non*-application of dispute settlement procedures. On this later point the SPS approach is the same as for TBT provisions.

A subcommittee on SPS measures is established with the mandate to ensure, *inter alia*, information exchange, notification, science-based consultation to identify and address specific issues that may arise from the application of SPS measures with the objective of obtaining mutually acceptable solutions, technical cooperation and cooperation in international forums. The subcommittee may, if necessary, establish ad hoc technical advisory groups to provide technical information and advice on specific issues.

The wording of the Japan–Malaysia PTA (Chapter 6, Arts 68–72) is identical to that of the Japan–Mexico PTA, with the one important addition of technical assistance. Here it states that both parties, through the subcommittee, shall cooperate in the areas of SPS measures, including capacity-building, technical assistance and exchange of experts, subject to the availability of appropriated funds and the applicable laws and regulations of each country.

Singapore

According to Chapter 7, Article 7.1 (SPS Measures), of the Singapore–Korea PTA, both parties reaffirm their rights and obligations under the WTO SPS Agreement. Other than reiterating provisions found in the WTO SPS Agreement, such as non-discrimination and the use of scientific principles, this agreement provides for consultation and exchange of information between the parties on SPS matters and obliges the parties to respond to queries on SPS matters within a reasonable time. Enquiry points are also established.

There is nothing in the Singapore–Jordan PTA on SPS measures.

Conclusions on TBT and SPS

At first glance, the approaches of the "core entities" to TBT/SPS measures in PTAs appear to be very similar, namely the use of the existing WTO approach through reference to the WTO agreements.[6] The WTO agreements provide a menu of options. They urge the use of agreed international standards, while at the same time providing an opt-out for parties that do not wish to be tied to such standards. In the case of the NAFTA approach, there is an explicit opt-out. In the case of the European Union, it is more a question of the interpretation of precaution – taking the EU approach would provide considerable scope to opt out. The WTO SPS rules also encourage the use of mutual recognition (of test results) for TBT and the use of "equivalence" in the field of SPS.

Much turns on how the WTO-plus procedural measures, discussed below, are used to apply these different principles. Virtually all the PTAs considered reaffirm conformance with the WTO rules. This is consistent with findings of other studies.[7] But there are clearly differences between the core entities on which of the various options available under the WTO rules is the preferred approach. The European Union and EFTA tend to use a comprehensive approach to addressing TBT and SPS. The texts of the provisions are more extensive in an effort to ensure that essential safety rules are really equivalent. This can then facilitate recognition of test results, trade and market access. The European Union and also, to a very large extent, EFTA place rather more emphasis on the use of agreed international standards, with centralized systems of accreditation for conformance assistance in order to facilitate mutual recognition (of conformance assessment) and relatively elaborate institutional arrangements to promote cooperation and deal with disputes.

The US approach, as reflected in its PTAs, places less emphasis on – and devotes fewer resources to – agreed international standards and prefers a less detailed approach that envisages a kind of organic emergence of compatibility or equivalence. The United States stresses the more general use of equivalence (unilateral recognition rather than mutual agreements), with safeguards to inhibit the use of the discretion to not recognize equivalence. For example, regulators must give reasons if they refuse to recognize equivalence. Rather than sophisticated institutional rules, the United States emphasizes the rights of legal persons from PTA partners to be involved in national standards-setting or regulatory processes and the use of individual "coordinators" to deal with disputes rather than committees.

Compared with the United States, Japan and Singapore tend to be more supportive of agreed international standards, and some of the PTAs they have negotiated, such as Singapore–Korea and the TPSEPA, suggest a more comprehensive approach to TBT and SPS measures. Japan and Singapore, however, appear to follow a pragmatic line of offering a range of options in their PTAs. Again, it is a question of emphasis here between the more institutional approach of the Europeans and the more organic approach envisaged by the Americans. Japan tends to be rather closer to the US approach, in that its PTAs adopt the equivalence concept, with competent bodies in the importing country being required to state why they have not accepted equivalence. But both Japan and Singapore have sophisticated and centralized domestic systems that can promote agreed international standards and verification and monitoring of conformance assessment. In the case of Singapore's PTAs, the level of sophistication varies with the level of development of the partner country, but is also in part the result of a pragmatic desire to offer its PTA partners the option of the institutional or the organic approach.[8]

In the texts of the PTAs there is little evidence of the difference between North America and other agricultural exporting countries and the Europeans over risk assessment in agricultural bio-technology. All the PTAs commit the parties to the WTO SPS Agreement, which is rather more science based than the European Union would like. The European Union has not pressed for – or not been able to get – explicit reference to the precautionary principle in its PTAs. Its PTA partners, such as Mexico and Chile, would be unlikely to agree to this given that they are being asked to adopt a rigorously science-based approach in their agreements with the United States. The EPA agreement with CARIFORUM also says nothing on the matter of precaution, so that one must assume that it is the WTO text (in Article 5 of the SPS Agreement) that is relevant. The divergence between Europe and the United States on this issue may, however, emerge over time if the respective EU and US PTAs diverge in how they implement the SPS rules.

The TBT and SPS provisions of the PTAs studied are not significantly WTO-plus. In almost all cases the PTAs reaffirm the existing WTO obligations under the TBT and SPS agreements negotiated during the Uruguay Round. Although remaining within the letter – and in most cases the spirit – of the WTO agreements, many of the PTAs elaborate on the TBT and SPS provisions, such as in the area of more explicit transparency provisions and more detail on how principles set out in the WTO agreements, such as mutual recognition, equivalence and harmonization of international standards, should be applied. This is also the case with regard to the cooperation measures in the various PTAs, which are often more extensive than is possible within the WTO. There are also bilateral or regional institutions established that promote cooperation and implementation and provide a venue for conciliation and dispute settlement.

The WTO-plus nature of some the PTAs negotiated by the core entities rests therefore in how various principles and instruments are applied. One could argue that the WTO agreements offer a menu of possible approaches for dealing with TBT/SPS issues because there is no agreement between the main protagonists on what the rules should be.

The WTO-plus nature of procedural rules in the PTAs is illustrated, for example, in the Annex IV provisions of the EU–Chile PTA. This provides a detailed text on how equivalence, regionalization, etc. should be implemented in practice. This and other PTAs are therefore within the letter of the WTO text but hold out the promise of more effective implementation of the principles. Much the same can be said of the use of mutual recognition in TBT. This is envisaged in the WTO TBT Agreement, so promoting mutual recognition (of conformance assessment) is within the letter of the WTO rules. But mutual recognition agreements are clearly WTO-plus (though not necessarily "better") in that they provide preferential benefits for parties signing up to them that are not available to general WTO members.

Another area in which the PTAs go beyond the WTO in TBT/SPS is in the establishment of specialist Joint Committees to oversee the implementation and application of the agreements. The establishment of specialist committees is widely used for SPS but rather less than complete for TBT. These specialist committees have the job of promoting the implementation of the principles and instruments envisaged in the agreements, but they also promote cooperation and provide a forum for addressing disputes. It is noteworthy that there have been very few WTO dispute settlement cases in TBT/SPS between signatories to PTAs. In the case of North–South PTAs, where the agreements are generally much less detailed, Joint Committees provide a channel for cooperation and the provision of technical assistance.

Asymmetry measures in the TBT and SPS field take the form of technical cooperation and assistance. The trend towards more sophisticated provisions implies greater capacity and compliance costs for developing countries. The core entities considered therefore all provide technical assistance, including financial support and exchange of expertise to help developing country PTA partners meet the requirements in terms of compliance with standards and technical regulation, testing and certification. The analysis of the PTAs covered in this study did not find any cases of the acceptance of lower standards being incorporated into the PTAs themselves.

The policy approaches to TBT/SPS of the core entities have clearly been shaped by their domestic policies and institutional capacities. This largely explains the more comprehensive EU and EFTA approaches and the more skeletal US approach. Japan and Singapore also have well-developed, centralized institutions dealing with TBT/SPS issues and have therefore been ready to negotiate fairly comprehensive agreements. In terms of the impact of PTAs on domestic policies, the obligations in the PTAs tend to commit the parties to more intensive cooperation than the WTO agreements do. In this sense they are more constraining on domestic policy autonomy. At the same time, the PTA provisions on TBT/SPS tend to be more soft law than binding hard law.

The link between domestic policy and PTAs goes both ways. On the one hand, consumer pressure for higher standards of, in particular, food safety has been a major factor driving the greater sophistication of TBT and SPS agreements. On the other hand, PTAs have probably contributed to the development of greater sophistication and better regulatory practices at the national level. This occurs as countries recognize the need for more domestic capacity in standards and conformance assessment in order to ensure access to export markets. The technical assistance measures offered by PTAs have also directly contributed to increase capacity.

The trend in treatment of TBT/SPS issues in PTAs suggests that these will remain an important element in trade relations and that PTAs will include more comprehensive provisions to deal with such non-tariff barriers. The WTO-plus provisions are, however, likely to be in terms of procedural measures and efforts to intensify transparency and cooperation between the parties to the PTA. Much turns on how such measures are used. Will they be used to "sell" the regulatory and voluntary standards of the "core entity" and, if so, will this lead to divergence between the various approaches? Or will the closer cooperation be used to implement the WTO rules more effectively and adopt agreed international standards? As most of the PTAs have not been established long, it is not yet possible to come to any firm view on these questions. The key thing to monitor will be how the various specialist Joint Committees established in PTAs are used.

Public procurement

Introduction

When considering the provisions on public procurement in the PTAs negotiated by the core entities it is helpful to distinguish between the *framework* agreements and the schedules specifying *coverage*. In most cases, the PTAs use the plurilateral Agreement on Government Procurement (GPA) of 1994 for framework rules. This means that the provisions in the PTAs on transparency of public procurement (laws and individual contracts); contract award procedures (open, selective and negotiated); selection criteria (lowest costs or the economically most advantageous bids); and compliance (bid challenge) are as set out in the GPA. The widespread use of the GPA as the framework means that there is a very large measure of consistency across all the core entities. Box 3.2 summarizes the elements of provisions on government procurement in trade agreements.

The second element of all procurement provisions is the *coverage*. This is set out in schedules of purchasing entities covered by the various agreements in category I (central government), category II (sub-central government) and category III (public enterprises and other purchasing entities). Here one finds a variation across the core entities in their PTAs, depending largely on the PTA partner and (as in the case of the GPA schedules) determined by reciprocity calculations. Coverage is also determined by the thresholds for coverage set to capture the most economically significant public contracts while minimizing the compliance costs for all purchasing entities. Broadly speaking, the thresholds are the same as those used in the GPA. In short, the main variation across the PTAs and core entities lies in the coverage of purchasing entities. Here there are some important differences that may be critical in specific sectors.

Box 3.2 Typical elements of provisions on public procurement

Coverage

Rules may cover procurement of supplies (goods), works (construction) and services. Coverage can extend to central government (on average one-third of all public procurement), sub-central government (roughly one-third) and public enterprise or parastatal organizations (roughly one-third). Coverage is also determined by thresholds designed to ensure that the most valuable contracts are open to competition, while avoiding the significant compliance costs of dealing with lots of smaller contracts.

National treatment

Public procurement was excluded from the GATT Art. III national treatment and most favoured nation provisions in 1947, and there remains no agreement to change this at a multilateral level. National treatment obligations in plurilateral or preferential agreements prohibit formal or *de jure* preferences for specific categories of suppliers unless there are explicit exemptions.

Transparency

Central to the aim of facilitating increased competition, more efficient purchasing and reduced scope for corruption in public procurement is the provision of information. This can encompass the statutory rules and implementing regulation as well as information on specific calls for tender and technical specifications. It can also include post-contract-award transparency, in which purchasing entities are obliged to explain contract decisions and/or provide statistics and reports. Without knowledge of contract award procedures or individual calls for tender, there can be no competitive tendering. Without information on decisions taken, there is unlikely to be effective monitoring and implementation of the procedures.

Contract award procedures

In order to ensure flexibility, procurement rules tend to provide for open, selective, limited and negotiated tendering. Open tendering is generally used for standard products and is based on price. Selective tendering is used when the purchasing entity wishes to ensure that suppliers are qualified (both technically and financially) to complete the contract successfully. This requires open and transparent procedures and criteria for the selection of suppliers. Limited tendering is

Box 3.2 (cont.)

when the purchasing entity invites specific suppliers to bid. Negotiated tenders involve negotiation between the purchaser and supplier over the terms of the contract. Contract award procedures can have more or less detailed rules on how calls for tender are made and what information is provided, and what time limits are set for bidding and for awarding contracts. Short time limits may put foreign bidders at a disadvantage, whereas long time limits may be detrimental to the service provided by the procuring entity.

Technical specifications

By specifying standards, a procuring entity can prefer certain suppliers over others. Rules on procurement therefore tend to require the use of performance standards in place of specific or "design" standards. Performance standards set out how the equipment or system should perform, not the details of its components or dimensions, and are thus less restrictive. Rules may also require the use of agreed international, regional or national standards rather than firm-specific standards, which can mean a de facto preference for the (national) firm that produces to that standard.

Technical cooperation

Technical cooperation can cover assistance with drafting laws or procedures, training officials or exchanges of experience. All agreements on procurement include some form of technical cooperation.

Special and differential treatment

Special and differential treatment in the case of procurement can take a number of forms. There can be specific development exemptions from the rules, and in particular from the national treatment commitments, to allow for preferences to be used to promote development aims or domestic suppliers. There may also be higher thresholds for developing countries to reduce the costs of complying with the rules, or lower thresholds in developed countries to facilitate asymmetric access to the more developed market.

Exclusions/safeguards

General exclusions from national treatment and other obligations under procurement rules are common for reasons of human health, national security and national interest. Most agreements also leave

Box 3.2 (cont.)

governments a residual safeguard in the form of the right not to award a contract. Although this is intended for cases in which there is doubt about the ability of the winner of a contract to deliver, it can be used to block the award of a sensitive contract to a foreign supplier. The GPA and bilateral agreements also provide scope for governments to retain discretion in the use of enforcement provisions, such as waiving contract suspension rules.

Compliance or bid challenge

Experience has shown that, without effective compliance, rules on public procurement will have little effect. Given the thousands of contracts awarded every day, central compliance monitoring has been deemed to be impracticable. Rules therefore tend to provide bidders who believe they have not been fairly treated with an opportunity to seek an independent review of a contract award decision. Penalties in the case of non-compliance may involve project cancellation or financial penalties (limited to the costs of bids or exemplary damages). Post-contract transparency rules requiring information on contracts awarded and the reasons bids failed can also been seen as facilitating compliance.

The trend in procurement is therefore the progressive application of the GPA framework to more and more countries, since the core entities include GPA-equivalent provisions on procurement in most of the PTAs they conclude.

The only real exception to this trend is that not all the core entities have sought GPA-like rules with developing countries. This does not really amount to asymmetric provisions favouring the developing countries because the weaker provisions on procurement provide no rights for developing country exporters to the developed country markets. However, a form of de facto asymmetry exists in that the transparency rules in the GPA framework rules ensure that information on the procurement procedures and specific contracts of the developed countries are put in the public domain and are thus open to all potential suppliers, including developing countries.

Comparison of approaches

The 1994 GPA was one of the few plurilateral agreements of the Uruguay Round. It was signed by a limited number of developed OECD countries and a few emerging markets, including Singapore. Thus all the core entities have signed the GPA. The PTAs concluded with non-signatories to the GPA are thus "WTO-plus" in the sense that they extend coverage of the WTO's GPA to more countries. The PTAs negotiated with Chile, for example, in effect extend the reach of the GPA framework rules to a country that had strongly opposed the GPA when it was negotiated in 1994.

The procurement rules in some of the PTAs are WTO/GPA-minus. For example, earlier EU PTAs with developing countries often included only a short article setting out the progressive liberalization of public procurement as an aim. These are far short of the fairly lengthy and complex provisions included in the GPA framework-type agreements.

The United States

The US PTA provisions in procurement are WTO-plus in the sense that the United States has included GPA-type provisions in the PTAs it has concluded with emerging markets (Mexico and Chile) as well as a string of developing countries (Peru, Morocco, Bahrain, Oman, etc.). The NAFTA agreement with Mexico was negotiated before the 1994 GPA and as a result has somewhat less coverage. For example, NAFTA does not include any category II entities (state or provincial government purchasing, which is probably worth more than the federal government purchasing in each of the three countries). NAFTA also includes only 53 central government entities compared with the 79 listed in category I in the GPA. Table 3.4 provides a schematic comparison of the provisions on procurement in the PTAs of the European Union and the United States. The NAFTA approach is that taken by the United States in all its PTAs, although coverage varies in order to ensure reciprocity.

The 2003 US–Singapore PTA was, in contrast, more or less identical to the GPA coverage.[9] Both the United States and Singapore were signatories to the GPA, so the PTA in effect had no impact in this policy area.

The US–Chile PTA (2003), on the other hand, extended the GPA to Chile[10] and was as such GPA-plus. The thresholds for category I and II purchasing were also set somewhat lower in the US–Chile PTA than in the GPA, thus opening rather more of the respective purchasing markets to competition.

The US–Peru PTA (2005) extended the GPA regime to another new country and is therefore WTO/GPA-plus. The full GPA framework was applied in the US–Peru PTA even though Peru is a developing country. However, the entity coverage offered by the United States was GPA-minus, with only 7 entities in category I (compared with 78 federal agencies in the GPA) and 9 in category II (compared with 37 states in the GPA) covered. The United States also excluded purchasing by US

Table 3.4 Comparison of procurement provisions in various agreements

	1994 GPA	EU–Chile	CARIFORUM EC text	NAFTA
Coverage	*Cat I: central government* Supplies and works negative list; services positive list Thresholds: supplies and services 130k SDR; works 5m SDR *Cat II: sub-national government* "Voluntary" on first sub-national level; no local government Thresholds: supplies and services 200k SDR; works 5m SDR *Cat III: other entities, e.g. utilities* Thresholds: supplies and services 400k SDR; works 5m SDR	Central, sub-central government and utilities as per the GPA for the EU and equivalent for Chile (Annexes XI and XII) Goods, services and works Thresholds: central government supplies 130k SDR; works 5m SDR; sub-central respectively 200k and 5m SDR; and utilities respectively 400k and 5m SDR (as GPA 1994)	Central government only for CARIFORUM; central, sub-central and public enterprise for the EU (but not some key utilities) (Annex 6) Goods, services and works covered Thresholds: as per GPA 1994 for the EU; for CARIFORUM 150k SDR for goods and services and 6.5m SDR for works	Central government; agreement in principle to first sub-federal level Goods, works and services through negative listing Thresholds slightly lower than GPA: US$50k for goods and services; US$6.5m for works; US$250k and US$8m respectively for public enterprises Private companies not covered, even regulated utilities
National treatment commitments	National treatment and MFN for signatories	National treatment and non-discrimination	Joint Committee *may* decide on entities and procurement to be covered (Art. 167 (3)) Encouragement for the provision of national treatment within CARIFORUM	National treatment and non-discrimination (Art. 10003)

Transparency	Information to be provided on national procurement laws and rules Contracts to be advertised to facilitate international competition	Provision of information sufficient to enable effective bids (Art. 142) Statistics on contracts to be provided only when a party does not comply effectively with objectives of the agreement (Art. 158) Information on why bids unsuccessful on request (Art. 154)	Provision of information sufficient to enable effective bids No requirement on statistics	Detailed information on tenders and decisions to facilitate private actions reviews Information on why bids were not successful
Contract award procedures	Option of open, restricted or single tendering	Open and selective (i.e. restrictive); single tendering possible in exceptional cases (Arts 143–146)	Open, restricted or limited tendering	Open, restricted and single tendering; detailed procedures vary slightly from GPA
Contract award criteria	Lowest price or most economically advantageous bid	Lowest price or most advantageous bid based on previously determined criteria	Lowest price or most advantageous bid based on previously determined criteria	Lowest price or most advantageous bid based on previously determined criteria
Technical specifications	Use of international standards encouraged Performance standards preferred to design standards	Performance rather than design or descriptive standards (Art. 149) International, national or recognized standards to be used, but exceptions possible	No mention	Performance standards rather than descriptive standards Encourages use of international standards, but exceptions always possible (Art. 1007)

Table 3.4 (cont.)

	1994 GPA	EU–Chile	CARIFORUM EC text	NAFTA
Exclusion/ safeguard	Public interest override (Art XXIII)			
Bid challenge	Bid challenge introduced in GATT for the first time	Bid challenge (Art. 155)	Bid challenge (Art. 179)	Elaborate bid challenge provisions
	Independent review	Independent review	Independent review with administrative or judicial body	Independent review body
	Interim remedies, but no contract suspension	Rapid interim remedies that may include contract suspension; compensation, but may be limited to costs of bid and protest	Effective, rapid interim measures	Rapid interim measures including suspension and termination of contract
			Procuring entities to retain records to facilitate reviews	
	National interest waiver on contract suspension			National interest waiver on contract suspension

Technical cooperation and special and differential treatment	Developing countries can negotiate exclusions from national treatment to support balance of payments problems; to support the establishment or development of domestic industries; or for regional preferential agreements (Art. V, 1–7) Non-binding technical assistance including help for developing country bidders (Art. V, 8–10) Developing countries may negotiate offsets (which are otherwise banned under Art. XV) such as local content at time of accession (Art. XVI)	Vague technical cooperation commitment (Art. 157)	Exchange of experience	Non-binding provisions on technical cooperation

Source: compiled by the authors from the texts of the agreements.

81

ports from category III. The thresholds for Peru were also a little higher than the GPA, thus providing some form of asymmetry, but not significantly.

In the US–Morocco PTA (2006), the United States also sought the full application of the GPA framework agreement for this developing country. As for US–Peru, the coverage of entities offered by the United States was less than the GPA. Although category I coverage was equivalent to the GPA, only 23 US states were covered under category II, compared with the 37 in the GPA. Purchasing by US ports was again excluded.

The PTAs with Bahrain and Oman (2006) also provided for the full application of the GPA framework. In these two cases, however, there was no coverage of category II (state purchasing) at all by the United States.

Finally, the US–Korea PTA involves two signatories to the GPA, so the agreement makes no substantive difference to the procurement sector.

To sum up, the US PTAs have been WTO/GPA-plus in the sense that they have extended the rules on public procurement to a number of the United States' PTA partners. They have also been WTO/GPA-plus in the sense that some of the thresholds have been (marginally) lower than those in the GPA. But the United States has offered less entity coverage than in the GPA with some PTA partners on reciprocity grounds, and has thus been GPA-minus in this sense.

The European Union and EFTA

The European Union has also adopted the GPA framework rules for all its PTAs with emerging markets, but until 2006 it had less extensive rules for PTAs with developing economies. In this sense it might be said that the European Union was rather less WTO/GPA-plus than the United States. The EU–Mexico PTA (2000) is NAFTA- and GPA-consistent. It was NAFTA-consistent because Mexico used the NAFTA text and coverage on procurement, which although similar to the GPA is not the same. Indeed, Mexico is not a signatory to the GPA. The PTA is GPA-consistent in that the European Union uses both the GPA framework and its schedules.

In terms of the EU agreements with developing countries, the EU–Morocco PTA has only one short article (Art. 41) that sets out the aim of progressive liberalization of procurement markets. This will have no effect until the EU–Morocco Association Council takes specific action to add some flesh to the provisions. This approach to developing countries was established with the Trade, Development and Cooperation Agreement (TDCA) between the European Union and South Africa negotiated in 1995. The same is true for the EU–Egypt Euro-Med Association Agreement of 2003, which has just the one short article (Art. 38) setting out liberalization as an objective.

The EU–Chile PTA (2003), on the other hand, applies the full GPA framework to the procurement practices of the two parties. Coverage is somewhat GPA-minus however, in that the European Union offers fewer category III entities (public enterprises and utilities) than under the GPA.

EU policy on public procurement in PTAs changed in 2006 with the adoption of the European Union's revised PTA strategy as elaborated in the *Global Europe* statement of 2006 (European Commission, 2006). This identified access to public procurement markets as a priority, along with more effective enforcement of intellectual property rights and the promotion of competition and investment provisions in PTAs. Since 2006, the European Union has thus sought more extensive coverage of procurement in its PTAs. Even in the EPAs the European Union is seeking the inclusion of procurement. The CARIFORUM has accepted fairly comprehensive provisions on procurement (see Table 3.4). The EU–CARIFORUM provisions on procurement are very close to the GPA framework rules but stop short of "liberalization". In other words, there is no national treatment requirement that would prohibit the use of preferential procurement for industrial or development policy purposes. The CARIFORUM still wishes to retain scope for such policies and has thus limited the agreement to transparency in procurement only.

None of the other ACP regions has (as of 2007), however, been ready to accept inclusion of procurement. The EU PTA being negotiated with South Korea is likely to pose few problems because both are signatories to the GPA. EU negotiations with ASEAN and India in particular are, however, likely to be a real litmus test of the ability of the European Union to include framework rules on transparency in government procurement in the next generation of PTAs.

There is little difference between the EU and EFTA positions on public procurement in their PTAs. The EFTA agreements negotiated with Mexico and Chile are the same as the EU agreements. In the case of Chile, the EFTA parties exclude electricity entities from the list for category III entities. EFTA agreements with developing countries such as Morocco have, like the EU agreements, simply included one short article (Art. 15 in the case of Morocco) that sets out the aim of progressive liberalization. EFTA has also negotiated PTAs with Korea (2006) and Singapore (2003). Because both these countries are signatories to the GPA there is simply a reference to the obligations of the parties under the GPA.

Japan and Singapore

Both Japan and Singapore are signatories to the GPA. Japan has followed the same pattern as the European Union and EFTA in its PTA with Mexico. In other words, Japan has used the GPA framework rules and offered the same coverage as for the GPA, and Mexico has used the NAFTA text. This has clearly been done with the intention of avoiding Mexico having to implement two slightly different provisions in its national law.

In the PTA between Japan and Singapore there is simply reference to the GPA obligations in terms of procedures, compliance, bid challenge, etc. But the two parties agreed to somewhat lower thresholds than those in the GPA, so the agreement could be said to be slightly GPA-plus. The same is true for the Singapore–Korea PTA agreed in 2006.

When it comes to agreements with less developed countries, Japan accepted the PTA with Malaysia (2006) without any reference at all to public procurement. In the case of Singapore's agreement with Jordan, provisions on procurement were left out, pending Jordan's negotiation of accession to the GPA. So both Japan and Singapore appear to be rather more flexible in leaving procurement off the agenda of PTAs than the European Union or EFTA, which seek some inclusion, or the United States, which seeks a full GPA-equivalent approach, albeit with major limitations on entity coverage.

Conclusions on public procurement

One distinction between the "core entities" is that, whereas the United States tends to expect all its PTA partners to adopt the full GPA framework, the European Union, EFTA and Japan have up to 2007 accepted simple, short provisions aiming at the progressive liberalization of procurement markets with their developing country PTA partners. The EU PTA with Chile included full GPA provisions but the TDCA with South Africa did not. However, the European Union appears to have switched to a policy of seeking more or less GPA-compatible framework rules in its PTAs even with developing countries such as the ACP states. Outside of the Caribbean there has, however, been significant resistance on the part of the ACP states, with countries such as South Africa adopting a firm opposition to such transparency rules. The question is whether the European Union will be able to include the GPA framework in its Asian PTAs.[11] In terms of coverage, the United States tends to lower its thresholds in its PTAs compared with the GPA, but excludes certain entities and/or federal states. The coverage largely depends on the partner country: US–Peru has very restrained coverage, US–Chile much larger coverage. For US–Morocco, US–Bahrain and US–Oman, the United States used a blueprint on procurement framework rules even if the schedules differed. EU coverage, on the other hand, appears to be more uniform, perhaps as a function of the internal liberalization within the European Union and perhaps as a result of somewhat less emphasis on reciprocity.

For example, the European Union is offering almost full GPA coverage of procurement to the ACP states.

The PTAs are GPA-plus in the sense that they extend the application of the GPA framework rules to more countries. There is, however, a significant GPA-minus feature in US agreements (notably with Peru, Morocco, Bahrain and Oman) and in the EU agreements (such as that with Chile) to the extent that entity coverage is less than in the GPA.

PTA schedules provide scope for asymmetry in the sense that developing or emerging market signatories can include fewer purchasing entities in their schedules than the developed countries. But in practice the developed parties to the PTAs have also varied the coverage of their schedules to satisfy reciprocity objectives. This appears to be particularly the case with the United States. The United States has, however, used some general asymmetry provisions in NAFTA, which allowed transitional measures for Mexico such as exclusion of PEMEX, Mexico's state-owned petroleum company (eight-year transition period), and a general "set-aside" for Mexican suppliers of around US$1 billion up to 2003 (Mexican purchasers could prefer domestic suppliers up to US$1 billion). Mexico was also permitted local content requirements of 40 per cent for labour-intensive contracts and 25 per cent for capital-intensive contracts. The agreements with Oman and Bahrain also allow two-year transition periods for the two countries to implement the agreement and set slightly higher thresholds. Following the precedent set with NAFTA, the EFTA and EU agreements with Mexico also offered Mexico the same asymmetrical benefits, as did the Japan–Mexico agreement. The European Union offered asymmetric access to the Single European Market to the accession states under the Europe Agreements in the early 1990s and appears to be offering asymmetric access for the ACP states in the EPAs. It remains to be seen how the European Union will deal with PTAs with larger emerging markets that will have more capacity to supply EU procurement markets.

As might be expected, there appear to be close links between the procurement provisions negotiated in international agreements and domestic policies. This holds for the European Union, where limited progress in intra-EU negotiations held back the plurilateral negotiations on the GPA.[12] With reference to PTAs, agreement to GPA-like rules generally requires the introduction of new legislation and administrative measures, bringing about more transparent procurement practices and driving out discriminatory practices and corruption in contract award procedures. There are therefore quite important implications for domestic policies.

As noted in the introduction, the trend in procurement is the progressive application of the GPA framework to more and more countries as the core entities include GPA-equivalent provisions on procurement in most of the PTAs they conclude. In this respect, preferential agreements might be seen as filling a vacuum left by the agreement at the Cancun WTO Ministerial Meeting in 2003 to exclude government procurement (as well as competition and investment) from the agenda of the Doha Development Agenda. The shift in focus towards preferential arrangements need not, however, mean more discrimination between foreign suppliers. If national purchasing is carried out in a transparent fashion following best regulatory practices, there is unlikely to be discrimination between different foreign sources. Equally, however, an extension of GPA principles need not mean improved access for foreign suppliers. The evidence from quantitative studies of the impact of rules on procurement is that changes in domestic policy tend to favour competition within the national market rather than increased cross-border provision (Evenett and Hoekman, 2005). This will be particularly the case where there is increased transparency but a carve-out of purchasing by sub-national authorities.

Notes

1. Much will depend, of course, on how the provisions in the PTAs are applied. Here, as in other aspects of the study, the assessment is based on the substance of the agreements as adopted.
2. Only PTAs with the Gulf or Middle Eastern states tend to exclude TBT and SPS measures. For example, the EU agreement with the Gulf Cooperation Council has nothing on TBT, nor do US and Singaporean agreements with Jordan. This contrasts with Israel, which has fairly highly developed provisions in its PTAs; this suggests that inclusion of TBT and SPS rules and their degree of sophistication correlates with the degree of development (Lesser, 2007).
3. In line with the TBT Agreement, this is binding only for the federal government. The United States is obliged to make "best endeavours" to ensure that state-level governments conform. In general, only mandatory regulations are covered under the WTO. The various private standards-making bodies are not bound to provide such notice.
4. The EU–Chile agreement provides a choice between mutual recognition and equivalence as the means of addressing TBTs.
5. See the DDA Trade Capacity Building Database (TCBDB), ⟨http://tcbdb.wto.org/⟩, cited in Lesser (2007: 20).
6. For those familiar with transatlantic differences over the use of precaution in SPS agreements, this statement may seem odd. But the precaution issue illustrates how different interpretations of a principle included in trade agreements can result in major trade disputes. Assessments of the text of agreements may therefore come to the conclusion that they appear very similar, but the devil is of course in the detail of how they are applied.
7. See, for example, for TBT rules, Lesser (2007) and Piermartini and Budetta (2006).
8. Chile is an analogous case in that it includes harmonization to international standards, mutual recognition and equivalence in the TBT rules it has agreed with the European Union and the United States.
9. Entity coverage of the GPA is negotiated on a bilateral basis.

10. In the US–Chile PTA, of course, an agreement on public procurement establishes a preference for the US and Chilean exporters to each other's markets. In reality, however, the degree of preference is not very great. Much of the GPA framework rules concerns promoting transparency and best practice in public procurement. If national purchasing is carried out in a transparent fashion following best regulatory practices, there is unlikely to be discrimination between different suppliers, let alone between different foreign supplies. In other words, the same purchasing procedures are often used regardless of the origin of the bid.

11. The EU–Korea PTA does not raise much of a challenge because both are signatories to the GPA. India has resisted inclusion of procurement in the WTO negotiations and the indications are that it will resist its inclusion in a PTA with the European Union.

12. The European Union could not agree that EU rules on procurement should cover the utilities, because these were privately owned in some member states and publicly owned in others.

4

Services and investment

One of the trends in preferential trade agreements (PTAs) that we identified earlier was the heightened pursuit of deep integration among members. Nowhere is this more apparent than in the inclusion of provisions in
PTAs dealing with trade in services and conditions applying to the admission and treatment of foreign direct investment (FDI). Both areas –
services and investment – go to the heart of domestic regulation, often
in fields of considerable sensitivity such as the provision of health or education services.

It is this sensitivity that has fuelled controversy in the GATT/WTO.
There was initially considerable resistance among developing countries
to the inclusion of trade in services in the Uruguay Round – resistance
that was eventually assuaged by putting the negotiation of the General
Agreement on Trade in Services (GATS) on a separate track from the
rest of the negotiations, by building considerable flexibility into GATS
commitments and by establishing a framework that has still to produce
commercially meaningful improvements in market access. In the case of
investment, although it is dealt with in a piece-meal way in many
GATT/WTO provisions, there is no comprehensive framework agreement and the pursuit of one was abandoned at the WTO Cancun Ministerial Meeting in 2003 when it was decided to drop three of the so-called
Singapore Issues (investment, competition and government procurement) from the Doha Development Agenda.

The question arises – why is it seemingly easier to make progress in
these two areas in PTAs than in the broader context of multilateral trade

The rise of bilateralism: Comparing American, European and Asian approaches to
preferential trade agreements, Heydon and Woolcock,
United Nations University Press, 2009, ISBN 978-92-808-1162-9

negotiations? A number of possible explanations can be advanced: that commitments on services and investment are less threatening among a smaller number of players; that commitments in a PTA, though they can entail dispute resolution, do not run the risk of triggering the full force of the WTO dispute settlement mechanism; or that inclusion of commitments on services and investment is the price to pay for other PTA advantages, such as improved market access for manufactured products. Each of these factors may play a part, underpinned by the recognition that freer flows of services and FDI bring with them considerable benefits.

On some counts, the potential gains from the liberalization of trade in services are five times higher than those from the liberalization of trade in goods. These potentially big gains follow directly from the fact that the service economy has the largest share of GDP in all country groupings; it has particularly high barriers to trade, embodied in domestic regulation; and it offers opportunities for welfare gains associated with improved factor mobility – capital, via commercial presence (GATS Mode 3), and labour, via the temporary movement of service providers (Mode 4).

Measures designed to foster the flow of FDI and its protection carry with them both increased opportunities for market access – retail banking services call for investment in a commercial presence – as well as associated flows of skills and technology.

In pursuing these potential gains, the members of preferential trade agreements frequently endorse PTA measures that go beyond provisions in the WTO. Among the WTO-plus features of services provisions in many preferential agreements are the pursuit of negative listing (whereby everything is liberalized unless explicitly excluded, rather than the positive-listing approach of the GATS) and inclusion of the right of non-establishment to accommodate service providers who do not wish to have commercial presence. In the area of investment, WTO-plus features found in PTAs include provisions dealing with investment regulation and protection, borrowed from – and it seems increasingly superseding – bilateral investment treaties.

It may well be that these WTO-plus features are implemented on a non-discriminatory basis. This will frequently be the case where the measures are achieved through increased transparency or flexibility in domestic regulation. But this is by no means guaranteed. Mutual recognition agreements in services (or elsewhere) are inherently discriminatory. And some PTA progress is made possible precisely because of its exclusivity – like the facilitation of Filipino and Indonesian nursing services in Japan. Similarly with investment, it is unlikely that all of the increased FDI flows associated with PTA provisions on investment are "additional" and it can be expected that at least part of these flows is the result of investment diversion away from third parties.

Services

Introduction

The growth in the number, and the pattern, of PTAs including provisions dealing with services (and investment) mirrors that of PTAs more generally. Since 1994, some 180 preferential agreements combining investment and trade in services rules have come into existence, compared with only 38 in the previous 40 years. Over 40 per cent of the cumulative total has come into existence since 2000, involving countries and regions increasingly further apart and more diversified in levels of development. The most active countries have been identified as Mexico, Chile, Singapore, the United States, Australia and New Zealand, with the European Free Trade Association (EFTA), the European Union and the Association of Southeast Asian Nations (ASEAN) standing out as the most active regional groupings (Houde et al., 2007).

Two factors explain the increased role of preferential agreements in addressing trade in services: the size of the potential gains from services trade liberalization and the slow pace of such liberalization at the multilateral level.

As noted, the size of potential gains is a reflection of the size of the service economy (now the biggest component of GDP in all country groupings), the relatively high level of impediments to services trade, usually in the form of behind-the-border regulatory constraints, and the fact that services trade liberalization acts as a proxy for improved factor mobility – of labour, through freer movement of service providers, and of capital, by facilitating establishment or commercial presence. Insofar as establishment is a proxy, or vehicle, for investment, the advantages deriving from this mode of services delivery are closely linked to those that derive from investment, and in particular from foreign direct investment.

Establishment, or commercial presence, can be essential for the effective delivery of a service. Establishment can also have important intermodal linkages with other forms of service delivery, notably through the movement of personnel (Mode 4) and the facilitation of cross-border service delivery (Mode 1). As such, important synergies can arise, of which establishment is an integral part. The FDI associated with establishment or commercial presence often brings with it related benefits in the form of human capital necessary for the effective functioning of branches or subsidiaries. And FDI is likely to bring with it related transfers of technology.

Although services loom large in developed country exports (see Table 4.1), there is a growing realization that the gains from the liberalization of trade in services will be shared by developing as well as by developed countries. This derives in part from their role as exporters, not simply in traditional areas associated with developing countries, such as tourism or construction, but in a wide range of other service activities such as port facilities, computer-related activities or media services. But perhaps the biggest welfare gains to developing countries from the liberalization of service trade will come via imports, given the crucial importance of services inputs for the efficiency of downstream users.

The General Agreement on Trade in Services has provided a valuable framework in which to achieve greater liberalization of trade in services, by incorporating the principles of transparency and non-discrimination within a negotiating modality in the form of requests and offers. Nevertheless, progress in the WTO to achieve commercially meaningful improvements in market access has been very slow. In examining the reasons for this lack of progress, it is possible to see why many countries feel that PTAs offer more hope of progress, albeit with discriminatory elements.

The attainment of services liberalization in the Doha Development Agenda (DDA) has been held hostage to the lack of progress in other areas, notably agriculture and non-agricultural market access (NAMA). It may be felt that the greater scope in bilateral deals to exclude sensitive products, and in some cases whole sectors, offers less risk of stalemate.

Progress in the DDA has also been impeded by stand-offs within the services negotiations, with some parties, mainly developing countries, reluctant to liberalize commercial presence (GATS Mode 3) until others, predominantly developed countries, show a willingness to liberalize the movement of service providers (Mode 4). Again, bilateral arrangements may be seen as offering better opportunities for breakthrough, such as with the provisions on the movement of nurses contained in the Japan–Philippines and Japan–Indonesia PTAs or even EU commitments under Mode 4 in the Economic Partnership Agreement (EPA) with the Caribbean Forum (CARIFORUM) of the African, Caribbean and Pacific (ACP) Group of States.

The GATS may be seen as somewhat dysfunctional to the extent that negotiators, using the long-established GATT focus on non-discrimination, have tended to place considerable negotiating emphasis and energy on improved national treatment (which yields benefits only to foreign service providers), whereas most estimates of the potential

Table 4.1 Trade in services of the core entities with the rest of the world, 2005 (US$ million)

	Total services			Transportation			Travel		
	Net	Credit	Debit	Net	Credit	Debit	Net	Credit	Debit
EU-25[a]	90,646.2	1,172,434.3	1,081,788.1	19,945.2	258,075.9	238,130.6	-3,782.3	289,173.9	292,956.2
USA	62,207.9	376,786.5	314,578.6	-24,998.0	63,175.0	88,173.0	28,253.6	102,014.6	73,761.0
Japan	-23,968.9	110,302.3	134,271.2	-4,555.5	35,789.1	40,344.6	-25,094.8	12,439.0	37,533.8
Singapore[b,c]	-2,876.0	51,200.0	54,076.0	–	–	–	–	–	–
Switzerland	23,750.9	47,110.5	23,359.5	1,485.0	4,358.7	2,873.7	1,737.0	11,040.4	9,303.4

	Communication			Construction			Insurance		
	Net	Credit	Debit	Net	Credit	Debit	Net	Credit	Debit
EU-25	225.2	29,293.9	29,068.7	7,258.6	25,787.2	18,528.6	-2,429.9	24,018.9	26,448.8
USA	-258.6	5,033.1	5,291.7	170.0	423.0	253.0	-21,652.4	6,831.3	28,483.7
Japan	-221.4	395.6	617.0	2,450.6	7,228.4	4,777.8	-1,061.5	868.3	1,929.8
Switzerland	205.4	1,156.0	950.5	–	–	–	4,267.0	4,534.3	267.3

	Financial services			Computer and related services			Royalties and licence fees		
	Net	Credit	Debit	Net	Credit	Debit	Net	Credit	Debit
EU-25	48,512.2	94,699.8	46,187.5	28,196.6	59,416.0	31,219.5	-14,155.0	47,344.9	61,500.0
USA	21,732.0	34,081.0	12,349.0	-730.0	8,239.0	8,969.0	32,909.0	57,410.0	24,501.0
Japan	2,366.2	5,070.9	2,704.6	-1,315.6	1,126.9	2,442.4	2,984.1	17,618.7	14,633.7
Switzerland	9,396.0	10,420.5	1,024.5	–	–	–	–	–	–

	Other business services			Government services (not included elsewhere)		
	Net	Credit	Debit	Net	Credit	Debit
EU-25	15,816.1	301,548.7	285,732.6	-1,170.7	21,203.6	22,374.4
USA	27,927.2	66,237.1	38,309.9	-10,639.9	22,767.4	33,407.3
Japan	824.7	27,347.6	26,522.9	671.4	2,320.9	1,649.5
Switzerland	5,581.5	14,285.2	8,703.7	1,161.0	1,310.3	149.4

Source: OECD Statistics on International Trade in Services, extracted from OECD Database.
Notes:
[a] EU-25 trade includes both intra- and extra-EU trade.
[b] Total commercial services for Singapore not including government services.
[c] Data for Singapore based on WTO Statistical Database and available only for total trade.

gains from liberalization suggest relatively greater opportunities arising from improved market access. Market access has the potential to bring benefits to both foreign and domestic service providers, through, for example, relaxed limits on the total number of service providers permitted in the domestic market. PTAs, by their nature, will be less focused on the principle of non-discrimination.

Finally, progress in the GATS has been impeded by concerns (understandable, though largely unfounded) about threats to regulatory sovereignty and a perceived weakening of the prerogative of governments to preserve standards in sensitive public services such as health and education. While PTAs offer little beyond the extensive provisions in the GATS for carve-out, bilateral agreements have not so far attracted the intense, and often unhelpful, attention of non-governmental organizations seeking to put a brake on liberalization.

There is no doubt that many preferential agreements have achieved a measure of liberalization of trade in services not so far seen in the GATS, including a tendency to use negative listing. There are nevertheless limits to the scope of this achievement, as witnessed, for example, by the fact that the EPAs recently negotiated between the European Union and certain ACP states do not cover trade in services.[1]

Comparison of approaches

United States

NAFTA

The services provisions of the North American Free Trade Agreement (NAFTA) go further and deeper than the GATS with respect to both substantive measures and sectoral coverage. Sector coverage is based on a negative-list approach, whereby everything is liberalized unless explicitly excluded, in contrast to the positive-list (or bottom-up) approach of the GATS. The negative-list approach is generally regarded as being more transparent than positive listing and as affirming an up-front commitment by signatories to an overarching set of general obligations. This approach, pioneered by the United States, Canada and Mexico, has since been spread by Mexico in the agreements it has signed in Central and South America.

The implementation of services provisions in NAFTA is also GATS-plus by virtue of procedural provisions that facilitate continuous consultation and review in various trilateral commissions and working groups. These procedural aspects of NAFTA have helped establish the integrity of the regulatory process in the countries concerned, and in Mexico in particular.

NAFTA was a pioneer in seeking to complement disciplines on cross-border trade in services (Modes 1 and 2 of the GATS) with a more comprehensive set of parallel disciplines on investment (Mode 3) and the temporary movement of business people (Mode 4).

NAFTA was also a pioneer in providing for the right of non-establishment (i.e. no local presence requirement as a precondition to supply a service) as a means of encouraging greater volumes of cross-border trade in services. This right, for which no GATS equivalent exists, may prove particularly well suited to promoting electronic commerce (Sauvé, 2003).

A sectoral focus

This section will examine the sectoral dimension of WTO-plus in US agreements. All US agreements, apart from the PTA with Jordan, advance on rule-making in financial services and telecommunications. In financial services, US PTAs advance on transparency measures, availability of insurance services, senior management and board of directors (Mode 4) requirements and dispute settlement procedures, as well as providing for detailed extension of the most favoured nation (MFN) clause (between signatories) to prudential recognition. It should be noted, however, that market access is provided with regard only to financial institutions, excluding, for example, insurance agents (thus limiting the scope of the PTA), and new financial services are defined differently than in the Understanding on Financial Services negotiated under the GATS in 1997. With regard to telecommunication services, the PTAs exclude cable and broadcast distribution of radio and television programming, but expand on access and usage of public telecommunication transport networks and services, interconnection with suppliers of public telecommunication services, submarine cable landing stations, universal service, licensing processes, scarce resources, enforcement, dispute settlement issues, independent regulation and privatization, as well as several other issues. Another GATS-plus provision is the introduction, definition and incorporation of express delivery services. In general, US PTAs in services exclude from their overall scope air transport services, government procurement, governmental services (covered under a separate chapter), subsidies, nationals seeking employment in the territory of the other party, and certain elements concerning investment.

The United States' PTAs also tend to advance on transparency issues and provide greater elaboration than is found in the GATS. Mutual recognition issues – of particular importance for the (Mode 4) movement of natural persons – also constitute GATS-plus elements, though no advancement is made on domestic regulation. On mutual recognition, US agreements provide criteria for professional services and encourage temporary licensing (such as in the Central America–Dominican Republic Free Trade Agreement). The PTAs with Chile and (*ad referendum*) with Korea liberalize legal consultancy services and provide a framework granting temporary licensing for engineers. Movement of natural persons is furthered beyond the GATS in the agreements with, for example, Chile and Singapore. These PTAs provide a chapter on the temporary entry of business persons, which sets principles and obligations concerning the provision of information, transparency rules and dispute settlement, as well as rules for the entry of business visitors, traders and investors, intra-corporate transferees and professionals. The agreements also go on to define minimum education requirements and alternative credentials in several professions. Lastly, the United States has committed to accept quotas of 1,400 and 5,400 business entry applications, respectively, in Chile and Singapore.

Competition rules constitute another development in the US PTAs, and the agreements include specific rules on anti-competitive behaviour and rules concerning major and dominant suppliers in the field of telecommunication, competitive safeguards, unbundling of network elements, and more.

Before concluding the discussion of the United States, a qualification is needed to what is otherwise a fairly positive assessment. There is an increasing tendency for US PTAs to contain negative-list reservations that exclude all measures affecting services maintained at the sub-national level.

European Union

EU–Mexico

All four modes of supply and all sectors are included in EU–Mexico, except for the usual exclusions (audio-visual, air transport and maritime cabotage). The agreement establishes a standstill clause, locking in the existing access that has in practice already been granted to EU companies. Insofar as Mexico's domestic liberalization is more comprehensive than the country's commitments under the GATS or NAFTA, which tends to be the case, the standstill clause therefore provides even more favourable treatment (*de jure* not *de facto*) for EU service providers (Reiter, 2003). EU–Mexico uses a positive-list approach, apart from financial services, which is negative list.

The services chapter of EU–Mexico provides for measures to be taken, within three years of entry into force of the agreement, with a view to additional liberalization (Article 7). This clause foreshadows the elimination of substantially all remaining discrimination, with maximum transition periods of 10 years. The services chapter also calls for the negotiation of mutual recognition agreements, particularly for the movement of natural persons, no later than three years after entry into force.

Finally, a committee on financial services is established that will negotiate further opening should either Mexico or the European Union agree to further liberalization with another party. In other words, if NAFTA's coverage of financial services is increased, the European Union has the right to seek equivalent access.

Euro-Med agreements

The Euro-Mediterranean Partnership (Euro-Med) agreements are WTO-plus in services to the extent that, for Mediterranean countries that are not members of the WTO and therefore not signatories to the GATS, a basic framework agreement similar to that of the GATS is established.

The European Neighbourhood Policy (ENP) sets the basis for future PTAs in services with Mediterranean non-member partners and will upgrade the current provisions on services found in the Association Agreements. The EU–Moroccan Action Plan calls for the opening of negotiations on a PTA in services, as well as exchange of information with a view to regulatory convergence with the European Union, capacity-building, and e-commerce development. Specific actions in the field of financial services are aimed at upgrading Morocco's regulatory system in line with that of the European Union and with international standards. Other specific measures to introduce greater competition in the Moroccan service sector include assessments of liberalization of airport ground handling services and sea-ports and liberalization of telecommunication services. It is not clear, though, whether reference to opening to competition is also an opening to foreign competition. The Action Plan with Israel proposes three complementary avenues for the integration and enhancement of trade in services: (I) liberalization of trade in services – the establishment of a PTA in services, cooperation on policy and regulatory issues in the field of services and cooperation on e-commerce issues, with an emphasis on a Mutual Recognition Agreement for digital signatures; (II) financial services – the possibility of Israel's participation in the Single European Market (SEM) for financial services, as well as closer cooperation on regulation, supervision and financial stability, with the aim of gradual convergence of the prudential regulatory and supervisory framework; (III) movement of natural persons through advancement on mutual recognition of professional services. The possibility of Israel's participation in the SEM for financial services (the only ENP country currently offered this possibility) is a development that, if implemented, would probably lead to greater liberalization measures in this field than are achieved by any PTA (seen by the European Union as offering a stake in the Internal Market).

It should be noted, however, that the EU approach to trade in services with the southern members of the ENP is based on the Euro-Mediterranean regional approach. Accordingly, liberalization of trade in services is to be based on a framework "Protocol on the Liberalization of Trade in Services and Establishment", which is very similar to the provisions of the GATS. This Protocol will provide the framework for individual PTAs with the European Union, which aspires to a regional Euro-Mediterranean PTA for services. One development beyond the GATS in this Protocol is the provision on progressive integration of services markets through alignment of partner countries to EU legislation when they sign a PTA and agreements on financial services.

Though the Protocol resembles the GATS in many respects, it contains a number of features that will need to be handled with care by developing country partners:

• The requirement in the Preamble to the Protocol that investment not be attracted by the lowering of labour or environmental standards. Although this requirement is unlikely to create unwanted constraints, it needs to be approached in a manner that does not impinge upon the partner government's sovereign responsibilities.

• The provision in the Protocol (Article 13) that, in order to achieve national treatment, treatment of the other party may be formally different from that afforded to nationals needs to be approached with care where this might involve treating foreign entities, say in the area of tax, more favourably (within the partner country) than domestic entities. (A similar consideration may arise with the GATS, though here the Exceptions provisions in Article XIV appear to grant considerable latitude with respect to tax policy.)

• The requirement (Article 15) to grant MFN treatment to Community services and service suppliers could dilute preferential treatment granted by a partner country to other developing countries. (In the case of the GATS, MFN exemptions have been tabled to deal with this eventuality. It is open to debate whether the square-bracketed reference to GATS Article V in the EU Protocol Preamble provides cover for regional preferences among EU partners.)

• The exclusion from MFN obligations (Article 15) of treatment afforded (by the European Union) to third parties that have undertaken to approximate their regulations to those of the European Union needs to be dealt with in a way that does not enshrine preferences granted to other parties that may be in conflict with Protocol signatories' interests.

- The requirement under regulatory cooperation (Article 22) that there be cooperation to ensure that legislation is progressively [aligned] [harmonized] or made compatible with that of the Community needs to be undertaken in a manner consistent with the interests of developing country signatories to the Protocol.

These observations may appear somewhat arcane, but they are a useful reminder of the complexities that can arise from preferential approaches to trade relations.

The European Union has recently negotiated an EPA with the CARIFORUM. This is seen by the European Union as a model for EPAs with other regions, so is important to consider.[2] The EU CARIFORUM text adopts essentially a GATS approach, with positive listing for commitments on national treatment and MFN. The CARIFORUM parties have made commitments on 60–75 per cent of all sectors. Each CARIFORUM member has produced its own schedule because of the diversity of interests between the countries concerned. The European Union has made commitments on 90 per cent of sectors and has in particular made more generous commitments in Mode 4 than it was ready to do in the DDA negotiations. The European Union offers in Mode 4 are important because they show that developing countries can achieve some results in bilateral negotiations with the European Union. The European Union's concessions in Mode 4 must of course be seen against other policy areas, such as government procurement, where the European Union was able to make progress towards its own aims.[3]

A sectoral focus

This section examines in more detail the sectoral aspect of WTO-plus in two EU agreements: EU–Chile and EU–Mexico. Both agreements advance beyond the GATS in their provisions on financial services, telecommunication services and maritime transport. In financial services, they incorporate and move beyond elements of the GATS Understanding on Financial Services, further elaborate on measures such as transparency and new financial services, prohibit key personnel requirements, provide disciplines on dispute settlement, and more. The provisions on maritime transport services extend to include door-to-door and intermodal transportation. They also provide for national treatment in relation to commercial presence, but, as noted above, exclude cabotage from the agreement. The PTA with Chile introduces measures in telecommunication services that include independent regulators, specific transparency measures and non-discrimination in the application of scarce resources (such as frequencies and numbers), and interconnection issues.

Domestic regulation is treated in the same manner as in the GATS. Nevertheless, concerning mutual recognition, the PTA with Mexico contains a soft commitment to negotiate mutual recognition agreements within three years. The agreement with Chile advances on the GATS in respect of movement of natural persons by providing for a specific review of rules in this area, including a change of the definition of a natural person.

Specific rules concerning anti-competitive behaviour and major and dominant suppliers in the field of telecommunication services exist in all PTAs with telecommunication provisions. The EPA with CARIFORUM includes competition provisions in the tourism sector that seek to ensure no abuse of market dominance by large EU investors in the Caribbean. The EPA also follows the EU–Chile model of including significant sections aimed at the promotion of e-commerce.

EFTA

Agreements signed by EFTA are mainly of a positive-listing nature. However, the PTA with Mexico is a negative-list agreement. Whereas GATS-plus provisions differ between the agreements, all PTAs contain commitments to eliminate further trade discrimination within given time-frames (for example, 10 years with Mexico and Singapore).

From a sector-specific perspective, most of the agreements provide for new commitments on rules in financial services and telecommunication services. In financial services, GATS-plus provisions apply to extensions of measures found in the Understanding on Financial Services (such as in respect of national treatment), senior management and board of directors requirements, further elaboration of prudential carve-outs, and the incorporation of transparency rules set by international organizations, such as the Bank for International Settlements. In telecommunication services, the agreements with Chile, Korea and Singapore expand the GATS framework to include new definitions, licensing procedures, treatment of scarce resources, minimum interconnection obligations and interconnection with dominant suppliers, independent regulation, universal service, and dispute settlement issues. The agreement with Mexico is noteworthy in including commitments and understandings on maritime transport services.[4] Air transport services are excluded from all agreements.

On domestic regulation, two PTAs go beyond the GATS. The agreement with Mexico treats regulation as a general non-trade barrier to trade in services, beyond bounded sectors as defined by the GATS. The agreement with Singapore is slightly GATS-plus by also applying international standards. Mutual recognition is an area advanced by almost all PTAs, which commit to a time-frame for the development of mutual recognition procedures and agreements on qualifications, requirements, licences and other regulations. The PTA with Singapore contains a specific (Mode 4) commitment to develop mutual recognition disciplines for engineering services.

Although competition elements, such as monopolies or exclusive suppliers, are either treated as in the GATS or not mentioned, most agreements provide for specific rules concerning anti-competitive behaviour and major and dominant suppliers in the field of telecommunication services.

In terms of new provisions that do not exist in the GATS, the agreement with Mexico provides for a standstill on new discriminatory measures, as well as another standstill in financial services.

Japan

Japan's PTAs have a mixed approach to listing. Its PTAs in Latin America follow either a hybrid approach consisting of an overall negative-listing framework, with positive listing in financial services (Chile), or a negative-list approach (Mexico). The agreements in Southeast Asia adhere to a positive-list formula.

On a sector-specific basis, all PTAs, excluding that with Thailand, mildly advance on financial services rules, notably in the sense that they provide for rules on dispute settlement and incorporate provisions from the Understanding on Financial Services. The treatment of new financial services is more restrictive than in the Understanding. Progress on rules in telecommunication services is found only in the agreement with Singapore, where the PTA goes beyond the Annex on Telecommunications and expands on scope and definitions, interconnection issues including their dispute settlement, independent regulation, universal service and scarce resources. All PTAs exclude air transport services, government services, maritime cabotage, subsidies and government procurement. Some PTAs also specifically exclude the other party's nationals seeking employment.

The agreement with Thailand slightly progresses on domestic regulation by including provisions in sectors where no specific commitments were undertaken in the GATS. Mutual recognition is advanced with Singapore, but only to the degree that a designated committee is tasked to develop rules in this area, and recognition of professional qualification is mentioned as a possibility. Excluding Malaysia, Japan's PTAs go beyond GATS provisions on the movement of natural persons. A specific chapter addresses the entry and temporary stay of nationals for business purposes. This chapter provides principles, definitions, means of information exchange and dispute settlement. It also defines categories for business purposes, namely intra-corporate transferees, investors and nationals of a party who engage in professional business activities on the basis of a personal contact with a public or private organization in the other party. Japan's agreement with the Philippines, which advances on the movement of natural persons, contains provisions designed to promote the movement of nurses from the Philippines to Japan. Under the agreement, Japan has agreed to accept 400–500 nurses and care-givers annually (*Bridges Weekly Trade News*, 21 September 2006). The PTA with Singapore also extends its scope to non-party juridical persons who have constituted in one of the parties, so long as they are genuinely engaged in this member's territory.

GATS-plus rules on competition are found in the agreement with Singapore, in addressing anti-competitive behaviour in the telecommunication sector and in providing for competitive safeguards.

Singapore

Singapore has three PTAs with non-core entities (Korea, Australia and Jordan) that are of all types: positive listing, negative listing and hybrid.[5] Whereas the PTAs with Korea and Australia advance beyond the GATS in several ways, the agreement with Jordan is not GATS-plus in any respect. PTA negotiations are currently under way with China and Canada. The PTA with China has been substantially concluded and will provide greater market access. The PTA with Canada has been under negotiation since 2001 and was projected to be completed in 2008.

The PTAs with Korea and Australia advance beyond the GATS in financial services and telecommunication services. The Korea PTA also includes progress on maritime services. The financial services framework includes services as well as investment, and further develops the GATS in transparency rules and definitions. It also has WTO-plus provisions on dispute settlement and incorporates several provisions from the Understanding on Financial Services. Whereas financial services are treated under a negative list in the PTA with Australia, they are positively listed in the agreement with Korea. The chapters on telecommunication services exclude from their scope cable and broadcast distribution of radio and television programming, while providing new measures and rules that extend beyond the GATS. These rules include definitions, transparency disciplines, access and usage of public telecommunications transport networks and services, independent regulation, universal service, licensing processes, treatment of scarce resources, enforcement and dispute settlement. In maritime transport, the PTA with Korea provides a list of sectors where additional commitments are taken. Overall, government services, transportation and non-transportation services, investment, subsidies and government procurement are excluded from the scope of the PTA.

GATS-plus provisions on mutual recognition in the Korean PTA provide for criteria in the development of professional standards, and also encourage temporary licensing of professional services. Furthermore, with regard to professional engineers, Korea committed to recognize 2 Singapore universities, and Singapore committed to recognize 20 Korean universities. The chapter in the PTAs on the movement and temporary entry of business persons goes beyond the GATS framework on the movement of natural persons. It lists general principles and obligations for common disciplines, grants temporary entry and deals with information provision and dispute settlement. Furthermore, it grants specific commitments on temporary entry categories of business visitors, traders and investors, and intra-corporate transferees, as well as specifying durations of stay. The PTA with Australia also defines service sellers and short-term services suppliers for the purpose of movement of natural persons. It also prohibits labour market testing on those persons permitted to move under the agreement.

Competition rules further develop the GATS framework in telecommunication services. These rules include specific disciplines concerning anti-competitive behaviour and major and dominant suppliers.

Conclusions on services

It should first be acknowledged that the similarities between country approaches to services liberalization are as pronounced as the differences. Most importantly, they share to a very large extent the same sectoral and modal sensitivities. Moreover, the different agreements to which each core entity is a party are by no means identical, depending as they do on the partner(s) in question.

Nevertheless, some broad characteristics, and differences, can be identified:

- *Singapore*, in keeping with its generally liberal approach to trade policy, is at the liberalizing end of the reform spectrum in its preferential agreements. As in other policy areas, Singapore shows a willingness to be flexible to accommodate the preferences of its PTA partners.

- The *United States* too seeks ambitious outcomes, as reflected in its use of negative listing, though this needs careful interpretation. Moreover, the United States departs significantly from its self-imposed "gold standard" by using negative-list reservations to exclude measures affecting services maintained at the sub-national level. The United States is also relatively cautious with respect to provisions on competition policy. In the area of investment, as will be noted elsewhere, US-style agreements (including NAFTA) tend to go beyond issues relating to the right of establishment (the principal focus of EU-style agreements) by building on the investment treatment and protection principles of bilateral investment treaties.

- The *European Union* is distinguished by its pursuit of regulatory harmonization. In the area of competition policy, agreements to which the European Union is a party tend to include coordination of specific competition rules and standards, in contrast to US-style agreements (including NAFTA), which tend to contain only general obligations to take action against anti-competitive behaviour without setting out specific standards or provisions. EU agreements (and those of EFTA) also tend to be distinguished from those of the United States by the use of positive (or hybrid) listing. It may be that positive listing helps facilitate internal coordination within a trading bloc. This will be a factor when the European Union is successful in negotiating region-to-region agreements as is its aim. For example, the CARIFORUM states have produced separate schedules of commitments.
- *Japan* tends to be distinguished by the intended use of preferential agreements to stimulate domestic reform efforts. Japan's agreements often share characteristics of those negotiated by the United States. Thus the investment chapter of the Japan–Singapore EPA has provisions similar to those found in NAFTA, and like NAFTA includes investor–state provisions. The Japan–Singapore disciplines, however, are weaker than those found in NAFTA and do not apply in full to investment in services (Sauvé, 2003). And the more recent Japan–Philippines PTA runs against the Japanese trend of including investor–state provisions because of Manila's concerns about the costs of international arbitration (*Bridges Weekly Trade News*, 21 September 2006). Japan's strategy with respect to positive and negative listing is not clear and the choice may reflect the preferences of Japan's partners as much as those of Japan.

In terms of going beyond the WTO, the United States has perhaps led the way in pressing for and largely achieving GATS-plus commitments in the PTAs it has negotiated. The US achievements have then provided the target for other core entities in their service negotiations. Given the slow pace of the services negotiations in the WTO, here is perhaps a case in which the motivation for a broad WTO agreement can be undermined by PTAs satisfying the offensive interests of some of the key sector interests in the core entities.

The desire to match the United States' successes in at least negotiating significantly GATS-plus commitments in services has been one of the factors behind the European Union's more aggressive push for better market access in – among other things – services since 2006. The European Union has therefore gone out to match what the United States has done in its PTAs. On the commitments side, the European Union interestingly was willing to make some GATS-plus commitments in Mode 4 in the EU–CARIFORUM negotiations at the end of 2007. As this agreement is seen by the European Union as a model, it suggests that other developing countries, and especially other ACP regions, should be able to get similar GATS-plus commitments.

Designating services provisions as being GATS-plus requires considerable care, however. This is nowhere more evident than in respect of positive and negative listing. Although it is generally accepted that negative listing is usually associated with more transparency and greater liberalization than is positive listing, this says nothing about causality. It may simply be that countries that are prepared to open up significantly are more likely to use a negative list. Nor is the balance of advantage always clear cut. This is nicely illustrated by Japan's agreements (Fink and Molinuevo, 2007). Positive listing (as in Japan–Malaysia) can offer advantages, such as status quo bindings, usually ascribed only to negative listing, while negative listing (as in Japan–Mexico) can bring disadvantages, such as effectively denying application of the agreement to future service activities, that are usually ascribed only to positive listing. The form of listing has implications for asymmetric provisions in PTAs, as discussed below.

An assessment of the extent to which PTAs go beyond the GATS should, ideally, involve measurement of the depth of commitments based on estimated tariff-equivalents. Such a measurement remains technically difficult. It has not been undertaken here and is not readily available in the literature on PTAs. However, an assessment has been made of the incidence of new and improved services commitments in East Asian PTAs (Fink and Molinuevo, 2007), which has enabled the following broad conclusions to be reached about two of our core entities:

- Singapore stands out with 86 per cent of sub-sectors and modes showing improved or new commitments across its 11 PTAs. The corresponding figure for Japan is 71 per cent (less than Korea, at 76 per cent).
- The main value-added of Singapore's PTAs is the widening of GATS commitments to cover additional sub-sectors. With the exception of the US–Singapore agreement there are few improvements relative to existing GATS entries, although Singapore's GATS commitment is already relatively liberal.
- Japan's PTAs offer value-added relative to the GATS in a large number of sub-sectors and modes, though the depth of PTA liberalization is sometimes modest. This partly reflects the already liberal commitments of Japan under the GATS. New PTA commitments cover, in particular, certain professional services.

A common feature of most of the PTAs examined is the extent to which the agreements advance beyond the GATS in financial and telecommunication services. This contrasts with an earlier finding (OECD, 2003) that progress in these infrastructure services was more likely in a multilateral setting, where critical mass is more present. It may in fact be the case that, in a form of reverse engineering, progress in the GATS has provided a stimulus to liberalization at the bilateral and regional level.

On a somewhat related point, it might also be observed that, although there is clear evidence of PTAs going beyond the GATS, there is a tendency for sectors that are difficult to liberalize multilaterally to be equally problematic at the regional level. In the Korea–US agreement (KORUS), for example, while Korea has agreed to open up accounting, legal and broadcasting services, it will not open the education and health sectors.

On the question of asymmetric liberalization, it is often observed that the positive-list/hybrid approach of the GATS contains built-in special and differential treatment, in that countries are able to determine the level of liberalization with which they are comfortable. It might also be observed that bilateral and regional agreements with positive listing are more amenable to asymmetric commitments geared to the levels of development of the participating parties. A positive list of sectors, together with the possibility of binding above status quo, might thus enable governments to tailor their commitments to meet regulatory concerns. It is noteworthy that three East Asian negative-list PTAs have fully or partially reverted to a positive list in scheduling commitments for financial services, a sector where regulatory concerns about foreign participation are often acute (Fink and Molinuevo, 2007).

The pursuit of services liberalization through preferential agreements reflects domestic priorities in terms both of sectors chosen for market opening – as was the case with Japan seeking an external stimulus to domestic reform of financial services – and of sectors shielded from opening – as is the case with maritime cabotage services in the United States and elsewhere. Liberalization of particular sectors or modes can also reflect particular domestic preoccupations. The agreement of Japan in the recent accords with the Philippines and Indonesia to allow greater access of Filipino and Indonesian nurses into Japan reflects concerns arising from Japan being one of the world's most rapidly ageing societies.

At a broader level, services liberalization is being carried out in all of the countries examined in recognition of the dominant and growing role of the service economy and of the benefits to be derived, via both exports and imports, from greater market opening. The focus on infrastructure services, as highlighted in this study, is a clear manifestation of this linkage.

Finally, it should be noted that the policy approximation fostered by some PTAs can have important implications for domestic policy in the less developed partner countries. The tendency for the regulatory norms of the United States and the European Union to become, by virtue of the economic size of these entities, the required standard (*de facto* and *de jure* for EU accession states) means that care is needed in ensuring that regulatory practices are appropriate for the level of development of partners. This is not a feature exclusive to services but it is of particular relevance in this sector. Moreover, notwithstanding the tendency for US and EU regulatory standards to become the *de facto* norm in bilateral agreements to which they are a party, the proliferation of PTAs nevertheless means a proliferation of standards. This has been identified as a particular challenge for developing countries (see OECD, 2005).

On the basis of observations emerging from this study, a number of trends might be expected to become more pronounced within preferential agreements. In some respects, there is likely to be a progression in the WTO-plus character of bilateral and regional agreements. Thus, in those sectors that are subject to liberalization commitments, a consolidation of WTO-plus elements relating to domestic regulation might be expected, whether through greater transparency (seen, for example, in US agreements), standstill provisions (in some EU PTAs) or the inclusion of sectors where no GATS commitments have been made (as in some Japanese agreements). Modest progress is likely in tackling Mode 4 liberalization, because the facilitation of service-provider mobility at the bilateral level is seen to be less threatening than a possible multilateral commitment. There may also be a greater focus on the competition policy dimension of service provision, though in the case of the United States on a very selective basis, as compensation for the absence of competition policy from the Doha Development Agenda. Finally, we can expect an increasing tendency to provide for the right of non-establishment (i.e. no local presence requirement) in order to facilitate cross-border trade via e-commerce. Such a provision is a common feature of agreements featuring generic investment disciplines.

However, sensitive sectors will remain sensitive and there will be measures to shield them from more intense competition. We are likely therefore to see greater use, particularly in North–South PTAs, of a hybrid listing formula, whereby overall negative listing is combined with positive listing in sectors where there are strong regulatory sensitivities. There is also likely to be a growing disparity between the treatment of those sectors subject to liberalization commitments and those (such as health, education and audio-visual) that preferential accords, no less than multilateral negotiations, tend to exclude.

Insofar as preferential agreements are increasingly bilateral, often involving countries that are widely separated both geographically and economically, the pursuit of regulatory harmonization and "legislative alignment" (discussed under EU, above) may become less pronounced (apart from in certain agreements to which the United States or the European Union is a party). Where countries are economically and socially disparate, the conditions for regulatory harmonization may be less than optimal (see work undertaken at the World Bank to establish criteria for "optimum regional harmonization areas"; Mattoo and Fink, 2002).

Investment

Introduction

International rules and provisions on investment have not followed a consistent development, and are the result of a patchwork of multi-level international investment agreements. These agreements range from bilateral investment treaties (BITs), to regional and bilateral trade agreements, and codes and decisions of the Organisation for Economic Co-operation and Development (OECD), as well as multilateral rules under the WTO and UN non-binding codes (Reiter, 2006). This section will focus on the treatment of trade-related investment provisions in PTAs by the core entities, and will thus concentrate on bilateral trade agreements, leaving other levels of rule-making in investment out of its scope. For the sake of coherence and clarity regarding the relationship with the international trading system, we will also briefly describe rule-making within the WTO.

Rules on investment and trade are among the current contentious areas of the WTO and are opposed by many countries, notably in the developing world. Despite this resistance, which led to the withdrawal of the Singapore Issues (apart from trade facilitation) from the current multilateral trade round, trade-related investment measures proliferate in PTAs formed by many countries, including some of those countries that oppose their adoption at the multilateral level. The inclusion of investment provisions in PTAs – arising in part, perhaps, from the greater flexibility of commitments in bilateral accords – is seen by some as highlighting the possibility that PTAs can complement the WTO framework.

As a consequence of the reluctance to negotiate a multilateral trade and investment agreement, rule-making on investment in the WTO is rather limited and patchy to the extent that the relationship between trade and investment is, on the one hand, not comprehensively covered and, on the other hand, spread over various agreements. Investments are covered in the GATS insofar as they constitute a part of Mode 3 (commercial presence), but can also be relevant under Mode 1 (cross-border supply) through provisions for non-establishment. The GATS applies the most favoured nation (MFN) principle to all services, and thus also to investments in services that fall within the scope of the agreement. Furthermore, the national treatment (NT) principle applies to those services where commitments have been undertaken in the schedules of specific commitments. The Agreement on Trade-Related Investment Measures (TRIMs) relates only to trade in goods. It prohibits quantitative restrictions and measures that are inconsistent with national treatment. It also provides an illustrative list, which deals mainly with local content and trade-balancing requirements. The Agreement on Trade-Related Aspects of Intellectual Property Rights (TRIPS) indirectly relates to investment, insofar as it covers intellectual property, an intangible asset that constitutes a significant part of many investments. The Agreement on Subsidies and Countervailing Measures (SCM) addresses investment insofar as it prohibits subsidies and similar measures, which are a practice of states in providing incentives to local and foreign investment. Provisions on government procurement can also have an indirect effect on investment. Enhanced transparency and openness in procurement promote competition because new suppliers believe there is a real chance of gaining access to markets that have otherwise been reserved for preferred suppliers. Even with comprehensive agreements on procurement, a presence in the market is generally required. Thus foreign suppliers will invest in order to gain *de facto* access to procurement markets. Table 4.2 summarizes the treatment of investment in WTO agreements.

Almost all the PTAs reviewed include investment provisions, which can be grouped under six issue areas: provisions related to establishment and non-establishment in sectors other than services; provisions dealing with non-discrimination in non-services sectors; the treatment of investment in services; investment regulation and protection; dispute settlement; and investment promotion and cooperation (Miroudot and Lesher, 2006). The following sections will analyse investment provisions covered in the PTAs of the core entities, keeping in mind the above taxonomy.

Table 4.2 WTO provisions on investment

Agreement	Coverage	Important rules
GATS	Services	MFN, NT in Modes 1 and 3
TRIMs	Goods	NT, prohibition of quantitative restrictions
TRIPS	Intellectual property	MFN, NT, other provisions
SCM	Goods	Prohibition of subsidies and countervailing measures

We will then reflect on the trends across time in this field and the strategies applied by each core entity.

Comparison of approaches

United States

In the OECD ranking of PTAs according to the extensiveness of their investment provisions (Miroudot and Lesher, 2006), NAFTA is placed high. The agreement is WTO-plus in many respects. NAFTA defines "investment" in broad terms. It provides (Chapter 11) for national and MFN treatment both for investment from all NAFTA signatories and for investments from non-partner countries that are located within the NAFTA territory. National and MFN treatment apply equally to both pre- and post-establishment phases of an investment project, and Chapter 11 requires that members provide the better of national or MFN treatment. Chapter 11 also states that members must provide "fair and equitable" treatment. NAFTA contains provisions that prohibit various types of performance requirements, such as import, export and domestic content targets, as well as obligations to transfer technology, many of which go beyond those found in the TRIMs Agreement. NAFTA was one of the first PTAs to provide for investor–state dispute resolution; it also contains provisions for state-to-state dispute settlement. Overall, NAFTA – together with Canada–Chile and Mexico–Japan – is found to have the most extensive package of provisions on investment regulation and protection. NAFTA is commonly considered to have established a "model" approach to the treatment of investment in PTAs (see Table 4.3).

Liberalization of non-services sectors is implemented according to the NAFTA model in the United States' PTAs with Chile (2004), Morocco (2006) and Central America (CAFTA, 2006). The PTA with Oman (2006) contains national treatment but does not extend the MFN clause. Investment in services is most commonly covered in the services section, although in some agreements (Chile, CAFTA) it is explicitly covered within the investment chapter. Regardless of whether investment in services is treated in the services or investment sections, almost all PTAs adopt MFN and national treatment on investment and apply a negative-listing approach. The only exception to this rule is the PTA with Jordan (2001), which uses positive listing. The PTAs with Jordan and Bahrain liberalize investment in services but do not apply to non-services liberalization. The relatively old agreement with Israel (1985) does not include any provisions on investment.

Table 4.3 The NAFTA models of investment agreements

Provision	US model BIT	NAFTA	US–Chile	US–Singapore
Definition of investment	Broad tangible and intangible assets "Every kind of investment owned or controlled"	Broad tangible and intangible asset based	Broad tangible and intangible asset based	Broad tangible and intangible asset based
Coverage	Investment agreement only	Chapter covering all investment (distinct from cross-border services)	Separate investment chapter	Separate investment chapter
Principles	Negative lists tailored to the country concerned	Negative list	Negative list	Negative list
	Pre- and post-investment national treatment and MFN	Pre- and post-investment national treatment (Art. 1102) and MFN (Art. 1103)	Pre- and post-investment national treatment and MFN	Pre- and post-investment national treatment and MFN
Transparency and due process	Some general measures	General rules under Articles 1800–1804	General rules for agreement as a whole	General rules for agreement as a whole
Liberalization	General ban on performance requirements Fair and equitable treatment	Seven performance requirements banned Ban on linking incentives to performance requirements Fair and equitable treatment	As in NAFTA	As in NAFTA
Investment protection	Classic and effective protection	Classic and "effective" expropriation rules and protection of capital transfers	As in NAFTA	As in NAFTA
Regulatory safeguards	Scope for exclusion of sectors General exemptions for security, etc.	Negative list exclusions; reciprocity	As in NAFTA	As in NAFTA
Enforcement / dispute settlement	Investor–state and state–state dispute settlement	Detailed procedural rules on investor state actions	Detailed procedural rules on investor state actions	Detailed procedural rules for investor state dispute settlement

Regulation and protection of investment in US PTAs is substantial to the extent that the agreements, as well as including TRIMs-plus provisions on the prohibition of performance requirements, also provide for the free transfer of funds, the temporary movement of key personnel and provisions on expropriation and specifically address the issue of fair and equitable treatment for investment. As in the modalities of liberalization, the PTA with Jordan differs from the general trend because it does not include any of these measures, with the exclusion of the temporary entry and stay of key personnel. This last measure is also absent from the PTA with Morocco.

Dispute settlement is addressed in most PTAs in the same manner. State–state disputes are settled on an ad hoc basis of consultation and arbitration. Investor–state disputes are to be resolved either through ad hoc arbitration or by permanent arbitration through the International Centre for the Settlement of Investment Disputes (ICSID).

Assessing the WTO-plus character of US PTAs is made difficult by the fact that whereas NAFTA, as well as US–Chile and US–Singapore, is ranked high, another agreement, US–Jordan, is not. It has been suggested (Miroudot and Lesher, 2006) that the absence of pre-establishment provisions in US–Jordan arises because the agreement is focused on investment promotion and cooperation rather than on investment liberalization.

In concluding, it might be observed that US investment provisions in its PTAs are linked closely with broader US foreign policy and economic goals. The United States has used PTAs to promote US investment abroad, as well as economic reforms. It puts considerable emphasis in its PTAs on securing access and protection for its investors in its partners' markets. For this reason, the United States pursues the extension of the NAFTA model to other countries in its PTAs. Similarly, investor–state dispute settlement provisions seek to safeguard US investors' interests abroad. Even so, the United States itself is willing to deviate from its model, as in the case of the US–Australia PTA, which does not include investor–state dispute settlement provisions, probably for fear of legal challenges.

European Union

The Treaty Establishing the European Economic Community (1957) was among the early efforts at introducing rules on investment at the regional level; it emphasized the issues of establishment and the free movement of capital (OECD, 2003). As part of the Single Market Programme, measures were adopted prohibiting restrictions on the movement of capital between member states that were extended to include restrictions between member states and third countries.

Agreements involving countries that have historically restricted capital movements have also tended to emphasize establishment and capital movement issues. For example, the Europe Agreements, concluded in the early and mid-1990s between the European Community and Central and East European countries, also focus primarily on establishment issues by providing for national treatment with regard to the establishment and operation of companies and nationals.

The EU–Chile PTA contains a number of WTO-plus features. The chapter on investment in goods provides pre-establishment national treatment, together with an undertaking to review the legal framework for investment in both Chile and EU member states by March 2008. The services chapter covers establishment with respect to Mode 3. Several sectors are nevertheless excluded from the ambit of the agreement, including audio-visual, maritime cabotage, air transport and government procurement (covered under a separate chapter). It has been observed that EU–Chile is the first PTA in which the European Union included rules on the establishment of investments with a non-EU-accession country and that, in this respect, it could represent a new EU model agreement in respect of investment. It might also be observed that EU–Chile can be distinguished from the NAFTA model in that it makes reference to existing obligations under OECD codes, and might be regarded as representing a progressive, or gradual, approach to investment rules (see Table 4.4).

The limited coverage of investment in EU PTAs is owing in part to the fact that foreign direct investment does not fall under European Union competence. Bilateral investment treaties have been negotiated at the member state level. The draft Lisbon Treaty, if ratified by the 27 member states, would bring FDI under European Union competence, with the result that more extensive investment provisions could be included in EU PTAs. It is of interest to note that some of the European Union's current and potential partners in PTAs would prefer a comprehensive investment agreement with the European Union as a whole.[6]

Whether or not EU–Chile represents a new departure will depend on the evolution of the relationship between the EU Commission and the member states.[7] On the basis of an agreement forged under the Swedish EU presidency between Sweden and France (representing the two poles of opinion), EU–Chile, unlike EU–Mexico, came to have meaningful commitments on pre-establishment. But post-establishment investment protection and enforcement through investor–state dispute settlement were once more left aside, with a reference to BITs between individual EU member states and Chile. In short, the Commission had to stay in line with the distribution of competence within the European Union, and was not given any mandate to negotiate provisions on protection similar to those found in BITs.

It is therefore not assured that the achievement of including pre-establishment commitments can be consolidated, and perhaps extended to post-establishment provisions. In the meantime, the Euro-Med agreements and the Cotonou Agreement between the European Union and the ACP countries, instead of directly incorporating the full range of investment provisions typically found in bilateral investment treaties, provide for the conclusion of such treaties between the parties. Until recently it was necessary to conclude (Reiter, 2006) that, in a post-NAFTA world and compared with many other countries, including some more advanced developing countries, the European Union's treatment of investment in PTAs remained fairly limited in scope. Adoption of the Lisbon Treaty would bring FDI under EU competence and thus clear one of the obstacles to the European Union including comprehensive investment provisions in PTAs, but even with this one must expect some of the member states of the European Union to wish to retain national BITs.

State–investor dispute settlement mechanisms are not included in any of the EU PTAs examined. State–state dispute settlement is solved through consultations (all agreements) and through the establishment of political bodies (Morocco, Jordan, Israel). The EU–CARIFORUM EPA, however, suggests the trend is towards more formal panel-based dispute settlement in EU PTAs.

EFTA

EFTA agreements are widely dispersed within the OECD ranking of investment provisions, with EFTA–Singapore highly ranked, EFTA–Mexico somewhat less so, and EFTA–Chile towards the end of the scale. Neither of EFTA's agreements with its Mediterranean partners – Morocco (2002) and Israel (1993) – contains provisions on investment. The declaration with the Gulf Cooperation Council (2000) has no concrete provisions on investment. And the PTA with the Southern African Customs Union (2002) deals only partially with investment promotion and cooperation.

Surprisingly, the PTA with Mexico (2001) is rather limited and mainly deals with liberalization and protection of certain payments and transfers related to foreign direct investment, as well as investment promotion. It has no provisions on the right of establishment or non-establishment with regard to non-services sectors. Investment promotion and cooperation are confined to information-enhancing mechanisms, cooperation procedures and harmonization of rules. The review clause foresees the

Table 4.4 The progressive liberalization model of investment agreements: An illustrative list

	WTO	OECD	EU–Chile	EU–CARIFORUM EPA
Definition	Provision of a service by means of establishment	Broad	FDI, real estate and securities	
Coverage	Services covered by GATS using positive and negative listing	Positive listing		Positive listing (Art. 66)
Principles	Post-investment national treatment for services and MFN subject to exceptions	National treatment (not binding for pre-investment) and MFN	Reference to existing obligations under OECD codes	National treatment (Art. 68) and MFN (Art. 70)
Transparency	Rules for services investment under Mode 3	Binding rules on transparency with ratchet mechanism	General transparency rules for the agreement	
Liberalization	Ban on six performance requirements in TRIMs	Progressively remove all restrictions	As under existing agreements	
Investment protection	None	Financial transfers protected	None, but reference to existing BITs that provide protection	No restrictions on capital movements (Art. 123); otherwise covered by BITs with EU member states

Obligations on investors	None	Non-binding provisions in the Code of Conduct for multinational corporations OECD codes on restrictive business practices	None	Anti-bribery obligation Obligation to core labour standards as per 1998 ILO Declaration on Fundamental Principles and Rights at Work (Art. 72 (a)) No undermining of environment agreements (Art. 72(b))
Exclusions/safeguards	Exclusion of sensitive sectors General exclusions (e.g. security, health, environment) Pursuit of "legitimate" regulatory policy objectives	Scope for exclusion of sensitive sectors Public policy, health and security exemptions Derogations in cases of economic disturbance	N/a	
Implementation and enforcement	General state–state under Dispute Settlement Understanding	Consultation and peer pressure	Bilateral state–state	State–state dispute settlement through conciliation in bilateral Trade and Development Committee with option of panels

Source: compiled by the authors on the basis of the texts of the agreements.

possibility of future liberalization within three years of entry into force. Investment is addressed in the services section covering national treatment and MFN on establishment and pre-establishment with negative-list schedules. In the EFTA–Chile PTA (2004), non-discrimination is not included for non-services sectors and the services section covers investment with national treatment and MFN, providing for market access using positive lists. The PTA also contains provisions that prohibit ownership requirements and allows for the free transfer of fees, but it is silent on expropriation, which is an important provision recurring in many PTAs. There is no investor–state mechanism. And investment promotion or cooperation mechanisms are absent from the agreement.

In contrast to those agreements, the PTAs with East Asian countries Korea (2006) and Singapore (2003) are further developed.[8] Liberalization of investment is quite extensive in the case of Korea, and the PTA provides for both MFN and national treatment for establishment (investment provisions are covered in a separate agreement to the PTA) and pre-establishment on a negative-list basis. Investment in services sectors is treated through the same instrument, although limited through positive lists. The PTA provides for provisions on free transfer of funds, expropriation and the temporary entry of key personnel as part of the investment regulatory setting. State–state dispute settlement is carried out through consultation and ad hoc arbitration, while state–investor dispute settlement in investment is subject to both an independent international arbitrator and the ICSID. Investment promotion and cooperation mechanisms are not provided for in the PTA.

EFTA countries have tended to follow the European Union in their PTA investment provisions for many years. However, as seen in their PTAs with Korea and Singapore, this has changed in recent years, and EFTA has gone beyond the European Union with relation to its investment provisions. This is to some extent a result of an amendment to the EFTA convention, adopted in 2001, which led to the internal adoption of key NAFTA provisions that later on facilitated more advanced PTAs with third countries.

Japan

As noted earlier, Mexico–Japan is ranked among the agreements having the most extensive package of provisions dealing with investment regulation and protection. It is ranked high in the OECD listing, as is Japan–Singapore.

Japan's agreements with Mexico (2005), Malaysia (2006), the Philippines (2006) and Chile (2007) all follow a negative-listing approach for pre-establishment, with MFN and national treatment provisions on establishment for non-services sectors. The PTA with Thailand (2007) is an exception, following a positive-listing approach to pre-establishment. Investment provisions in services are addressed in the PTAs within the services sections. In these chapters, MFN and national treatment are accorded, and limitations and commitments are provided in positive listing. The PTA with Mexico is an exception, and applies a negative-list approach, following the NAFTA model. Furthermore, liberalization of investment in services is covered in this PTA in the investment chapter.

All of Japan's PTAs surveyed here include provisions that prohibit performance requirements. However, these provisions extend beyond the TRIMs only in the case of the Philippines, Mexico and Chile. Whereas prohibition of an ownership requirement is specifically covered solely in the case of Mexico, all of the PTAs include measures on the freedom of transfer of fees and on expropriation and guarantee the temporary entry or stay of key personnel.

Dispute settlements are treated through ad hoc consultations and arbitration in the case of state–state disputes. Investor–state disputes are resolved through international arbitration or referral to the ICSID.

The framework for investment promotion and cooperation does not include measures dealing with harmonization of legislation and rules or lock-in prospects for future liberalization. However, investment promotion provisions are included in the Mexican and Malaysian PTAs. In addition, these two PTAs include mechanisms for cooperation in investment.

Singapore

The investment provisions in PTAs to which Singapore is a party tend to be ranked relatively high.

The New Zealand–Singapore PTA is found to be among the most extensive in terms of investment liberalization, with pre- and post-establishment national treatment of goods and services (Miroudot and Lesher, 2006). The absence of an MFN clause in the services chapter causes the agreement to be ranked a little behind NAFTA. Provisions on investment regulation and protection are also absent, although, interestingly, they are included in more recent Singapore PTAs with the United States and Japan.

Singapore's PTAs tend to follow the NAFTA model. Investment in services, however, is covered in a more varied way. The PTAs with the United States and with Korea (2006) address investment in services within the investment chapter. Other agreements – with Japan (2002), Australia (2003), EFTA and Jordan (2005) – include investment within the services section. National treatment is always granted, yet MFN is extended only in the case of PTAs with EFTA and the United States. The PTAs with Korea, Australia and the United States use a negative-list approach, whereas other agreements follow positive listing.

Provisions on the prohibition of performance requirements tend to extend beyond those in the TRIMs, with the exception of the PTA with Jordan. The agreement with Australia includes a specific prohibition on ownership requirements. The free transfer of funds, which is common to almost any PTA with investment provisions, is not prescribed in the PTA with Korea. Temporary stay or entry of key personnel, fair and equitable treatment, and expropriation measures are addressed in all agreements.

Dispute settlement is addressed in a similar manner across the PTAs. For state–state disputes, the PTAs provide for ad hoc consultation and arbitration. Investor–state disputes are to be resolved through either the ICSID or international and independent arbitration.

In principle, Singapore's investment provisions do not address investment promotion, cooperation, harmonization of rules and legislation or future liberalization. However, investment promotion measures are provided for in the PTAs with Japan and Jordan. Furthermore, cooperation in investment mechanisms is addressed in the PTA with Japan.

Following the Asian financial crisis, Singapore decided to accelerate its liberalization processes beyond the ASEAN Investment Area. Although a part of ASEAN, it considered the grouping's processes to be slow, in particular with regard to consensus-building concerning trade agreements with third countries. Singapore's active bilateral trade policy following the Asian financial crisis prioritizes its main trading partners, as well as trying to achieve a first-mover advantage with countries that are not yet linked with Southeast Asia and are interested in becoming so. Singapore's strategy in investment is based on a small and open economy perception aimed at attracting inward investment, and its PTA investment rules put an emphasis on the benefits of foreign-owned investment. Singapore's conclusion of PTAs with Egypt and Jordan was motivated by the goal of inducing investors in third countries to channel their investments in Jordan and Egypt via subsidiaries to be established in Singapore, rather than in places such as the United States or the European Union.

Conclusions on investment

A recurring theme of this section has been the variety of ways in which countries deal with investment in their own agreements. Such differences may in fact be simply the result of differences between the countries. Nevertheless, some distinctions among countries might be suggested.

A distinguishing feature of the investment provisions of the United States, and its NAFTA partners, is the relative emphasis placed on investment regulation and protection. The three agreements found (by the OECD) to have the most extensive provisions in this area all involve NAFTA parties.

A distinction might also be drawn between the NAFTA practice of combining all investment provisions (goods and services) in one chapter, with cross-border services in another chapter, and the preference of the European Union to have separate chapters for provisions dealing with, respectively, goods and services. However, it has been found (Houde et al., 2007) that, in terms of investment protection, the determining factor is not the configuration of the chapters within PTAs, but rather the scope and coverage of the investment protection provisions themselves.

A distinction can also be drawn between those agreements that tend to use a negative-list approach and those employing a positive list. The former are essentially NAFTA inspired and include US–Mexico, US–Morocco and Japan–Mexico. The latter are GATS based and include EU–Chile, EFTA–Singapore and Japan–Singapore, which we have termed the progressive liberalization model (see Table 4.4). As with the services discussion earlier, however, care is needed in drawing implications about the liberalization potential of these two approaches. Although negative listing is seen as being relatively comprehensive and transparent, and positive listing as flexible and gradual, both approaches in the area of investment in PTAs are found to be WTO-plus. Furthermore, elements of flexibility can be introduced into negative listing, just as positive listing can be made more transparent (Houde et al., 2007).

The tendency to cover investment provisions in side-BITs would also seem to be a distinguishing feature of EU – or, more precisely, EU member states' – practice.

A difference is also evident between the United States and the European Union in terms of resort to sequential negotiations at different levels or forums (Woolcock, 2006). The United States first forged progress through linking the investment protection principles of bilateral investment treaties with the plurilateral rules developed at the OECD. The resulting model was then applied at the regional level in the Canada–US Free Trade Agreement and perfected in NAFTA, before efforts were made to have the model adopted at the plurilateral level in the negotiations over the Multilateral Agreement on Investment (MAI). When the MAI failed, the United States opted to promote the NAFTA model in preferential agreements, rather than in the multilateral setting of the WTO, because of developing country opposition to high-standard rules. In contrast, the European Union has (to date) made less use of such sequential negotiations and has not used PTAs to promote a coherent model for investment rules. As seen above, this is largely because of "domestic" factors related to which level of policy-making in the European Union – the Commission or the member states – has competence over investment in international negotiations. As discussed in the section on EU motivations however, there has been a noticeable shift in EU policy since 2006, and the European Union's negotiating partners, in PTAs at least, see the European Union as pursuing more of a sequential negotiation strategy in which the current PTAs under negotiation play a central role.

Rules on investment found in PTAs usually go beyond the WTO by providing provisions for the right of establishment (OECD, 2003). One of the most comprehensive examples is the 1957 Treaty Establishing the European Economic Community, which addresses investment primarily through provisions on freedom of establishment and free movement of capital. The European Union seems now to be extending this approach beyond the confines of the Union. The EU–Chile PTA was the first agreement in which the European Union included rules on the establishment of investments with a non-EU-accession country. Freedom of establishment objectives are also a common feature of many African PTAs – such as the Common Market for Eastern and Southern Africa and the Economic Community of West African States.

A number of PTAs have gone beyond issues relating to establishment by building on the investment treatment and protection principles of bilateral investment treaties. For example, NAFTA requires parties to accord the better of national treatment and MFN treatment to investors of another party. The investment chapter of the Japan–Singapore Economic Partnership Agreement has provisions very similar to those found in NAFTA and, like NAFTA, the agreement includes investor–state provisions. The agreements that have the most extensive "packages" of provisions on investment regulation and protection are NAFTA, Canada–Chile and Mexico–Japan. Because of questions of competence, EU agreements tend to be accompanied by BITs, negotiated by the member states, which deal with post-establishment investment protection.

Finally, in respect to WTO-plus, several regional agreements aim at fostering cooperation between the firms of member states by establishing a special legal regime for the formation of regional business enterprises. For example, the Cartagena Agreement provides for the formation of Andean Multinational Enterprises.

It has been found that, compared with the GATS, there is a tendency towards bilateral reciprocity in investment provisions in PTAs, particularly in agreements between developed countries and developing countries that have made fewer commitments under the GATS (Houde et al., 2007).

In short, very little evidence has been found of asymmetry in provisions dealing with investment. And where there is evidence it needs to be interpreted with care. It may even be that, where there is asymmetric treatment, it could be seen as favouring the developed partner. For example, in EU–Jordan, EU foreign direct investment gets both MFN treatment and national treatment in Jordan, whereas Jordanian investment in the European Union receives only MFN. This raises the question, however, of whether in talking about asymmetric treatment it is necessary to distinguish between the legal provisions and the economic effects of such treatment. In this particular case, asymmetric *legal provisions*, which give better treatment to EU investment in Jordan than to Jordanian investment in Europe, may, because of the benefits of inwards FDI, in fact serve the *economic interests* of Jordan. In this case, Jordan stands to "gain more by giving more", which suggests that asymmetric treatment that serves to limit liberalization commitments does not necessarily promote national self-interest (Heydon, 2008).

The tensions between, on the one hand, fostering and protecting investment and, on the other, preserving governments' right to regulate are a clear manifestation of the link to domestic policy. This is reflected, for all of the core entities, in the way in which PTA provisions seek to foster the growth of FDI and its attendant benefits while at the same time excluding sectors, such as audio-visual or coastal shipping, where domestic sensitivities remain high.

In terms of policy trends, a clear tendency has become apparent (Miroudot and Lesher, 2006) whereby investment, which has traditionally been covered in BITs, is increasingly – with a question mark for the European Union – being incorporated into PTAs. All North–South PTAs with investment provisions have been signed within roughly the past 15 years, starting with NAFTA in 1994. As long as investment remains outside the scope of the DDA, this trend might be expected to continue. However, the counter-argument to this is that, precisely because investment has been taken out of the Doha Development Agenda, public opinion in both developed and developing countries will come to question the inclusion of comprehensive investment provisions in PTAs. Parts of civil society in the European Union have already voiced concerns that Economic Partnership Agreement negotiations aim to establish rules in areas that have been taken off the agenda in the WTO. In Canada and the United States, the number of politically sensitive investor–state disputes, and the associated fines imposed upon governments, could generate a public backlash against ambitious investment provisions in PTAs (Reiter, 2006). The jury is out on this, and for the moment the view that PTAs can bring a more coherent approach to the promotion and protection of investment is likely to prevail.

Notes

1. One reason for the non-inclusion of services in the EPA negotiations is that the original Cotonou Agreement refers only to goods and a main motivation for negotiating EPAs was to comply with Article XXIV of the GATT.
2. The other ACP regions are reluctant to see the EU–CARIFORUM EPA as setting a precedent because it is more comprehensive in many respects, including services, than many ACP states are comfortable with.
3. The Mode 4 commitments by the European Union include fairly generous provision for temporary entry of professionals and contract workers from the CARIFORUM states and even include access for Caribbean artists in the cultural industry, where the European Union has been especially defensive in the GATS with its insistence on a "cultural exclusion" (see Chaitoo, 2008).
4. In the GATS, Mexico, Liechtenstein, Norway and Iceland have not listed any commitments on maritime transport. Switzerland has two sectors committed.
5. This section will not review Singapore's PTAs with the core entities, which are covered in other sections.
6. This was, for example, the case in the EU–CARIFORUM negotiations (see Commonwealth Secretariat, 2008).
7. The following observations draw on Reiter (2006).
8. The PTA with Singapore will be analysed later. A PTA containing investment provisions is currently being negotiated with Thailand.

5

Intellectual property rights, the environment and core labour standards

The seemingly disparate group of issues concerning intellectual property rights (IPRs), the environment and core labour standards has in common one important characteristic – a concern about "market failure". It is said that, without limits on imitation, the private returns on innovation would be lower than the public returns, and the supply of innovation correspondingly reduced. There is concern that, without corrective action, production in one country can have negative environmental effects, or externalities, on other countries because the prices of the resources used (such as air or water) are too low. Similarly, there is a concern that the market cannot be relied upon to give a correct "price" to the practice of child labour or the denial of trade union rights.

Related to concerns about market failure are those about a perceived race-to-the-bottom that would arise were countries deliberately to breach standards relating to IPR protection, the environment or labour conditions in order to gain an unfair competitive advantage. Although clearly there are abuses in each of these areas, there is no evidence of a race-to-the-bottom. Rather the contrary; compliance with internationally agreed standards in each of these fields is seen to rise as countries become more prosperous. Nor is it clear that trade policy has a role in seeking to enforce such compliance.

Underpinning doubts about the role of trade policy is the principle established by the Dutch economist Jan Tinbergen that, for policy to work, there must be as many independent effective instruments as there are feasible targets (Tinbergen, 1956). Hence trade policy measures are

The rise of bilateralism: Comparing American, European and Asian approaches to preferential trade agreements, Heydon and Woolcock,
United Nations University Press, 2009, ISBN 978-92-808-1162-9

unlikely to be the most effective way of protecting IPRs or improving labour or environmental standards. It is this uncertainty about the role of trade policy that fuels ongoing debate about the treatment of these three issues in the WTO.

The protection of intellectual property rights is covered in the World Trade Organization (WTO) through the Agreement on Trade-Related Aspects of Intellectual Property Rights (TRIPS), though some trade economists have questioned whether IPRs belong in the WTO, in part because IPR protection is seen as a device for transferring income from poor to rich countries and because bringing in IPRs makes it harder to resist the inclusion of other "non-trade" issues, such as core labour standards. A continuing focus of attention is the need for the flexible application of WTO provisions in order to improve developing countries' access to medicines.

The environment is covered extensively in different GATT/WTO provisions – including via Article XX, key findings of dispute settlement panels and the Appellate Body, and ongoing efforts to liberalize trade in environmental goods and services. However, apart from cases where environmental damage is intrinsic to the trade (such as the transport of hazardous waste), attempts to use trade restrictions to enforce environmental standards (for example, suggested restrictions on imports from non-signatories to the Kyoto Protocol) have so far been strongly resisted.

Similarly, apart from sanctions against trade in products of prison labour, attempts to use trade restrictions to help enforce labour standards have been avoided in the WTO. Among the reasons for the failure of the WTO Ministerial Meeting in Seattle in 1999 was the push by the American Federation of Labor and the Congress of Industrial Organizations (AFL-CIO), backed by then President Clinton, to have trade sanctions used to enforce compliance with the provisions of the International Labour Organization (ILO).

Given the lack of agreement about how intellectual property rights, the environment and labour standards should be treated in the WTO, it is perhaps not surprising that, in each of these three areas, preferential trade agreements (PTAs) are frequently WTO-plus. It is striking, however, that the PTAs in question are essentially those to which the United States is a signatory, with the European Union perhaps moving in this direction with regard to labour standards. US preferential agreements are TRIPS-plus in many respects, including by extending the minimum term of protection for copyrights, trademarks and patents. And, as a result of an agreement reached in May 2007 between the US administration and the Congress, US agreements will henceforth be required to contain provisions dealing with the environment and labour standards, which if breached in a way that demonstrably affects trade or investment will trigger dispute settlement.

This leads to the final characteristic shared by these three issues: being WTO-plus does not necessarily mean being "better".

IPR protection undoubtedly brings benefits, not least for developing countries. If intellectual property rights are not enforced in a particular country, foreign rights holders will be discouraged from making their intellectual property available, whether by trade (through licensing) or by investment. It is thus found that a 1.0 per cent increase in patent protection in developing countries is associated with a 0.5 per cent increase in the stock of foreign direct investment (FDI) (Park and Lippoldt, 2003). Nevertheless, the relationship between patent protection and FDI is found to be positive, *but diminishing*. Beyond a certain point, the protection of intellectual property rights becomes counter-productive. By granting producers of intellectual products excessive market power, IPRs may negatively affect trade and investment. PTAs, particularly those of the United States, that extend IPR protection risk entering the zone of diminishing returns.

The danger with associating trade policy with the pursuit of improved environmental and labour conditions – in themselves laudable goals – is that trade policy itself will succumb to protectionist capture. This too is a risk inherent in the PTAs that incorporate this linkage.

Intellectual property rights

Introduction

Many of the recent bilateral agreements implemented by the United States, the European Union, the European Free Trade Association (EFTA), Japan and Singapore include provisions on intellectual property rights that go beyond the requirements of the WTO Agreement on Trade-Related Aspects of Intellectual Property Rights. However, with few exceptions, the majority of these "TRIPS-plus" provisions are to be found in the PTAs of the United States and the European Union (see Table 5.1 for an overview). Many of the PTAs negotiated by Japan and Singapore do not even include sections concerning IPR. Furthermore, the PTAs of the United States are significantly more "TRIPS-plus" than those that have been negotiated to date by the European Union, which tend to focus narrowly on the protection of European geographical indicators (GIs). The PTAs negotiated by the United States contain extensive "TRIPS-plus" requirements for copyrights, trademarks, patents, civil

Table 5.1 TRIPS-plus provisions in preferential trade agreements

	USA	EU	EFTA	Japan	Singapore
Copyrights	X	*			
Trademarks	X	*			
Patents	X	*	X		
Data exclusivity	X		X		
Geographical indicators		X			
Industrial design			X		
Satellite signals	X				
Rights management information	X				
Internet domains	X				
Civil proceedings	X				
Border measures	X				
Criminal proceedings	X				

Notes: X = findings from the current study; * = observations from Pugatch (2006).

and criminal proceedings, and border measures, which are the most comprehensive IPR provisions contained in PTAs.

Comparison of approaches

The United States

The PTAs negotiated by the United States include many "TRIPS-plus" provisions over a range of areas.[1]

Copyrights
US PTAs have extended the minimum term of protection for copyrights from the 50-year term established by TRIPS. Although the North American Free Trade Agreement (NAFTA) required only 50 years of protection, subsequent agreements with Singapore, Chile, Morocco, Bahrain and Peru have all extended this term to a minimum of 70 years.[2] US–Oman, signed by President Bush in late 2006, extends the period of protection, when not calculated on the life of a person, to an astounding 95 years.[3] US PTAs also provide rules and penalties for the circumvention of technological protection measures.

Related rights
US PTAs are also TRIPS-plus in their obligations concerning rights management information and the protection of satellite signals and Internet domain names.[4]

Trademarks

US PTAs extend the term of protection for trademarks from the 7 years established in TRIPS to a minimum of 10 years. US agreements also strengthen the protection of well-known marks and eliminate a loophole in TRIPS that allowed countries to require that the generic name of a pharmaceutical product be displayed larger than the trademark name (Article 20 of TRIPS).[5] US PTAs provide detailed provisions for the creation of an efficient and transparent trademark registration process, which includes electronic applications, refusals of protection to be written and reasoned, and the opportunity for interested parties to contest decisions.[6]

Geographical indicators

US PTAs are not TRIPS-plus in their provisions for GIs; in fact, they may be "TRIPS-minus" (Vivas-Eugui and Spennemann, 2006). US PTAs seek to protect GIs through incorporating them into trademark systems, whereas TRIPS established GIs as a potentially separate IPR from trademarks.[7]

Patents

US PTAs are TRIPS-plus in three important ways. First, every US PTA since Singapore has carefully prohibited the "Bolar provisions" that allow for the use of technology from a patented pharmaceutical to aid in the production of generic versions. The use of such Bolar provisions to produce generic drugs has been ruled consistent with TRIPS obligations.[8] Second, US PTAs require the extension of the term of patent protection if the life of the patent has been curtailed owing to delays in patent registration or authorization.[9] Third, some US PTAs prohibit the parallel importation of pharmaceutical products – a practice allowed under the international exhaustion provisions of TRIPS.[10]

Data exclusivity

US PTAs have all been used to clarify the vague terminology of Article 39 of TRIPS, which merely stated that undisclosed data for the approval of pharmaceutical products or agricultural chemicals should be protected. After NAFTA required a period of protection of 5 years for such data, all subsequent US PTAs have required 5 years of data protection for pharmaceutical products and 10 years for agricultural chemicals.[11]

Civil proceedings

US PTAs contain careful legal wording in order to better define TRIPS provisions that were left vague and difficult to enforce. For instance, US

PTAs attempt to preclude the possibility of "innocent infringement" by excluding the TRIPS wording that punishable infringement must be done "knowingly, or with reasonable ground to know". In contrast, US PTAs simply state that "in judicial proceeding, the judicial authorities shall have the authority to order the infringer to pay the right holder",[12] without any qualifications as to what type of infringement occurred.

TRIPS-plus provisions also include:

- the option for pre-established damages to be paid to rights holders, in excess of losses, in order to provide a deterrent against future infringement;[13]
- the destruction of infringing goods in civil proceedings, despite the domestic law of most countries only allowing such action in criminal proceedings;[14]
- the extension of civil proceedings to all IPRs, not just those mentioned in the agreement;
- the destruction of any materials used in the infringement – whereas TRIPS holds that materials can be destroyed only if the "predominate use" is for infringement;[15]
- the provision that sanctions be applied to any party of the proceedings that does not protect confidential information;[16]
- the provision that government experts who must be paid by the litigation shall not be prohibitively expensive.[17]

Border measures

Since the implementation of TRIPS, US PTAs have progressively tightened the requirements on border control. Although TRIPS requires *ex officio* action only for the importation of infringing goods, the PTA with Singapore requires such action for the importation and the exportation of infringing goods, as well as cooperation for infringing goods found in transit. All subsequent agreements have explicitly required *ex officio* action for infringing goods imported, exported and in transit.[18]

Criminal proceedings

The most notable provisions in US PTAs include: the right of authorities to initiate legal action without the need for private complaint;[19] forfeiture of assets traceable to the infringing activity;[20] and the need for criminal proceedings in the absence of wilful wrong-doing.[21]

The European Union

Although the EU agreements may be TRIPS-plus in their requirement for all parties to accede to several international conventions, the focus of the EU agreements is clearly on the protection of geographical indicators for EU wine and spirits.[22] However, the protection of wine and spirits is not always sought as an integral part of Association Agreements. Although the Agreements for the Protection of Wine and Spirits are included in an annex of the agreement with Chile, the Agreement for the Protection of Spirit Drinks with Mexico is a separate document.

Geographical indicators

The European Union has used bilateral agreements to protect its interest in international protection for GIs. Specifically, the European Union has used such agreements to eliminate the exceptions granted in Article 24 of TRIPS, which allows for the continued use of GIs that had been used in good faith for a period of time before TRIPS.

Level and means of protection

Both the Spirits Agreement with Mexico and the Wine and Spirits Agreements with Chile stipulate that the use of GIs must follow the laws and regulations of the party in which the GI originates.[23] This requires Mexico and Chile to respect EU laws concerning GIs.

Automatic protection for GIs

Both the Spirits Agreement with Mexico and the Wine and Spirits Agreements with Chile require "reciprocal" or "mutual" protection for GIs.[24] This requires Mexico and Chile to provide protection for all EU GIs listed in the PTA. This eliminates the ability of domestic authorities to decide that certain uses of GIs do not "mislead the public" sufficiently to infringe upon rights holders.

Exceptions allowed in TRIPS Article 24

The Agreement with Mexico explicitly eliminates the exceptions allowed for in TRIPS.[25] The Agreement with Chile accords protection to a list of designated GIs, thus eliminating the exceptions to TRIPS.[26] For instance, all trademarks deemed in violation of EU GIs must be cancelled within 12 years for domestic use, within 5 years for use for export, and immediately upon entry into force for small-quantity exports.[27]

Protection of "traditional expressions"

Regulation of "traditional expressions" is present in the PTA with Chile only because of its apparent specificity to wine.[28] Similar regulations can be found in the EU PTA with South Africa, another major wine producer. This is a major TRIPS-plus regulation, since "traditional expressions" do not qualify as GIs under TRIPS.

EFTA

Preferential agreements implemented by EFTA include TRIPS-plus provisions in three main areas. First, the extension of protection for industrial design. All EFTA agreements require a potential period of protection of 15 years, longer than the 10 years required by TRIPS.[29] Second, the extension of patent protection owing to curtailment by delays in the marketing approval process. Agreements with Singapore, Chile and Korea require TRIPS-plus extension of patent life.[30] And, third, the protection of confidential information. The agreement with Chile requires 5 years of protection for information concerning pharmaceuticals and 10 years for agricultural chemicals.[31]

EFTA agreements have progressively deepened protection for industrial design. In early agreements with Morocco and Singapore, protection was required for periods of 5 years, renewable two consecutive times. Later agreements all require a 15-year term of protection.

Japan

Of the Japanese agreements examined in detail in this study, only those with Singapore and Malaysia contain TRIPS-plus provisions. However, these provisions are limited to the establishment of a Joint Committee for Singapore and Malaysia, enhanced patent registration systems, and the limitation of liabilities for service providers in the agreement with Malaysia.[32]

Singapore

Of the agreements examined in detail here, only Singapore's PTA with Japan includes provisions for intellectual property rights. The agreement calls for the creation of a Joint Committee, co-chaired by government officials from both parties, to monitor the implementation of the agreement and to foster cooperation between the two countries.[33] The only other substantive requirement provides that Singapore shall designate the Japanese Patent Office as a prescribed patent office in order to facilitate the patent process for applications filed jointly in Japan and Singapore.[34]

Conclusions on intellectual property rights

Recent PTAs have been TRIPS-plus in areas ranging from the extension of patent and copyright terms, to the protection of undisclosed information, to the protection of geographical indicators for wine and spirits. However, these TRIPS-plus provisions have been largely limited to the PTAs negotiated by the United States. Although the European Union has used PTAs to eliminate the exceptions for GI protection allowed in TRIPS, the European Union has not negotiated TRIPS-plus provisions in other IPR areas. The most notable exception to this dominance of IPR provisions by the United States and the European Union is the extension of protection terms for industrial design included in all agreements negotiated by EFTA. For the most part, agreements negotiated by Japan do not address IPR issues in a way that goes beyond TRIPS.

Though US, and to a lesser extent EU, PTAs are found to be TRIPS-plus, this does not necessarily mean "better". It is generally agreed that, although the protection of IPRs is beneficial up to a certain point in encouraging innovation, once that point is exceeded and protection becomes stricter, there can be negative effects on the development of new ideas and processes.

All US PTAs allow for transitional periods in order to ratify certain international conventions and agreements. Transition periods are also often allowed for enforcement, criminal proceedings, electronic applications for trademarks, the extension of patent terms, border measures and civil proceedings, as well as other regulations.[35] It is worth noting, however, that there is not a single instance of a transitional period allowed for the United States, because TRIPS-plus regulations in US PTAs appear to be an extension of US domestic law. The European Union allows for differing transitional periods during which to accede to international conventions.

The United States can most clearly be seen to be advocating domestic-type regulations in the field of geographical indicators and trademarks. Although TRIPS provides for geographical indicators to be protected as a separate type of IPR, US PTAs have attempted to classify GIs as types of trademark. The US conception of GIs is based on a common law system, or private law conception, which grants trademark protection to persons or corporations. Other countries or regions, especially the European Union, can be seen to advocate a public law conception of protection for GIs, which are technically owned by the state rather than by a person (Vivas-Eugui and Spennemann, 2006). By including GIs in the trademark sections of many PTAs, the United States has attempted to spread its domestic conception of GIs and trademarks abroad.

The European Union's focus on GIs is a direct link to domestic protection. The EU approach to GIs is the opposite to the US approach, because EU trading partners must cancel all existing trademarks that are similar to EU protected GIs. EU PTAs eliminate the ability of trading partners to decide that certain trademarks do not "mislead the public", as allowed for in TRIPS.

What can we say about trends? US PTAs follow a standard approach that is nearly identical in most agreements. Although NAFTA does go beyond TRIPS in some important ways, the contemporaneous negotiation of the two agreements led to many similarities. However, US PTAs after NAFTA have all followed a very similar format. In this way, most US PTAs are equally "TRIPS-plus", although there are a few notable exceptions:

- The extension of copyright protection, not based on the life of a person, from 50 years in NAFTA, to 70 years in PTAs with Singapore, Chile, Morocco, Bahrain and Peru, and 95 years with Oman.
- The civil proceedings provision of sanctions against parties not protecting confidential information, which is found only in more recent PTAs such as those with Bahrain, Peru and Oman.
- The increase of border measures from NAFTA's requirement of *ex officio* action for imported infringing goods,[36] to US–Singapore's requirement for such action on imports and exports, to the subsequent requirement in all following PTAs of *ex officio* action on infringing goods imported, exported or in transit.
- The requirement of criminal proceedings for infringing activity, even in the absence of wilful wrong-doing for trafficking in counterfeit labels for computer programs, motion pictures and other audio-visual works.

It can be expected that the EU approach to IPRs in successive PTAs will continue to evolve in a way that reflects the perceived competitive strengths of respective partner countries. For instance, wine and spirits producers such as Chile and South Africa have agreements on both wine and spirits, Mexico has only an agreement concerning spirit drinks, and Morocco, a Muslim country with little production of alcohol, does not have an agreement on either wine or spirits.

The environment

Introduction

Many PTAs, especially the more recent ones, mention the resolve of parties to promote sustainable development, and most of them specifically refer to the environment (Tebar Less and Kim, 2006). This applies to NAFTA and all subsequent agreements adopted by the United States, a majority of agreements signed by the European Union, and a number of Asian treaties, including Japan–Mexico.

Comparison of approaches

United States

General requirement
In the Trade Act of 2002, Congress calls upon negotiators, among other things, "to ensure that trade and environmental policies are mutually supportive" and, in particular, to ensure that a party to a trade agreement with the United States does not fail to effectively enforce its environmental laws in a manner affecting trade; to seek market access for

US environmental technologies, goods and services; and to ensure that the labour, environmental, health or safety policies and practices of the parties to trade agreements with the United States do not arbitrarily or unjustifiably discriminate against US exports or serve as a disguised barrier to trade.

Enforcement of environmental laws
Since the passage of NAFTA, all PTAs concluded by the United States include an obligation to enforce existing domestic environmental laws. They usually provide that "[a] Party shall not fail to effectively enforce its environmental laws, through a sustained recurring course of action or inaction, in a manner affecting trade between the Parties". Agreements recognize that lowering environmental regulations in order to attract investment is inappropriate.

Clarifying the relationship between trade and environmental rules
NAFTA (Art. 104) has addressed an issue that remains unresolved in the WTO by stating that, in the case of an inconsistency between NAFTA provisions and the obligations set out in certain multilateral and bilateral environmental agreements, such environmental obligations will prevail. However, in subsequent bilateral agreements, the United States took a different approach. In US–Singapore, for example, the parties simply recognize the "critical importance of multilateral environmental agreements". Similar wording is found in US agreements with Morocco, Australia and Central America (CAFTA).
   As a result of a bipartisan agreement reached on 10 May 2007 between the US administration and the Congress, parties to US PTAs will henceforth be required to implement seven multilateral environmental agreements (MEAs), including the Montreal Protocol on Substances That Deplete the Ozone Layer, the Convention on International Trade in Endangered Species, the Convention on the Prevention of Marine Pollution, and the Ramsar Convention on Wetlands. The agreement has been interpreted as meaning that, in the event of any difference, the provisions of the MEA would prevail over trade provisions in the relevant PTA. These environmental obligations, and those on core labour standards described below, will be subject to the same dispute settlement procedures as the core commercial rules on tariff cuts. However, violations of these two sets of provisions will become subject to dispute settlement only if they demonstrably affect trade or investment.

Enforcement mechanisms and remedies
US agreements typically provide for state-to-state dispute settlement via binding arbitration, allowing parties to initiate formal dispute settlement

proceedings in the case of alleged persistent patterns of failure by a party to enforce its environmental law effectively. In a particularly interesting form of WTO-plus, some agreements provide for remedies other than retaliation. These agreements, including US–Chile and US–Morocco, provide that a party in breach may have to contribute monetary assessments to a fund for appropriate environmental initiatives.

Public participation
Some of the more recently concluded PTAs, such as US–Australia and US–CAFTA, make specific provision for open dispute settlement hearings and public participation.

Enhanced environmental performance
US agreements tend to include suggestions for improving environmental performance. US–Chile identifies specific goals that both parties will work towards, such as reducing mining pollution, developing a pollutant release and transfer register, and reducing methyl bromide emissions.

The 10 May 2007 accord between Congress and the administration directed the United States Trade Representative to negotiate with Peru a new annex to the US–Peru PTA on forest sector governance, aimed at preventing trade in endangered forest products.

European Union

Collaboration and dialogue
EU agreements, particularly those negotiated with developing countries and transition economies, commonly provide for cooperation aimed at preventing deterioration of the environment, controlling pollution and ensuring rational use of natural resources. EU–Egypt is a case in point.

Exceptions clauses
Most of the agreements concluded by the European Union (and some by EFTA) include exceptions clauses that largely reflect the language used in Article 30 of the Treaty Establishing the European Economic Community. The construction of this exceptions clause differs from that of Article XX of the GATT in that it requires exceptions to be "justified on specified grounds". Moreover, the requirement of Article 30 that exceptions should not "constitute a means of arbitrary discrimination or a disguised restriction on trade between Member States" has been interpreted by the European Court of Justice (ECJ) to include the requirement to examine whether the measure is proportionate to its aim and necessary to achieve the aim – i.e. a necessity test.[37]

Public participation

As with a number of US agreements, some EU arrangements, such as EU–Chile, provide that dispute settlement panel hearings may be open to the public if both parties agree. The agreement also specifies that the panel may receive *amicus curiae* submissions, unless the parties agree otherwise.

EFTA

The preamble of EFTA agreements contains references to promoting conservation, protecting the environment and promoting sustainable development.

Japan

Japan's agreement with Mexico states that it is inappropriate to encourage investment by relaxing environmental standards and allows for consultation among the parties in the event of such action. This is the NAFTA approach. The agreement with Malaysia states that encouraging investment through such actions shall not be done, but does not provide for the possibility of consultation between the parties.

Singapore

Agreements with Japan, India and Korea all contain references to protecting the environment and state that parties retain the right to enact laws to protect human, animal and plant life, as well as the environment. The agreement with Korea is accompanied by a Memorandum of Understanding to further cooperation between the parties.

Conclusions on the environment

Notwithstanding the similarity of approaches to PTA environmental provisions among the core entities, a number of differences can be identified.

Collaboration and dialogue among parties, though by no means exclusive to EU agreements (see, for example, US–Jordan or Japan–Singapore), could be seen as featuring more prominently in EU PTAs than in other agreements. While agreements recently concluded by the United States lay out some general principles on the relationship between trade and environment, leaving the particular objectives to be elaborated in side agreements (such as the North American Agreement on Environmental Cooperation), many recent agreements concluded by the European Union refer to environmental cooperation, priorities and objectives. The latter approach means that the principles of environmental cooperation are present in the agreement as a cross-cutting theme, thus covering a wide range of issues. EU agreements also tend to be distinguished by their provisions for the approximation of laws as a condition of strengthened economic links between the parties. As already noted, EU agreements, and some EFTA agreements, are also distinguished by their reference to Article 30 of the EC Treaty in dealing with exceptions, as an alternative to invoking GATT Article XX.

A particular feature of Japan's approach to the environment in PTAs is the inclusion of more elaborate provisions on cooperation for the implementation of MEAs. In the Japan–Mexico agreement, cooperation in the field of the environment is focused on capacity- and institution-building to foster activities related to the Clean Development Mechanism under the Kyoto Protocol and exploration of appropriate ways to encourage the implementation of projects related to this mechanism.

A number of features of the treatment of the environment in PTAs can be considered as WTO-plus: the obligations in respect of MEAs set out in the accord reached between the US administration and Congress; the introduction of a necessity test in EU PTAs; provision for the use of fines in dispute settlement in US agreements; and provisions for regulatory harmonization in EU agreements.

It seems that environmental cooperation is more prevalent in PTAs between countries with different levels of development. The European Union, for example, although it includes provisions on environmental cooperation in the agreements with developing countries (such as the Cotonou Agreement), generally does not incorporate such provisions in agreements negotiated with developed countries. It may thus be that such cooperation is seen as a way of mitigating potential negative environmental effects resulting from trade provisions, which are often greater in developing countries.

A common feature of PTA treatment of the environment is an express recognition that each party has the right to establish its own levels of domestic environmental protection. Correspondingly, for the most part, it is the domestic environmental law that parties undertake to comply with. This characteristic has met with criticism from environmental non-governmental organizations, which lament the absence from these agreements of provisions to enforce core environmental standards.

Three broad trends can be distinguished. Notwithstanding the WTO-plus character of environmental provisions in many PTAs, these trends tend to reaffirm the importance of developments in the WTO. First, there has been a clear tendency for a number of countries to use Article XX of the GATT as a model for their environment-related exceptions clauses, though the precise language varies – in some agreements the language is broader than that in the GATT; in a few cases it is narrower. Second, in a number of the more recent agreements (for example, US–Chile and US–CAFTA) there is a tendency, in dealing with the relationship with multi-lateral environmental agreements, to refer to ongoing negotiations in the WTO. Third, as in the WTO, the facilitation of public engagement seems to be growing. For example, whereas NAFTA states that all dispute panel hearings are to remain confidential, NAFTA trade ministers in July 2004 instructed their officials to develop rules governing open hearings. US–Australia, US–CAFTA and EU–Chile all provide for open hearings.

Labour standards

Introduction

The exclusion of core labour standards from the work of the WTO, other than through institutional cooperation with the International Labour Organization (ILO), tends to put the spotlight on PTAs – essentially those of the United States – that cover this issue. With the agreement reached on 10 May 2007 between the US Congress and the administration, US emphasis on labour standards can be expected to strengthen.

Comparison of approaches

United States

All of the US PTAs examined in this study contain sections on labour standards. NAFTA and its accompanying North American Agreement on Labor Cooperation (NAALC) are clearly the most comprehensive labour provisions required by any US PTA to date. The NAALC established the Commission for Labor Cooperation, which oversees the implementation of the agreement, reviews public letters on enforcement matters, and provides for an arbitral panel process to resolve disputes between parties. However, the dispute mechanism of the NAALC, as is the case with all US PTAs, allows only for disputes over a party's failure to "effectively enforce its labour laws".[38] Such limitations are usually stated as: "Neither Party may have recourse to dispute settlement under these Agreements for any matter arising under any provision of this Chapter other than Article 16.2.1(a)."[39] US PTAs after NAFTA have all reaffirmed the parties' obligations as members of the ILO and the ILO Declaration on Fundamental Principles and Rights at Work and its Follow-up (1998). They also contain provisions on the following:

- *Enforcement*: each party shall enforce its own domestic laws and recognizes that lowering domestic labour laws to attract investment is inappropriate.[40]
- *Procedural matters*: "Each Party shall provide for appropriate access by persons with a legally recognized interest in a particular matter to impartial and independent administrative, quasi-judicial, or judicial tribunals for the enforcement of its labor laws."[41]
- *Public participation*: vague requirements that recognize the importance of public participation and state that each party shall take into account public comments.
- *Labour consultations*: each party may request consultations over disputes, but only in respect to the failure of a party to enforce its own domestic laws.
- *Creation of a labour cooperation mechanism*: parties shall work jointly on initiatives such as establishing priorities for cooperative activities on labour matters, exchanging information and promoting compliance with ILO Convention 182 on child labour.

It is worth noting that the US agreements on labour and the environment are nearly identical, with the word "Labor" often being substitutable for "Environment".

As a result of the accord reached on 10 May 2007, parties to US PTAs will henceforth be required to enforce worker protection as set out in the ILO's 1998 Declaration on Fundamental Principles and Rights at Work, including:

- freedom of association and the effective recognition of the right to collective bargaining;
- the elimination of all forms of forced or compulsory labour;
- the effective abolition of child labour; and
- the elimination of discrimination in respect of employment and occupation.

Although falling short of invoking the ILO's eight Conventions, which the United States has not signed, this new undertaking clearly goes beyond the current requirement in US PTAs that parties shall enforce their *own domestic laws*. As with the provisions on the environment arising from this accord, violations of these labour provisions will become subject to dispute settlement only if they demonstrably affect trade or investment.

The European Union

For the most part, EU PTAs do not contain substantive requirements for labour standards. However, the PTA signed with Chile makes direct reference to such standards. This agreement holds that the European Union and Chile will cooperate to promote ILO Conventions dealing with issues such as the freedom of association, the right of collective bargaining, non-discrimination, the abolition of forced and child labour, and equal treatment for men and women.[42] PTAs negotiated with Morocco and Egypt both contain provisions on the fair treatment of nationals of another party legally working in the European Union.[43] The PTA with Morocco holds that such treatment shall be non-discriminatory and that workers and their families shall be eligible for social security dealing with issues such as sickness, industrial accidents and unemployment benefits.[44]

For some time the European Union has included provisions on labour standards in its enhanced Generalized System of Preferences scheme, but the Economic Partnership Agreement (EPA) between the European Union and the Caribbean Forum (CARIFORUM) of the African, Caribbean and Pacific Group of States represents the first case of labour provisions in a PTA with developing countries. In Article 191(1) of the EU–CARIFORUM text, the parties reaffirm their commitment to the "internationally recognized core labour standards, as defined by the relevant ILO Conventions, and in particular the freedom of association and the right to collective bargaining, the abolition of forced labour, the elimination of the worst forms of child labour and non-discrimination in respect to employment". The parties also reaffirm their obligations as members of the ILO and their commitments under the ILO Declaration on Fundamental Principles and Rights at Work and its Follow-up (1998). In Article 191(2), the parties reaffirm their commitment to the 2006 Ministerial Declaration by the United Nations Economic and Social Council on Full Employment and Decent Work, promoting the development of international trade in a way that is conducive to full and productive employment and decent work for all, including men, women and young people. There is also a general recognition of the beneficial role that core labour standards and decent work can play in economic efficiency, innovation and productivity, but an obligation in Article 191(4) not to use labour standards as a means of protection.

EFTA

PTAs negotiated by EFTA do not contain substantive requirements for labour standards. In fact, of all the EFTA agreements examined in this study, only those with Mexico, Singapore and Chile make reference to labour in any way. Even in these agreements, the only mention of labour standards is the allowance – also provided for in the GATT/WTO – of trade barriers in order to protect against the products of prison labour.[45]

Japan

PTAs negotiated by Japan do not contain substantive requirements for labour standards. Of the agreements examined here, only the PTAs with

Singapore and Mexico make reference to labour standards of any kind. In these agreements, both parties are allowed to use trade barriers in order to protect against the products of prison labour.[46]

Singapore

Similarly, PTAs negotiated by Singapore do not contain substantive requirements for labour standards. Only the PTA with Japan makes reference to labour standards of any kind. In this agreement, both Singapore and Japan are allowed to use trade barriers in order to protect against the products of prison labour.[47]

Conclusions on labour standards

The commitments made in respect of labour standards relate, for the most part, to the domestic legislation of the parties.

As noted above, concern with labour standards has, up to now, been a distinguishing feature of US PTAs. As such, it might be expected that, in light of the 10 May 2007 accord, even greater emphasis will be sought on the inclusion of labour provisions in US PTAs. Any associated strengthening of the influence of organized labour in the United States could be expected to have a similar result, recalling the influence of the AFL-CIO at the Seattle WTO Ministerial when advocating trade sanctions for non-compliance with internationally agreed core labour standards. The EU–CARIFORUM EPA does, however, include provisions on labour standards geared to existing ILO commitments. It remains to be seen whether this precedent will be followed by other EPAs but, if it is, labour standards could become more of a regular feature in EU PTAs.

The success of WTO members in keeping labour standards off the multilateral trade agenda, other than through cooperation between the WTO and the ILO, means that PTA provisions on this subject are, by their very nature, WTO-plus.

Given the nature of concerns about compliance with core labour standards, they do not lend themselves to PTA provisions favouring the less advanced party. Indeed, if anything, monitoring of compliance is likely to be more rigorous in respect of the developing country partner.

Notes

1. The foundation for this analysis comes from Pugatch (2006) and Roffe (2004).
2. US–Singapore, Art. 16.4:4; US–Chile, Art. 17.5:4; US–Morocco, Art. 15.5:5; US–Bahrain, Art. 14.4:4; and US–Peru, Art. 16.5:5.
3. US–Oman, Art. 15.4:4.

4. Articles 15.4 and 15.8 of US–Bahrain deal with Internet domain names and satellite signals, respectively. The provisions are identical in other US PTAs.
5. Article 15.2:3 of US–Morocco offers a good example of this provision, which is nearly identical in all US PTAs.
6. Articles 14.2:7 to 14.2:9 of US–Bahrain offer a good example of the standard system of registration.
7. For differing approaches to geographical indicators in US preferential trade agreements, see US–Peru, Art. 16.3, and US–Bahrain, Art. 14.2.
8. See, for example, US–Bahrain, Art. 14.8:5, US–Morocco, Art. 15.9:6, or US–Peru, Art. 16.9:5, for identical provisions.
9. The definition of an "unreasonable delay" differs from agreement to agreement. For variation, see US–Peru, Art. 16.9:6 (a), and US–Morocco, Art. 15.9:7.
10. US–Singapore, Art. 16.7:2, and US–Morocco, Art. 15.9:4.
11. See, for example, US–Morocco, Art. 15.10, or US–Peru, Art. 16.10.
12. See, for example, US–Singapore, Art. 16.9:8, or US–Morocco, Art. 15.11:5.
13. See, for example, US–Bahrain, Art. 14.10:7, or US–Oman, Art. 15.10:7, which establishes a maximum penalty of three times the assessed injury.
14. See, for example, US–Chile, Art. 17.11:12 (a), or US–Oman, Art. 15.10:10 (a).
15. Compare TRIPS Article 46 with US–Oman, Art. 15.10:10 (b).
16. See US–Morocco, Art. 15.11:12 (b); US–Bahrain, Art. 14.10:12; and US–Oman, Art. 15.10:12 (b).
17. See US–Bahrain, Art. 14.10:16; US–Peru, Art. 16.11:17; and US–Oman, Art. 15.10:16.
18. Compare US–Singapore, Art. 16.9:19, and, for example, US–Peru, Art. 16.11:23.
19. See, for example, US–Peru, Art. 16.11:27 (d).
20. See, for example, US–Bahrain, Art. 14.10.27 (b).
21. See, for example, US–Bahrain, Art. 14.10:28.
22. This analysis draws on Vivas-Eugui and Spennemann (2006).
23. See Article 5.1 of the EU–Chile Agreement on Trade in Wines and Article 4.1 of the EU–Mexico Agreement on Spirit Drinks.
24. See Article 5.1 of the EU–Chile Agreement on Trade in Wines and Article 4.3 of the EU–Mexico Agreement on Spirit Drinks.
25. See Article 4.4 of the EU–Mexico Agreement on Spirit Drinks.
26. See EU–Chile, Annex VI, Art. 5.
27. See Article 7 of EU–Chile, Annex V and Annex VI.
28. See EU–Chile, Annex V, Art. 3(c).
29. Compare EFTA–Chile, Art. 5, and EFTA–Morocco, Art. 3.1, for differing approaches to protection.
30. EFTA–Singapore, Art. 3(b)(i); EFTA–Chile, Art. 3(b); and EFTA–Korea, Art. 2(b).
31. EFTA–Chile, Art. 4.
32. Japan–Malaysia, Art. 122.
33. Singapore–Japan, Art. 4.10.
34. Singapore–Japan, Art. 4.11.
35. See NAFTA, Arts 1701.3 and 1718.14; US–Singapore, Art. 16.10; US–Chile, Art. 17.12; US–Morocco, Art. 15.12; US–Bahrain, Art. 14.11; and US–Peru, Annex 16.1.
36. NAFTA, Art. 1718:1.
37. The ECJ is unlikely to rule on the interpretation of a provision in a PTA, but precedent set in European law will clearly have a bearing on the European Union's approach to such a provision in any Joint Committee procedure.
38. For instance, US–Singapore, Art. 17.2:1(a), US–Chile, Art. 18.2:1(a), and US–Morocco, Art. 16.2:1(a).
39. US–Morocco, Art. 16.6:5.

40. For instance, US–Peru, Art. 17.2:2, US–Bahrain, Art. 15.2:2, US–Morocco, Art. 16.2:2.
41. US–Morocco, Art. 16.3:1.
42. EU–Chile, Art. 44.
43. EU–Egypt, Art. 62, and EU–Morocco, Art. 65.
44. EU–Morocco, Art. 65.
45. EFTA–Mexico, Art. 17(e); EFTA–Singapore, Art. 19(e); EFTA–Chile, Art. 21(e).
46. Singapore–Japan, Art. 19(e), and Japan–Mexico, Art. 126(d).
47. Singapore–Japan, Art. 19(e).

Part III

Goals and outcomes: US, European and Asian approaches compared

6

The United States

After obtaining Trade Promotion Authority in 2001 (which gave it fast-track negotiating authority), the administration of George W. Bush adopted a more offensive policy on preferential trade agreements (PTAs). In the course of the administration, a total of 18 countries or groups of countries participated in PTA negotiations with the United States, ranging over nations as diverse as Australia, Oman, Morocco, Colombia and Korea (for details, see Annex 1). Notwithstanding the agreement on trade issues reached between the Congress and the administration on 10 May 2007, the subsequent expiry of Trade Promotion Authority brought some uncertainty to US policy on PTAs, though, as discussed below, it is unlikely that the United States will abandon the pursuit of bilateral trade deals.

US motivations for pursuing PTAs

The motivations of the United States in pursuing preferential trade agreements are highly diverse. In a speech to the Institute for International Economics in May 2003, the then United States Trade Representative (USTR) Robert Zoellick identified no fewer than 13 factors that guide US evaluation of the suitability of starting negotiations with a foreign party. Also in May 2003, the National Security Council issued guidelines to "improve the process of assessing potential parties by, among other things, expanding the number of inter-agency groups involved

The rise of bilateralism: Comparing American, European and Asian approaches to preferential trade agreements, Heydon and Woolcock,
United Nations University Press, 2009, ISBN 978-92-808-1162-9

with the assessments" (GAO, 2004: 13, cited in Evenett and Meier, 2007). As we shall see, motivations differ not only from agreement to agreement but also between the Congress and the administration. There are nevertheless seven key elements that have governed, and will continue to govern, US pursuit of PTAs. These will be dealt with, briefly, in turn.

A fear of being left out

A concern about being left behind has been very clearly expressed by former USTR Zoellick, fearful of "other nations seizing the mantle of leadership in trade from the United States" and observing:

> The United States has been falling behind the rest of the world in pursuing trade agreements. World wide there are 150 regional free-trade agreements and customs agreements; the United States is a party to only three. Each one sets new rules and opens markets for those that signed on and creates hurdles for those outside the agreement. (Editorial in *New York Times*, 14 April 2002)

This particular motivation has been mirrored, and in a sense confirmed, by the comment of EU Trade Commissioner Peter Mandelson that the negotiation of the US–Korea agreement (KORUS) "strengthens the prospects for the planned EU–Korea free trade agreement" (*Financial Times*, 3 April 2007).

The US fear of being left out is now most clearly manifested in Asia. The Director of the Peterson Institute for International Economics, Fred Bergsten, has observed that a full East Asian free trade area (including the Association of Southeast Asian Nations, China, Japan and Korea) would carry substantial trade diversion costs for the United States (Bergsten, 2005). He cites a study estimating that the creation of such a grouping would cause US exports to fall by US$25 billion annually (Scollay, 2001).

Dissatisfaction with progress in the multilateral trading system

Fears about being left behind in the pursuit of preferential deals have been compounded by a range of factors that have weakened US commitment to the multilateral trading system.

The onset of multi-polarity has undoubtedly contributed to a moderated commitment on the part of the United States to multilateral approaches to economic diplomacy and, correspondingly, to reduced US leadership of such approaches.

Compared with US support for the Bretton Woods institutions in the post–World War II period, a number of factors have reduced US engagement in multilateral economic diplomacy. Not least is the reduced relative economic power of the United States, meaning that it is less able to control institutions and their decisions. The evolution of the Kyoto Protocol on climate change and the questioning of the "Washington Consensus" are each evidence of this. In the area of trade, reduced influence has been augmented by ongoing US preoccupations, including concerns about "free-riding" in the multilateral trading system and periodic disenchantment with the dispute settlement system of the World Trade Organization (WTO). A moderated US commitment to multilateralism has also been fuelled by the need to keep things simple, given the transparency of US domestic politics and the requirement for the administration to engage and be accountable to Congress and to work within the constraints imposed by US domestic interests (Bayne and Woolcock, 2007).

But the biggest US frustration with multilateral approaches arises from concern about the slow pace of progress. This is not new; the faltering of the Uruguay Round in the late 1980s was one of the triggers for launching the North American Free Trade Agreement (NAFTA). More recent was the call by the House Ways and Means Committee Chairman Bill Thomas in April 2006 for the Bush administration to take its focus off the Doha Development Agenda, which he said was stalled because of European intransigence, and instead focus its energies on completing ongoing bilateral free trade agreements (*Inside US Trade*, 17 April 2006). Such a view may strike a chord with business interests, as product cycles get shorter and multilateral negotiating rounds longer. In contrast, the US–Peru agreement took less than two years from the first round of negotiations to signature.

The forces moderating support for multilateral action tend to promote bilateralism, rather than unilateralism, because the relative decline in US economic power also limits scope for unilateral pressure. Although, in principle, as a large trader the United States could impose an "optimum tariff", obliging foreign suppliers to reduce their price, thus improving US terms of trade, freedom to do this is constrained by the threat of retaliation, as well as by commitments to bind tariffs in the WTO. And although the United States can and does implement unilateral defence measures through safeguard and anti-dumping action, this too is subject to greater discipline as a result of the Uruguay Round.

Opportunities for deeper integration

Among the "pull" forces for US engagement in PTAs are the economic opportunities arising from deeper integration. This has been documented in Part II, where WTO-plus elements are seen to be common and wide-ranging.

The US approach to deeper integration has been described as "policed non-discrimination" (Woolcock, 2006).

> The US approach tends to eschew policy approximation in favour of non-discrimination, policy competition and national treatment. In this sense the degree of integration is not especially deep, although there are specific sectors or policy areas where US-centred FTAs contain binding obligations to apply specific standards, such as in the case of IPRs [intellectual property rights], investment and some specific aspects of services. Outside of these sectors there is no attempt to lay down standards or rules, which leaves full scope for regulatory autonomy, but policy competition implies that there will be policy emulation, and the case of investment shows that this may well follow the US-determined norms. In other words, non-discrimination leaves the US Congress with policy autonomy by virtue of the asymmetric relationship between the United States and its partners in PTAs, but the size and importance of the US market obliges de facto policy approximation to the US rules on the part of the smaller parties. (Woolcock, 2006: 19)

In line with the concept of "policed non-discrimination", US-centred PTAs tend to have strong enforcement mechanisms that are significantly more elaborate than those found in EU-centred agreements, except where EU accession is involved. A good example is provided by the investor–state dispute settlement provisions in US PTAs. These are so detailed and comprehensive that they take up half of the "model" chapter on investment in NAFTA and US–Singapore. But investment is by no means the only example. In IPRs and telecommunications, PTAs involving the United States have included strong enforcement provisions. And in government procurement the United States has championed "bid challenge" mechanisms that provide companies that believe they have been badly treated with direct access to reviews of contract award decisions.

Advancing trade-related issues

Another aspect of WTO-plus, which is a particularly American feature of PTAs, is the use of bilateral and regional arrangements to exert pressure on partners to maintain or improve standards relating to public health, the environment or labour standards.

The provisions on access to medicines arising from the 10 May 2007 accord between Congress and the administration are likely to foreshadow a heightened focus on health matters in US PTAs. In response to Democrats' concerns that the intellectual property protections in US PTAs were restricting access to lifesaving medicines in developing countries,

the new template for preferential agreements will allow US trading partners to bring generic drugs to market more quickly. Pharmaceutical test
data will not be protected in partner countries beyond the period that
they are in the United States, which will make it possible to bring generics to market at the same time in both. A public health exception
from data exclusivity obligations will also be introduced. Furthermore,
patent extension requirements for pharmaceutical products will be soft-
ened, and drug regulatory agencies will be allowed to approve generics
without having to first establish that no patents have been violated. Finally, the new policy calls for making side letters on public health concerns part of the formal text of the PTAs, along with a reaffirmation of
countries' right under WTO agreements to suspend patents in order to
expand access to essential medicines.

Provisions dealing with the environment and labour standards are not
new. Side agreements on labour and the environment were necessary to
save NAFTA from congressional defeat. Echoing concerns about US
leadership, USTR Zoellick, speaking in May 2001, said:

> we need to align the global trading system with our values. We can encourage
> open and efficient markets while respecting national sovereignty. We can en-
> courage respect for core labour standards, environmental protection, and good
> health without slipping into fear-based campaigns and protectionism. And we
> must always seek to strengthen freedom, democracy, and the rule of law. (Zoel-
> lick, 2001b).

With the changed composition of the US Congress, the issue of labour
standards in US PTAs came to centre stage. In an attempt to ensure congressional approval of pending Peru, Colombia and Panama PTAs, USTR
proposed that the parties pledge to adopt either International Labour
Organization (ILO) codes or the equivalent US labour laws. This, however, was not enough to satisfy Congress. House Trade Subcommittee
Chairman Sander Levin (D-MI) said in March 2007 that anything short
of strict compliance with ILO standards simply would not pass Congress
(*Washington International Business Report*, March 2007). The result was
the accord reached between Congress and the administration on 10 May
2007.

It is not the purpose here to pass judgement on core entities' motivations, but it should nevertheless be noted that this particular feature of
US agreements has prompted criticism – that inclusion of provisions on
labour and the environment causes US PTAs to bear the weight of too
many objectives (Evenett and Meier, 2007) and, moreover, that these
particular objectives go beyond the realm of trade policy and are motivated by, or could become hostage to, protectionist sentiment (Bhagwati,

2003). Their inclusion, while in part reflecting humanitarian concerns, is founded on fears about countries gaining an unfair competitive advantage from low standards, leading to a "race-to-the-bottom". There is, however, no strong theoretical or empirical support for such a race (OECD, 2000a).

A stimulus to domestic reform

For some countries, such as Japan, bilateral and regional agreements are invoked as a way of stimulating domestic reform through external pressure. This motivation is mentioned here, for completeness, though in fact there is little documentary evidence of this being a strong motivation in the case of the United States. Indeed, the basic US assumption is that its market is essentially open. Robert Zoellick again: "American openness is high and our trade barriers are low, so when we negotiate free trade agreements with our counterparts we almost always open other markets more than we must change our own" (Zoellick, 2001a).

There is, however, one feature of the 10 May accord between the Congress and the administration that bears on the question of domestic reform. The agreement provides for expanded worker assistance and training in the United States, along with support for making health and pension benefits portable between different employers. These policies, through a Strategic Worker Assistance and Training Initiative, are intended to soften the blow of trade-related adjustment and make it easier for workers to change jobs without losing benefits.

A stimulus to the multilateral trading system

US disenchantment with the multilateral trading system does not mean abandonment. There is in fact a very carefully articulated view from Washington that a particular virtue of PTAs is that they can provide a stimulus to the successful conclusion of multilateral negotiations. It has thus been suggested (by Fred Bergsten, amongst others) that it was the threat of Asia-Pacific Economic Cooperation (APEC) coming to fruition that persuaded the European Union of the benefits of concluding the Uruguay Round. An updated version of this (untested and uncertain) view is that it could be the threat of APEC being converted into a preferential free trade area of the Asia Pacific that would provide the necessary stimulus to conclude the Doha Development Agenda.

The intellectual framework within which this notion of complementarity is placed is called "competitive liberalization", a concept dating from the 1990s but developed during the Presidency of George W. Bush. It has been described in the following terms by a former Chief Agricultural Negotiator of USTR, Mr Allen Johnson:

> Our strategy is to incite competitive liberalization by negotiating regional and bilateral agreements to complement our global strategy in the WTO. If others are ready to open their markets, America will be their partner. If some are not ready, or want to complain but not lower their barriers, the United States will proceed with countries that are ready. This competition in liberalization strengthens the United States' already considerable leverage, including in the WTO. (Testimony before the US Senate's Committee on Foreign Relations, 20 May 2003; cited in Evenett and Meier, 2007)

Robert Zoellick sought to make competitive liberalization the framework for US trade diplomacy at its broadest:

> When the Bush Administration set out to revitalize America's trade agenda almost three years ago, we outlined our plans clearly and openly. We would pursue a strategy of "competitive liberalization" to advance free trade globally, regionally and bilaterally. By moving forward on multiple fronts the United States can: overcome or bypass obstacles; exert maximum leverage for openness; target the needs of developing countries, especially the most committed to economic and political reforms; establish models of success, especially in cutting-edge areas; strengthen America's ties with all regions within the global economy; and create a fresh political dynamic by putting free trade on the offensive. (GAO, 2004: 57)

A complement to foreign policy objectives

For the United States, and indeed all of the core entities, a long-standing and pervasive motivation for the conclusion of preferential trade agreements has been to serve broader foreign policy or strategic goals.

In the formative stage of US pursuit of bilateral and regional accords, NAFTA was driven in part by the desire to foster the growth and development of Mexico and so address the underlying causes of illegal migration.

In subsequent accords, there is evidence of US bilateral agreements serving US strategic aspirations. Bilateral agreements with countries such as Oman and Jordan have demonstrable foreign policy goals, as do those with Peru and Colombia. In both these pairs of bilateral agreements, there is an important geopolitical dimension, linked in the one case to strategic and economic interests in a highly volatile environment, in the other case to the exercise of US influence and the containment of that of Venezuela, in its immediate neighbourhood.

A key motivation for KORUS is to help foster stability on the Korean peninsula. In writing to the Democratic leadership of Congress on completion of negotiations with Korea, President Bush said the deal would "further enhance the strong US–Korea partnership, which has served as a force for stability and prosperity in Asia" (*Financial Times*, 3 April 2007). USTR did not shy from the strategic link, saying that "this FTA [free trade agreement] will strengthen the more than 50-year-old alliance ... and will underscore the substantial US engagement in and commitment to East Asia [and] promote strong economic relations with the region" (*Washington International Business Report*, April 2007). Washington's view that KORUS assures the United States' continued clout in the area can also be seen as implying a restraint on China, as well as on the idea of an East Asian preferential bloc, first espoused by former Malaysian Prime Minister Mahathir and now characterized as ASEAN+3 (Association of Southeast Asian Nations, plus China, Japan and Korea).

US bilaterals may also provide an opportunity to reward partners for their strategic support. The United States' preparedness to enter an agreement with Australia but not with New Zealand was in part driven by the wish to recognize, and consolidate, the role of Australia as an ally in US engagement in Iraq.

In terms of possible future US bilaterals, a recent study of a possible US–Indonesia PTA stresses the role that such an agreement could have in helping stymie radical Islam (Hufbauer and Rahardja, 2007).

Beyond bilateral accords, US regional trade activities also have an important strategic dimension. Washington's advocacy, at the 2006 APEC Leaders' Meeting, of the transformation of APEC into a preferential bloc can be seen as a way of exerting US influence more broadly in the Asia Pacific region and, again, of containing – within APEC – the growing influence of China. APEC trade ministers, at their meeting on 5–6 July 2007, discussed "the possibility of developing a Free Trade Area of the Asia-Pacific (FTAAP) as a long term prospect" (*Bridges Weekly Trade News Digest*, 11(25), 12 July 2007).

Though all motivations play a part, the relative importance of these seven key elements clearly differs from agreement to agreement. Their importance also differs depending on whose US motivations one is talking about. Concerns about the foreign policy impact of bilateral and regional deals are likely to loom larger in the Office of the President than in Congress.[1] On the other hand, concerns about core labour standards are more pronounced in Congress than in the administration; it has been observed (Hufbauer and Schott, 2005) that, although side agreements on environment and labour were added to NAFTA as a condition for congressional approval, they were not backed by meaningful financial resources or authoritative judicial mechanisms.

There is, however, one underlying objective that seems to be shared equally by Congress and the administration, and that is the desire to use PTAs as a lever for improved market access for the goods and services produced and exported by the United States. If one accepts that the last three of the seven listed motivations (promoting, respectively, US domestic reform, the multilateral trading system and US foreign policy) are essentially "tactical" uses of PTAs for other ends, and that the first four motivations are all related in some way to market opening, then market access emerges, perhaps not surprisingly, as the single most important direct driver of US PTA policy. The United States' high ambitions in respect of investment provisions – a feature of this study – can be seen in this light. Thus the goal of using investment provisions in PTAs to promote pro-market reform in partner countries and to protect US investment overseas can be seen as related to the broader goal of advancing the United States' global market access interests. Similarly, concerns about a race-to-the-bottom in environmental and labour standards are rooted in fears about unfair competition – not least from China.

The pursuit of market opening has been a consistent theme of all three United States Trade Representatives of the Bush administration. We have seen how Robert Zoellick saw moving forward on multiple fronts as a way of exerting maximum leverage for openness. His successor, Ambassador Portman, stressed that, even with Bahrain and Oman, "we have real export opportunities" (20 January 2006).[2] More recently, USTR Susan Schwab said that she did not "preclude bilateral agreements with either big countries or small countries where there is – and here is the key – the ambition to do a gold-standard free-trade agreement.... The way we negotiate FTAs, everything is on the table. And that includes our sensitivities and their sensitivities" (*National Journal*, 15 July 2006).

On the basis of the earlier analysis, how successful has the United States been in achieving "gold standard" PTAs and what does the content of US PTAs tell us about America's revealed preferences?

America's revealed preferences

Is improved market access the primary driving force of US PTAs?

Tariffs

US PTAs are generally, but not universally, characterized by comprehensive liberalization of tariff lines by both parties. In the four PTAs closely analysed in this study, 100 per cent of tariff lines in the US schedule were liberalized entirely by the end of the transition period. Although 2–3 per cent of US tariff lines were subject to tariff rate quotas, all such quotas were eliminated by the end of the transition period. US agreements are thus highly WTO-plus with regard to US tariff elimination, albeit from a low initial level of tariff protection. US agreements also seek comprehensive tariff elimination by trade partners. Partners generally have not made use of longer transition periods than the United States, and have introduced the fewest tariff rate quotas as a percentage of tariff lines of all the studied agreements.

The negotiation of KORUS has demonstrated the bipartisan importance for the United States of this aspect of market access. Concerns about autos and rice were the most important sticking points for US negotiators. And, on the side of Congress, Senate Finance Committee Chairman Max Baucus (D-MT) declared that he would oppose KORUS until Korea fully opened its beef market (*Washington International Business Report*, April 2007).

Nonetheless, it should be noted that US objectives, however clear and firm, are not always realized. Although it has been estimated that, under KORUS, over US$1 billion worth of US farm exports to Korea will become duty-free immediately, rice is not among them. And, in the US–Australia FTA, the United States itself falls well short of full coverage of agricultural products.

Rules of origin

Even with comprehensive tariff coverage, a question arising is the extent to which an ambitious approach to tariff reductions can be negated by restrictive rules of origin (RoO). The NAFTA regime is distinguished by its complexity, specificity and detail, and the US–Mexico RoO regime has been found to have the highest level of restrictiveness in the world (Garay and De Lombaerde, 2004). However, the United States is considerably more flexible in more recent agreements, notably in the PTAs with Bahrain and Morocco, where the RoO regime is much less restrictive and simpler than in NAFTA.

Safeguards

US PTAs have consistently applied time limitations on the use of safeguard action that are tighter than those found in the WTO, with no re-application possible on the same product. Additionally, the US–Chile PTA provides that, on the termination of a safeguard, the rate of duty shall not be higher than the rate that would have been in effect one year after the initiation of the measure according to the agreed tariff schedule.

Sanitary and phytosanitary measures and technical barriers to trade

Many US PTAs are among those that require members to consider the technical regulations and standards of other parties as *equivalent*. Commonly within these US PTAs parties need to give an explanation when not applying the principle of equivalence to the regulations of other parties, hence going beyond WTO rules. Many US agreements also encourage parties to mutually recognize the results of their conformity assessment procedures and to explain the reasons when they do not do so. In addition, many US agreements – for example, with Australia, Bahrain, Central America (CAFTA), Chile and Morocco – call on the parties to recognize the conformity assessment bodies in the territory of the other party "on terms no less favourable than those it accords to conformity assessment bodies in its territory". Finally, several US PTAs, such as CAFTA, encourage the recognition of suppliers' declarations of conformity, which do not require a third party to assess whether a product conforms to technical regulations and standards, and promote the conclusion of voluntary arrangements between conformity assessment bodies from each party (Lesser, 2007).

Government procurement

NAFTA, like other US agreements, goes beyond the plurilateral Agreement on Government Procurement (GPA) by adopting lower thresholds and a negative-list approach to the coverage of services procured by the listed entities. NAFTA has influenced other PTAs concluded on its periphery, including several of Mexico's bilateral agreements (OECD, 2003).

Services

The relative impact of negative and positive listing needs to be assessed with care but, if it is agreed that a negative-list approach tends to promote greater transparency, then consistent US support for this approach can be seen as a commitment to ambitious services liberalization. US agreements tend to go beyond the General Agreement on Trade in Services (GATS) in rule-making in financial services, advancing on transparency measures, dispute settlement procedures, and detailed extension of the most favoured nation (MFN) clause to prudential recognition. In telecommunication services, US agreements expand on access and usage of public telecommunications transport networks and services, and are GATS-plus in respect of licensing processes, dispute settlement, independent regulation and privatization. The provision in US agreements prohibiting local presence requirements – pioneered in NAFTA – goes beyond the criteria defined in Article XVI (e) of the GATS on market access.

Investment

As noted above, US agreements, particularly NAFTA and the PTAs with Chile and Singapore, tend to be ranked high in terms of the comprehensiveness of their treatment of investment. More recently, we have seen investment provisions in KORUS that will ensure that US investors in Korea have the same rights as and enjoy an equal footing with Korean investors.

Intellectual property rights

The present study finds that, with few exceptions, the majority of provisions going beyond those of the Agreement on Trade-Related Aspects of Intellectual Property Rights (TRIPS) are found in the PTAs of the United States (and the European Union). US PTAs have thus progressively extended the 50-year term of copyright protection required by TRIPS, extended the minimum term of trademark protection from 7 to 10 years, and eliminated the "innocent infringement" clause in TRIPS that precludes penalties for "unknown violation".

In summary, the track record of the United States' PTAs seems to support the proposition that the attainment of improved market access, broadly defined, is the primary driving force of US preferential arrangements. Whether the resulting agreements constitute "gold standard" PTAs is, however, a matter for debate.

How successful has the United States been in achieving "gold standard" PTAs?

Comprehensive coverage – a condition for maximizing welfare gains – is often lacking, even in US-based agreements. Agriculture stands out; in US–Australia, for example, whereas the Australian list has no agricultural tariff lines excluded, the US list has 196 lines that will not be completely liberalized at the end of the transition period and 83 tariff lines that are totally excluded from liberalization commitments (Tsai, 2006). And domestic subsidies in agriculture – the United States' greatest area of vulnerability in the Doha Round – are not susceptible to effective discipline in PTAs. In services, too, coverage is incomplete, not least because of the growing tendency in US PTAs to use negative-list reservations to exclude all service measures maintained at the sub-federal level. Moreover, even where PTA coverage is comprehensive, the resulting improvements in market access are still on a preferential, and therefore discriminatory, basis. And, because of preferences, vested interests are created in opposition to multilateral liberalization.

In the rules area, although US PTAs oblige parties to use international norms for standards-setting, given US antipathy towards agreed international standards such measures will not result in much pressure to improve compliance.

In the area of government procurement, although WTO-plus in some respects, some US PTAs have less coverage than in the GPA. US municipalities and many states are not covered by the public procurement obligations of the United States, and it can be hard to get a single licence for service provision across the whole of the country.

The importance of market access as a motivation for US PTAs is mirrored by US reluctance, notable in the area of tariffs, to accept asymmetric liberalization commitments from its PTA partners. At first sight, there is a significant element of flexibility in agreements to which the United States is party. Unlike the European Union, the United States is not inclined to pursue regulatory harmonization in its agreements. It has thus been observed that the US-centred model places less importance on approximation or policy harmonization, as reflected in the limited standards-harmonization working groups established under NAFTA (Woolcock, 2003). As regards technical barriers to trade, US PTAs – unlike those of the European Union – aim to promote *equivalence* rather than harmonization of technical regulations and standards. Moreover, the relatively recent CAFTA includes important provisions of the special and differential treatment type, such as longer transition periods for developing members.

Before concluding, however, that the United States is actively engaged in promoting asymmetric commitments or that CAFTA might represent a model for future US agreements, some qualifications are in order. First, although there may be no formal pursuit of harmonization in NAFTA, the US model appears to assume that market factors will bring about *de facto* approximation to US regulatory norms and standards (Woolcock, 2003). This would be borne out by the fact that the United States resisted asymmetric liberalization commitments in the negotiation of NAFTA. Second, the US commitment to reciprocity was very clearly demonstrated in the (now abandoned) negotiations with the members of the Southern African Customs Union (SACU). SACU concerns that it lacked the institutional capacities to meet US expectations were met with the response that ways should be explored to strengthen the trade and investment relationship in the hope that SACU "could undertake the obligations of a US-style FTA in the future". In other words, the US preference appears to be to defer conclusion of a PTA rather than to dilute the reciprocal character of its agreements. In this light, the asymmetric elements of CAFTA might be seen as the product of particular economic, political and strategic factors. Although going beyond the scope of this study, it is nevertheless worth noting that asymmetric commitments, by permitting a reduced commitment to market opening and structural reform, will not necessarily serve the interests of the beneficiary.

Conclusion

As a focus for summing up, it is useful to reflect on the significance of the accord on PTAs reached between the Congress and the administration on 10 May 2007 and of the subsequent expiry of Trade Promotion Authority (TPA). One commentator believes that the 10 May agreement "portends great changes for US trade policy" (Stokes, 2007). This is an exaggeration. But the agreement does contain some important features that should be welcomed. The accord is bipartisan and, by focusing on worker training, it addresses a key requirement of successful adaptation to globalization, namely that labour and capital should be allowed to move from declining to expanding areas of activity. And, by addressing access to medicines, the agreement has an important humanitarian focus.

Indeed, the accord contains a large measure of continuity and as such needs to be assessed with caution. The strengthening of PTA provisions on core labour standards and the environment is driven by fears of unfair competition, and as such is a confirmation of the overriding, if not exclusive, importance of market access as the driver of US PTAs. Should the Congress seek to extend the scope of the May agreement to the multilateral sphere, by reopening the question of labour standards and the WTO, the impact on multilateral cooperation in trade – already under strain – would be highly adverse.

The practical impact of the 10 May accord is likely to remain an open question for some time. In what is arguably the most critical of the areas covered – trade and labour – there are reasons to believe that the direct impact will be modest. The labour unions' contribution to the Democrats' campaign funding is in decline, falling from 15.6 per cent of the party's funding in the 2000 election cycle to 12.4 per cent in 2006. The administration for its part has shown no willingness to test the labour provisions in US–Jordan. And, perhaps underpinning this unwillingness, it is by no means clear how, in dispute resolution, a causal link could be established between injury to US interests and a PTA partner's non-compliance with core labour standards. But the labour issue has been revived and the indirect consequence is likely to be heightened apprehension on the part of developing countries, whether as PTA partners or as participants in multilateral trade negotiations.

It had been hoped by the administration that the 10 May 2007 accord would ease passage of the PTAs in the pipeline and help ensure renewal of fast-track authority. This was not to be. In a statement released on 29 June 2007, House Democrats said that implementation of the agreements with Korea and Colombia would be dependent on, respectively, improved access for US motor vehicle manufacturers and strengthened labour laws. On 10 April 2008, House Democrats voted to eliminate the requirement to approve or reject the Colombia PTA within 90 days, thus indefinitely postponing action on the agreement.

With growing public concern about the effects of globalization, the Democratic leadership has said that "our legislative priorities do not include the renewal of fast-track authority" (*Washington International Business Report*, July 2007). None of the leading Democratic presidential candidates supported extension when TPA expired at the end of June 2007. It should not be assumed, however, that the United States is about to vacate the field. It is not excluded that Trade Promotion Authority will be granted. And, even if it is not, there are a number of reasons for believing that the United States will continue its pursuit of bilateral PTAs:

- as is often observed, the absence of fast-track authority, although it may complicate the conclusion of agreements, does not preclude the commencement of negotiations;
- US policy on PTAs requires that US partners, rather than the United States itself, initiate PTA proposals, and such initiatives can be expected to continue;
- as a result of the 10 May 2007 accord, there is bipartisan agreement on the goals and conduct of PTA negotiations, with a strong focus on congressional concerns related to the environment, labour and public health, underpinned by a shared pursuit of improved market access;
- as long as other major traders continue, as they will, to negotiate PTAs, the US fear of being left out will help ensure that Washington continues to seek trade and broader foreign policy advantage from bilateral arrangements.

It is unlikely therefore that there will be a retreat from US bilaterals; rather, in a phrase used on the Democrat side during the 2008 presidential campaign, there will be "a little time out".[3]

In short, we might conclude that, apart from foreign policy or strategic objectives, the United States will continue to be attracted to PTAs as a way of improving market access, while at the same time addressing the political economy dilemma in trade liberalization (concentrated losses and dispersed gains) by excluding difficult sectors; focusing on a narrow range of selected partners; avoiding MFN commitments, and therefore free-riding by third parties; securing reciprocity from partners; addressing concerns about a race-to-the-bottom in labour and the environment; and expanding Trade Adjustment Assistance to help those who lose. Successful passage of a Trade Adjustment Assistance bill through the Congress could well be the key to unlocking future, and pending, PTAs.

Notes

1. This is not to say that foreign policy considerations are not important for congressional approval. It has been pointed out that most major US trade initiatives, including NAFTA, have been sold to the Congress on foreign policy grounds (Schott, 2007).
2. "Roundtable Discussion with Rob Portman", 20 January 2006, at ⟨http://www.ustr.gov/ Document_Library/Transcripts/2006/January/Roundtable_Discussion_with_Rob _Portman.html⟩ (accessed 17 September 2008).
3. As a possible pointer to Democrat thinking, Senate Finance Committee Chair Max Baucus (D-MT), in a speech on 2 October 2007, called for bilateral agreements with "Malaysia, Taiwan, Indonesia, India and Japan", as well as bilateral services agreements with the European Union, Japan and other large economies (*Washington International Business Report*, October 2007).

7
The European Union

The European Union has shifted to a more offensive policy on preferential trade agreements (PTAs) in recent years. This has come after some
debate among the member states and within the European institutions
on the advisability of such a shift. In May 2006 the European Union announced it would be negotiating with Central America, and in October
2006 it set out the objective of negotiating PTAs with a number of Asian
countries, including in particular the Association of Southeast Asian Nations (European Commission, 2006). This followed various studies of the
pros and cons of negotiating PTAs with Asian partners, and was followed
in March 2007 by the adoption of negotiating mandates for PTAs with
ASEAN, Korea and India.[1]

The European Union is not new to preferential agreements. Indeed,
until the surge in negotiations of preferential agreements during the
1990s, the European Union was by far the biggest user of such agreements. The European Union also has a number of PTA negotiations "in
the pipeline". The European Union is negotiating Economic Partnership
Agreements (EPAs) with the African, Caribbean and Pacific (ACP)
states in order to replace the Lomé preferences and to fulfil the conditions of the Cotonou Agreement of 2000.[2] Since 1999, the European
Union has been negotiating an Association Agreement with Mercosur
(the Common Market of the Southern Cone). It is also negotiating Stabilisation and Association Agreements (SAAs) with the states in the western
Balkans and has agreements with Syria and the Gulf Cooperation Council ongoing. See Annex 2 for details of the EU PTAs and negotiations.

*The rise of bilateralism: Comparing American, European and Asian approaches to
preferential trade agreements, Heydon and Woolcock,
United Nations University Press, 2009, ISBN 978-92-808-1162-9*

Existing EU PTAs

As in the case of all PTAs, EU policy has a number of driving forces. In broad terms, it is possible to differentiate between three categories of PTA with somewhat differing motivations.

Near neighbours

First, there are the European Union's near neighbours with which the European Union negotiates Association Agreements, in which political and strategic factors tend to be the predominant motivation. These include, for example, the agreements with the Central and East European states in the 1990s before these became accession states, the SAAs with the western Balkans and the Euro-Mediterranean Partnership (Euro-Med) agreements with the European Union's southern near neighbours. The Association Agreements with these countries include political and financial elements as well as trade liberalization and are seen as a means of promoting economic development and thus political stability. By promoting economic growth and employment in these partner countries, such Association Agreements are seen as contributing to the European Union's (and the wider Europe's) security. The Association Agreements also seek to promote regulatory best practice and thus contribute to good governance in the countries concerned.

The ACP states

Notwithstanding a shift towards greater reciprocity as ACP states are now required to open their markets to EU exports, the predominant motivation is development policy. Of course, the Euro-Med agreements also promote development, but agreements with the Caribbean or African states under the current EPA negotiations are more driven by a general desire to promote development in countries that are linked to Europe through the legacy of colonialism. From a commercial perspective, very few of the ACP markets are significant for EU exporters and, although there are sensitive sectors in agriculture, there is no significant, general (i.e. outside of a few narrow sectors) competition from the ACP exporters in industrial products, with the possible exception of South Africa.

Other distant partners

The third category of PTAs is primarily driven by commercial considerations. Into this category fall the agreements negotiated with Mexico and Chile and the PTAs that the European Union is now seeking to negotiate

with the Asian countries. The commercial considerations can take a number of forms. They may come in the shape of a desire to neutralize trade
diversion resulting from other PTAs. EU–Mexico was such a case. Following the negotiation of the North American Free Trade Agreement
(NAFTA), EU exporters and investors lost market share in Mexico, so
the EU–Mexico agreement was negotiated to gain access to the Mexican
market equivalent to that gained by US (and Canadian) companies. The
European Union was also motivated to launch negotiations with Mercosur (and as a result with Chile) by the prospect of the Free Trade Area of
the Americas. The situation is similar with the current negotiations with
Central America and the Andean Community, following the conclusion
of the Central American Free Trade Agreement and the US–Peru and
US–Colombia agreements; with Korea, following the KORUS PTA; and
with ASEAN, following US PTAs with Singapore and negotiations with
Thailand and Malaysia. In addition to the threat to EU markets from
trade diversion, there appears to be a second commercial motivation in
the shape of strengthening commercial links with regions undergoing
economic growth, such as Latin America in the 1990s and South and
East Asia today.

This general categorization of EU PTAs should not disguise the fact that
there are multiple motivations for negotiating preferential agreements.
Clearly, there will be foreign policy considerations in all PTAs, especially
given the nature of EU foreign policy and its heavy reliance on economic
and commercial instruments. Equally, commercial and economic considerations will also play a role in all PTAs, so that the potential for conflict-
ing interests is always present.
   Before closing on the topic of motivations there are two other general
drivers that have shaped EU policy rhetoric on PTAs, if not so much the
substance. These are both to do with projecting a European approach to
economic relations and integration. The European Union represents a
distinctive model for deep economic integration. This finds expression in
EU trade and thus PTA policy in a number of ways. First the European
Union pursues a policy of negotiating region-to-region agreements. In
other words, the European Union prefers, in principle, to negotiate with
partner regions, such as Mercosur, Central America, the Southern African Development Community, the Economic Community of West African States, the Caribbean Community (or the Caribbean Forum of ACP
States – CARIFORUM) and ASEAN, than with individual countries.
The aim here is to use the leverage of access to the EU market to promote regional economic integration in other parts of the world. The
EU experience with economic integration has been that it has promoted
economic development and political stability. The member states and

European institutions therefore see it as natural to promote such integration elsewhere. The promotion of the distinctive European approach to economic (and thus political) integration is also seen as a major element of EU "soft power".

The record in region-to-region negotiations to date has, however, not been very good, largely because the policy is held hostage to the ability of the European Union's partners to make progress towards regional integration. The region-to-region policy is aimed at promoting regional integration among the European Union's partners, but it is also partly motivated by reciprocity. If the European Union offers preferential access to the whole EU market, it wants equivalent access to the partner region. If Mercosur is slow in realizing an integrated market or even a genuine customs union, EU exporters and investors will not get regional access to the whole of Mercosur, whereas the Mercosur countries get access to the whole EU market. Delays in regional integration in Latin America, the ACP regions in Africa and especially Asia (ASEAN) therefore create difficulties for the region-to-region policy. Individual members of certain regions may also prefer bilateral agreements with the European Union. The recent spate of interim Economic Partnership Agreements with ACP states, which have been a condition of the ACP countries' continuing to receive preferential access to the EU market, has in fact served to weaken rather than strengthen regional cooperation among the developing countries concerned. In the absence of agreements with Brussels, ACP states would find themselves subject to the less generous Generalized System of Preferences (GSP), potentially putting them in direct competition with countries such as Brazil and India.

The other motivation related to the European Union's experience with regional integration in Europe is a desire to promote framework regulation for international trade and investment. The European Union does not seek to export its domestic *acquis communautaire*, because it is clearly not appropriate or feasible in most instances. The EU *acquis* does, however, shape EU policy, just as domestic policies shape all trade negotiations. Indeed, the nature of the *acquis* means that it is more important in shaping EU policy because it has been arrived at through sometimes arduous internal negotiations within the European Union. The European Union does nonetheless favour international regimes for trade that mirror the European experience in that they establish a clear, consistent regulatory framework for international trade. This is one of the reasons the European Union has pushed the "Singapore" issues in the Doha Development Agenda (DDA) and why it is likely to seek analogous comprehensive agendas in its PTAs. Although not mirroring the EU *acquis*, there is a desire to see agreed norms and standards for trade that would serve a similar purpose in the international trading system to that served by the (constitutional) rules of the *acquis*. Like the region-to-region objective, this has not proved very successful, as the European Union's effort to promote a comprehensive agenda in the DDA has shown, but it remains a factor that can shape EU PTA policy.

In order to focus political attention on the aim of negotiating a comprehensive multilateral (millennium) Round in the World Trade Organization (WTO), the European Union maintained a *de facto* moratorium on new PTA negotiations from 1999 until 2006. This was not a formal position, in that it was not set out in a political decision of the Council, but the policy held because of a consensus among the member states and the Commission. The policy held despite setbacks in the effort to negotiate a comprehensive Round in Seattle and especially in Cancun, and in November 2003 a Commission position on trade policy after Cancun held to the view that the DDA should retain the priority. This was supported by the European Parliament and by the member states, especially the United Kingdom, Sweden and the other more liberally inclined governments. The November 2003 position did not, however, rule out new PTAs if there was an economic or business case to be made for them and if the European Union's PTA partners were making progress towards regional integration in cases of region-to-region negotiations.

The shift to a more activist EU pursuit of PTAs

The European Union's formal policy position on PTAs was set out in the October 2006 policy statement on the European Union and globalization, *Global Europe* (European Commission, 2006). This states that the European Union seeks to pursue multilateral negotiations in the DDA as well as negotiate PTAs and that these two objectives are complementary. At the same time, the European Union stresses the aim of ensuring that the PTAs offer improvements on the existing position, which implies WTO-plus provisions, if a business case for PTAs is to be made. Whether these two aims are compatible will depend very much on the detailed substance of agreements discussed in this volume and on the degree of progress made in multilateral negotiations. We will return to this question in the concluding chapter.

Apart from the declared policy aims there seems to be little doubt that the European Union's shift in policy has to do with a concern to match what others, and in particular what the United States, are doing in terms of PTAs, the lack of progress in multilateral negotiations and a desire to strengthen links with Asia as a centre for future regional growth.

As noted above, it is no coincidence that the European Union has sought PTAs with countries that have concluded agreements with the

United States. Although the United States has been pursuing a form of competitive liberalization for some time, it was not able to make progress, as we saw above, until the George W. Bush administration had Trade Promotion Authority. The more offensive US policy on PTAs from 2001 onwards made it harder and harder for the European Union not to respond. US policy on PTAs has therefore been a major factor in tipping the balance in favour of a more activist policy on preferential agreements on the part of the European Union. This appears to be especially important in Asia, where the United States has been negotiating a string of PTAs with ASEAN countries and Korea.

A second factor in the European Union's shift towards preferential agreements has clearly been the progressive reduction in the ambition of the DDA. Not only has the agenda been reduced by removing three of the Singapore issues that the European Union had a particular interest in (investment, competition and government procurement), but the more conventional agenda in terms of non-agricultural market access and services in the DDA does not hold out much for EU offensive interests in industry and services. The option of moving ahead in PTAs is therefore seen as holding out more promise for the EU aims of including Singapore issues in the trade agenda and for the EU offensive interests in enhancing EU market access to some key markets. Of course, much will depend on whether the European Union can achieve more through the PTA route than through the WTO.

A third factor could be a desire to seek to shape the rules and standards that will influence future access to some major markets. To date, deeper integration has been mainly something for the European Union and the United States in their PTAs. But a growing number of preferential agreements are now beginning to include deeper integration issues in their agendas. To date, Asian governments have eschewed standards for safety or environmental protection, or rules for competition or investment. As the Asian economies develop, however, one can expect to see such measures assume greater importance. This is beginning to be reflected in the content of the intra-Asian PTAs. The European Union therefore has an interest in ensuring that the standards and rules developed are consistent with European standards and rules, otherwise European exporters may face future barriers to market access throughout the region.

The EU's revealed preferences

The shift towards a more active EU policy on PTAs has not been controversial in the European Union. A broad consensus has emerged among the member states and between the member states and the Commission on the desirability of negotiating more PTAs. The main debate was on timing, with some member states such as the United Kingdom, Sweden and other more liberally inclined member states wishing to hold back longer in order not to undermine the prospects for the DDA.

The EU policy objective is thus to ensure compatibility between its PTAs and the multilateral system. At the same time, it is seeking PTAs that make business sense, which implies provisions that extend beyond the scope and depth of WTO liberalization. There are also other objectives such as the promotion of regional integration, the development of the European Union's PTA partners and wider political and strategic considerations. The aim of this section is to assess whether there are any clear policy trends in the substance of EU PTA policy. In the general debate on EU policy towards preferential agreements, there is a tendency to stop at generalizations. The aim here – and in the other sections of this chapter – is to get beyond this.

WTO-plus?

The substance of the European Union's PTAs to date has not been very WTO-plus. It has tended to stick to the framework rules as set out in the WTO, where these exist. This is, for example, the case for technical barriers to trade (TBT), sanitary and phytosanitary measures (SPS), public procurement and services. There are not very many cases of the European Union going significantly WTO-plus in its agreements. This contrasts with the United States for example, whose PTAs are significantly WTO-plus in intellectual property rights (IPRs) and in the inclusion of comprehensive investment measures. The EU PTAs have, however, included procedural measures that are WTO-plus, such as detailed provisions applying WTO principles and the establishment of relatively strong institutional provisions, such as specialist committees, to ensure implementation of the PTA and promote bilateral cooperation on a range of functional issues.

Turning to the coverage of agreements, there has up to now been little evidence of the EU PTAs including commitments on liberalization that are significantly beyond the WTO. The European Union offers tariff liberalization for industrial goods, but does not offer much by way of greater access to agricultural markets in PTAs than in the WTO. Even in services the PTAs to date have not gone much beyond the General Agreement on Trade in Services (GATS), although the expectation must be that the European Union will seek to match the level of commitment in the US PTAs in services and thus go GATS-plus. The European Union has investment provisions only in the EU–Chile agreement, and these are modest compared with the comprehensive nature of investment rules in the US PTAs. Recent developments in EU PTA policy, however, point to greater ambition as the European Union seeks to pursue the aims of the Global Europe strategy through both PTAs and multilateral negotiations. One clear illustration of this shift in policy is the comprehensive nature of the EPA negotiated with the CARIFORUM. This is far more ambitious than the previous PTAs the European Union had signed with developing countries and included fairly ambitious market access provisions as well as far more developed provisions on the Singapore issues. The PTA with South Korea should be ambitious in many respects, if not perhaps in agricultural liberalization. The litmus test of the European Union's ability to succeed in negotiating WTO-plus provisions in PTAs will then be in the negotiations with ASEAN and India.

Another observation that can be made about the substance of EU PTAs is that they stress the use of existing international standards. This is the case for TBT, public procurement and intellectual property, in which the EU PTAs seek to promote the effective enforcement of the various international standards for the protection of intellectual property, rather than introducing new standards through PTAs. The one major exception to this is geographical indicators.

The EU PTAs also place importance on developing agreed international standards, where these do not exist, as a means of facilitating trade and investment. Here the PTA policy reflects the "domestic" experience of the European Union.

The "domestic" *acquis* of the European Union has shaped its approach to PTAs, but the European Union has by no means sought to export the EU *acquis* through PTAs, except for potential accession states. If anything, the European Union has been rather "flexible" in the content of its PTAs, compared, for example, with the United States. This flexibility means that the European Union has excluded sensitive sectors from liberalization, such as a number of agricultural sectors. The European Union has also been flexible in what it asks of its PTA partners. Another way of putting this is to say that the European Union tailors the contents of PTAs to the particular circumstances of the agreement. Various agreements offer a number of options rather than requiring a specific policy. For example, the TBT provisions in the EU–Chile agreement offer mutual recognition or equivalence.

Asymmetric provisions

This brings us to the EU policy on asymmetry. The European Union has not used a set agenda for PTA negotiations, as appears to have been the case with the US use of NAFTA as the starting point for all PTAs. On the other hand, the EU PTAs show greater uniformity than Japan (at least in its early PTAs) or Singapore in terms of what they expect of the PTA partner.

On tariffs, the European Union offers asymmetry to developing countries on industrial goods. The Euro-Med agreements, for example, include provision for the developing country partner to reintroduce tariffs if these are needed as part of an infant industry strategy. As suggested above, however, this flexibility works both ways in the sense that the European Union has some asymmetry in its favour, such as in agricultural tariffs in the EU–Chile agreement. And, by seeking a sufficient measure of reciprocity from its EPA partners to satisfy the requirements of Article XXIV of the General Agreement on Tariffs and Trade, the European Union is reducing the asymmetry of its agreements with developing countries.

In the field of rules of origin, the current EU reform proposals for preferential rules of origin include simpler rules of origin based on a 45 per cent (ex factory price) value content. This would constitute a form of asymmetry because it should simplify rules of origin for developing country PTA partners.

On a range of deeper integration issues the European Union has been willing to accept modest commitments on the part of its developing country partners. For the Euro-Med there are a number of commitments for the European Union's partners to adopt European standards (TBT, SPS and competition), but these are long-term aims without any specific implementation phase. Beyond the Euro-Med, the European Union has been happy to accept asymmetric commitments on some of the Singapore issues, no doubt as a means of getting something on these topics into the EPA. In the EU–CARIFORUM EPA, for example, the European Union offers commitments on national treatment in procurement that are close to those of the Agreement on Government Procurement (GPA), whereas CARIFORUM partners must accept only transparency rules.

Trends

Based on the European Union's PTAs to date, it is difficult to identify any clear trends. The content of EU agreements varies between partners, depending on the level of development of the partners, how important they are for European security (i.e. near neighbours are treated differently) and in which sectors they constitute a competitive challenge. So variations over time are difficult to pick out.

As witnessed by the push for comprehensive coverage in the EPAs compared with previous PTAs with developing countries as well as countries such as Korea, the shift in EU policy clearly points to rather more ambition in future PTAs. Certainly the expectation is that the content of any EU–Korea PTA will be an advance on the EU–Chile agreement, which has to date been seen as "the model" for EU PTAs. It is significant that, in its negotiations with Korea, the European Union has said that with respect to trade in autos it seeks the same terms as those granted to the United States under KORUS, and that Korea should accept international standards as being equivalent to domestic standards. In its negotiations with India, the European Union has also said that it will not be rushed into finding solutions to problematic areas, notably in services, IPRs and government procurement (*Bridges Weekly Trade News Digest*, 12(9), 12 March 2008).

It remains to be seen, however, whether the European Union will be successful with a more ambitious agenda.

- On *tariffs*, it will be hard pressed to overcome the domestic opposition to significant liberalization of the sensitive agricultural sectors that have to date been excluded from preferential liberalization as well as non-preferential liberalization in the WTO. Although the European Union is likely to be able to offer near to 100 per cent coverage for industrial tariff liberalization in its PTAs, the exclusion of sensitive sectors by the European Union clearly opens the way for its PTA partners likewise to exclude sensitive sectors.

- On *rules of origin* (RoO), the European Union has been active in harmonizing its own preferential rules of origin. But the Pan-Euro rules remain complex. The current review of EU preferential rules of origin is aimed at simplifying the RoO for developing countries. But this might paradoxically introduce a two-tiered system for EU rules of origin, one for the developed economies and one for developing countries.[3]

- In *TBT and SPS*, the trend appears to be to use PTAs to apply the policies and principles in the WTO agreements. In this the European Union should for the most part facilitate trade. But there may be a degree of WTO-minus application of the rules when it comes to precaution, which the European Union wants to interpret in such a fashion that risk assessment and especially risk management should include social as well as scientific assessments of risk.

- The trend in *public procurement* is clearly to use the PTAs to extend the number of countries that effectively apply the GPA. Here the European Union has been successful in its PTA with Chile, but the test will be whether the European Union can succeed in extending coverage of at least the GPA framework rules to include the more advanced ASEAN countries and India.

- For *services*, the European Union is likely to seek to match the sector commitments achieved by the United States in its PTAs. This will be the case for EU–Korea and for those ASEAN countries that have concluded agreements with the United States. It will also be the case for Central America.

- For *investment*, the European Union can be expected to be rather more ambitious in its future PTAs. Within the European Union there is work under way to define a minimum platform for investment rules for PTAs. This could well find application in some of the future agreements, but will stop short of the kind of comprehensive investment rules that the United States includes in all its PTAs.

- Finally, in *intellectual property*, the EU trend will be to seek more effective enforcement of existing IPR standards through its PTAs and to press for inclusion of protection for geographical indicators, where it is likely to have much less success.

Notes

1. A negotiating mandate has also been adopted for the negotiation of an Association Agreement with Central America/Andean Community.
2. At the end of 2007 a series of interim EPAs were negotiated in order to avoid a position in which the European Union would impose tariffs on imports from ACP states that had previously benefited from preferences. Only one comprehensive EPA was negotiated with CARIFORUM. Hence the discussion of the EPA provisions in the respective sections above. There remain therefore significant negotiations if the European Union is to agree comprehensive EPAs with all the ACP regions or states, as is its aim.
3. In October 2007 the European Commission produced a review of rules of origin for the GSP schemes, which was under discussion in 2008. Wider application to PTAs with developing countries is likely to take longer. The EPA negotiated with CARIFORUM in December 2007 (Art. 10) provides for a review of the rules of origin included in that agreement within five years, with a view to further simplification.

8

The European Free Trade Association

The European Free Trade Association (EFTA) is one of the oldest and most successful examples of a regional trade agreement as foreseen by Article XXIV of the General Agreement on Tariffs and Trade (GATT). Membership has waxed and waned since its creation in 1960 and today is constituted by two Nordic members (Iceland and Norway) and two Alpine members (Liechtenstein and Switzerland). EFTA was once considered a serious alternative to integration through the European Communities, eschewing supranational governance structures while preferring a more flexible and understated free trade area. This holds true for its members today, which prefer a more flexible intergovernmental structure and a more limited scope of issues – mainly economic and trade related – as compared with the European Union. The reasons for rejecting EU membership are varied, depending on the member state, but EFTA's identity today is a legacy of its evolution vis-à-vis Europe. Most people's conception of EFTA is linked to its deep relationship with the European Union through the European Economic Area (EEA) Agreement. Switzerland is not a member of the EEA and manages its relationship with the European Union through a number of sectoral bilateral agreements. Most of EFTA's budget and personnel resources are devoted to the Secretariat in Brussels. However, the management and coordination of EFTA's so-called third-country policy (i.e. countries outside of the European Union) in Geneva are one of the most important functions of the organization. In the past decade, the EFTA states have slowly and deliberately built one of the largest and most dynamic free

The rise of bilateralism: Comparing American, European and Asian approaches to preferential trade agreements, Heydon and Woolcock,
United Nations University Press, 2009, ISBN 978-92-808-1162-9

trade networks in the world. Their agreements cover some 50 countries and territories, in four continents, reaching a population that is fast approaching 1 billion.

The EFTA approach to its bilateral and regional trade agreements is characterized by flexibility, pragmatism and a desire to gain market access for its economic operators. Its approach is governed by its own institutional structures and working methods. An overall direction is promulgated twice yearly at EFTA Ministerial meetings, and a six-month rotating presidency of the Council guides this work via a Chair's priority work programme. Negotiations are conducted by a Council-appointed chief negotiator, usually the head negotiator of one of the member states, and positions and strategies are continuously coordinated throughout the course of negotiations. However, it is important to keep in mind that member states retain full and complete control over their own fate and a consensus must be reached before any decision is taken.

The Liechtenstein Chair published EFTA priorities in January 2007. The paper called for the conclusion of negotiations with Canada, Thailand, Egypt and the Gulf Cooperation Council (GCC). It aimed to start negotiations on preferential trade agreements (PTAs) with Algeria, Indonesia, Colombia and Peru, and prepare the ground for immediate negotiations with Ukraine once its accession to the World Trade Organization (WTO) was finalized. In addition, the paper mentioned deepening economic relations with a select number of partners via Declarations on Cooperation – often a first step towards PTA negotiations – and mentioned 11 possible partners for the future.[1] These agreements would supplement EFTA's current global network and signal an upsurge, in both ambition and scope, in an already dynamic process. Before we can postulate on the general trends and stated aims of the EFTA states, it is useful to look at how their third-country policy has developed over the past 15 years.

The development of EFTA's third-country policy

Following the end of the Cold War, the EFTA states began to negotiate preferential agreements with countries outside of the European Union. The evolution of its third-country policy since 1990 can be divided into three phases.

The first phase entailed a network of free trade agreements (FTAs), limited to trade in industrial goods, signed with the Central and Eastern European countries (CEECs). The EFTA states were, according to the Secretariat, firstly guided by a desire to re-establish pan-European ties by contributing to the reconstruction of the former command economies and to supporting their transition towards market-based economies and democracy. Second, the agreements with the CEECs were in response to the European Agreements initiated by the European Union in order to ensure that important economic interests in the EFTA states were not discriminated against or placed at a competitive disadvantage vis-à-vis their EU competitors.

Phase two began at a Ministerial meeting in Bergen in 1995, when EFTA ministers announced a change in third-country policy by stating their intention to expand EFTA's network of PTAs beyond Europe to include the southern and eastern rim of the Mediterranean. This was very much a response to the Barcelona Process, launched by the European Union in 1995 to create a Euro-Med free trade area. The EFTA states, although not formally part of the process, clearly indicated their intentions to contribute to it. The creation of the Euro-Med cumulation zone was an important outcome of this phase.

The first two phases are distinguished from the third phase in that they were mostly defensive and based on a policy of *parallelism*, or negotiating with partners *after* the European Union to mitigate any economic disadvantages. The next phase portended a much more offensive strategy, negotiating with partners worldwide to secure economic advantages and preferential market access over EU and other competitors. In this third phase, the EFTA states went global. Starting with Canada in 1998, negotiations with overseas partners have increasingly become a significant component of EFTA's third-country activities. As the global market became more integrated and technological advances decreased transaction and transportation costs, geographical proximity was no longer central to trade flows. In adapting to this reality, the EFTA states have concluded PTAs with Mexico, Singapore, Chile, Korea and the Southern African Customs Union (SACU). In addition to being transcontinental, these agreements tend to be broader in scope in that they cover new areas such as services, investment, public procurement and competition. These so-called second-generation policy areas are particularly important to the EFTA states and reflect underlying national economic interests.

An argument can be made that the EFTA states are now moving into a fourth phase. This current phase foresees preferential agreements with some of the largest markets outside of the transatlantic area. The EFTA states will continue to push for second-generation agreements where possible but, as the impulse to complete PTAs strengthens, the EFTA states will have to compete for the attention of potential partners, which might be more interested in larger markets. In this case, it is likely that the EFTA states will continue their flexible approach and scale down their level of ambition depending on the partner. This phase also poses the most existential threat to EFTA since its three largest members –

Austria, Finland and Sweden – left in 1994. Larger partners mean higher stakes, and individual member states might prefer negotiating without their EFTA partners. In these circumstances, any minor differences in approaches and interests become more pronounced and cannot as easily be compromised away. Although the official rhetoric is that EFTA coordination is preferred, evidence to the contrary indicates that negotiating with larger PTA partners could seriously damage EFTA unity. For example, Iceland is now negotiating bilaterally with China, which to this point has deflected efforts to include the other EFTA states, and Switzerland has undertaken feasibility studies bilaterally with the United States and Japan, the latter leading to the commencement of negotiations in May 2007. The EFTA states have been successful in avoiding becoming "spokes" to the European Union's "hub". And they do have common interests and characteristics, not least the advantages of attracting potential partners because of their economic weight as a group. However, these benefits of membership are likely to be tested in the years to come. This, of course, fits into the larger picture developed in this study whereby regionalism is under pressure from the growth of bilateral accords.

The EFTA states have consistently affirmed their commitment to the multilateral trading system in general, and the Doha Development Agenda in particular. However, frustration with the pace and ambition of the Round has increased EFTA reliance on the PTA option.

As mentioned, the EFTA states are pragmatic, flexible and opportunistic in their third-country policy approach. They are similar to the European Union in that they do not approach negotiations with a standard "blueprint", such as some elements of the NAFTA model, and their agreements more often than not reflect the economic conditions and interests of their partners. For example, the PTA with the SACU states had to be scaled down considerably in scope and ambition once it became clear that the SACU states were not ready and willing to take on second-generation commitments. In addition, the EFTA Agreements with the Euro-Med countries are very similar to the EU Association Agreements, reflecting the broad objectives of exporting the European regulatory model and integrating these countries into the Single Market. Much of the language of these agreements is identical to that of the European Union agreements. Even with global partners, the EFTA states aim to receive concessions equivalent to those given to the European Union, if such agreements exist. However, the EFTA states do share interests and negotiating positions that, in general, favour a broader scope and deeper commitments.

The negotiating strategy is based on a quid pro quo. As small developed nations highly dependent on trade and investment and with low overall industrial tariffs, the EFTA states take a very offensive position on industrial goods, services, investment, procurement, intellectual property rights (IPRs) and competition. They desire a strong rules-based trade regime that takes into account a wider scope of issues than is currently available under the WTO. On the other hand, the EFTA states are all members of the highly protectionist agriculture group, the G10, and take a defensive position on agriculture. The EFTA states also negotiate bilaterally on agriculture, because, unlike the European Union, there is no common EFTA policy on agriculture. This allows them more flexibility. An important distinction here is that fish products (Chapter 3 of the Harmonized System) are considered by the EFTA states to be an industrial good and are therefore included as part of the more liberalized main agreement.

The EFTA states do not possess the political and economic clout to dictate terms or strongly influence partner country concessions in trade agreements. The agreements themselves are also not subject to the kind of scrutiny and political pressures one tends to find in the EU and US contexts. As a result, the EFTA negotiators have more flexibility and room for manoeuvre to conclude agreements.

Often, the EFTA states will offer technical assistance to ensure that their negotiating partners can benefit from the new opportunities offered by the PTA. This is especially the case with developing partner countries, where technical assistance comes mainly in the form of bilateral assistance. It also comes in the form of institutional assistance and training programmes through the Secretariat, but the yearly budget for these programmes is minimal. Before analysing evidence and revealing policy preferences based on the substance of particular agreements, let us examine some of the general motivations of EFTA's third-country policy.

General motivation of EFTA's PTA policy

In the case of EFTA PTAs, a number of factors have motivated each initiative. However, unlike EU or US PTA motivations, the EFTA states are almost wholly motivated by economic considerations. One could argue that other considerations – political, developmental or institutional – are also taken into account, but these are undoubtedly secondary motivations and will be dealt with briefly at the end of this section. First, however, we will look at the EFTA rationale for choosing potential PTA partners and the process this entails.

The choice of potential partners

The process of choosing PTA partners takes place on multiple levels. Potential partners are vetted by each individual member state in consultation with domestic partners and legislative bodies and discussed at the EFTA level in the Council of Ministers. This can occur as a result of partner country interest in the EFTA states, as seems to be the case with Peru, Colombia and Pakistan, or through EFTA initiatives, as seems to be the case with China and certain ASEAN countries. As a general rule, EFTA does not actively attempt to quantify the potential economic benefits of its preferential agreements through rigorous analysis such as computable general equilibrium modelling. Specific economic studies might take place within individual member states, but this remains outside of the EFTA context. The Secretariat does produce reports on potential partners, if requested by member states, but these reports tend to be descriptive in substance.

Preliminary work towards PTA negotiations with selected partners tends to take on one of two forms: either a Declaration of Cooperation is signed or a feasibility study is launched. The latter appears to be increasingly favoured by the EFTA states and was used in the Korea and Indonesia cases and now in the Malaysia context. Both methods foresee expert group consultation in specific sectors to gauge the ambition level of the agreement and the scope for possible action. In the framework of the EFTA–Korea feasibility study, the Korean side commissioned an econometric analysis to measure predicted commercial benefits and to justify PTA negotiations to sceptical domestic groups. The EFTA states do not appear to share such political constraints and are happy to justify partner choice based on potential market access opportunities and qualitative dynamics. In fact, many of these feasibility studies take place after a political decision has been taken at the EFTA level and – unless serious complications emerge – merely serve to support this decision. However, the third-country policy evolution towards ever larger countries and important markets indicates that these studies will take on a possibly more important role. In fact, the comprehensive Swiss–US feasibility study highlighted the political economy difficulties and divergent ambitions for the Swiss agricultural sector in particular, resulting in the decision not to pursue a PTA between the partners.

Overall, the EFTA approach in choosing partners is ad hoc and opportunistic. Despite the fact that the EFTA states, as a single entity, represented the tenth-largest global trading group in 2006, they are perceived by others as junior partners in Europe and have to compete to attract the limited negotiating resources of partner countries.

Economic considerations

As a commercial trading area the EFTA states are naturally motivated in their third-country policies by economic considerations. Indeed, Joseph Deiss, the former Swiss Economics Minister, succinctly articulated

EFTA's main motivation when he stated that "the main objective of
EFTA's FTA policy is to improve market access and to maintain the
competitiveness of EFTA economies".[2]

One can identify three broad economic considerations: limiting trade
diversion as a result of third-party agreements; securing market access
and economic competitiveness in fast-growing markets; and enforcement
of international trade rules.

Limiting trade diversion

The first consideration was the main driving force of EFTA's third-
country policy in the 1990s. As noted above, these early agreements
were motivated by parallelism – a defensive posture vis-à-vis the European Union. Most of these agreements were with small trading partners
around the Euro-Med region and the objectives were twofold: to mitigate
any potential competitive disadvantages vis-à-vis the European Union
and to link these agreements into the wider European strategy of integration. The scope of these agreements was minimal, limited to traditional
trade liberalization, and can be characterized as first generation.

The agreements with Mexico and Chile were motivated by these same
"defensive" commercial considerations because domestic economic operators were concerned that they were losing market access not only to EU
competitors but also to the United States and other partners. The EFTA
states demanded and largely received equivalent concessions – including
in services, investment and government procurement – to those offered
to the European Union. And although trade between the EFTA states
and Mexico/Chile was marginally increasing, the EFTA states were wor-
ried about their relative position vis-à-vis their main competitors. The
fact that the market size of most of these early partners was rather limited and the motivations were so closely tied to EU objectives is clearly
illustrated in the following trade statistics: in 2005, EFTA's total exports
to PTA partners were 76.8 per cent and its imports were 79.6 per cent of
total trade. However, if we discount the EU25, the numbers become
much less impressive. Total trade with PTA partners outside of the European Union was only 3.7 per cent of total trade. The EFTA states have
thus far been unable, or unwilling in the case of Norway especially, to
complete PTAs with some of their largest trading partners outside the
European Union, namely Japan, Canada, China, Russia, India, ASEAN
and Brazil. There is considerable pressure from business interests in the
EFTA states to move in this direction.

Improving market access and economic competitiveness

The second consideration is perhaps the most important driving force of
EFTA's third-country policy today. EFTA's approach towards the fast-

growing Asian region is at the forefront of its policy goals. Indeed, if you exclude Russia and count ASEAN as one entity, then 7 out of the possible 11 partners mentioned in the Liechtenstein priorities are in Asia. It is in Asia where the EFTA states bypassed the European Union and successfully completed PTAs with Singapore and Korea. As mentioned, they are negotiating with Thailand and the GCC and have announced their intentions to start negotiations with Indonesia. Contacts are ongoing with India and Malaysia, and there is an interest in deepening trade ties with other potential partners in Southeast Asia. The bilateral initiatives between Iceland and China and between Japan and Switzerland and the implications contained therein for EFTA unity have already been addressed in this chapter.

Market access and competitiveness objectives are manifested not only in industrial goods but also in other sectoral issues. The ambition is to follow the Singapore and Korea models and negotiate comprehensive second-generation agreements to foster EFTA's competitive advantage in services, investment and intellectual property. The main motivation for the EFTA shift towards Asia can be traced to a political economy dynamic, namely strong pressure from domestic and EFTA-based business lobbies. Indeed, the Icelandic, Swiss and Liechtenstein Chambers of Commerce have all pressed for an active policy for EFTA in Asia. The Icelandic Chamber of Commerce noted that, "for Icelandic businesses, it is therefore important to have comprehensive second generation FTAs not least in the rising markets in Asia".[3]

Overall, the Asian dimension of EFTA's third-country policy has generally been the most active and dynamic, driven by the EFTA states' interest in getting a solid toe-hold in the region and taking advantage of Asia's new-found affinity for preferential trade agreements.

Strengthening trade rules

Finally, the EFTA states are economically motivated to strengthen the implementation of existing trade rules through their preferential trade agreements. For example, the Swiss are very offensive minded when it comes to strengthening IPR provisions because of the size and influence of their industrial and pharmaceutical sectors. Indeed, the benefits of the second-generation agreements are of a qualitative nature, difficult to measure and assess, but nevertheless an important element of EFTA's third-country policy.

Other considerations

As a result of EFTA's institutional structure and limited mandate, other motivational considerations are subservient to economic interests.

Indeed, domestic pressures to include provisions for social, environmental or core labour standards in EFTA's PTAs are weakly articulated and have largely fallen on deaf ears. The fact that the built-in Consultative and Parliamentary Committees, whose mandate it is to guide member state policy, are more focused on EEA issues and EU matters attests to this claim. However, this is slowly beginning to change as the profile of the EFTA PTA network has changed in the past few years.

Regarding social matters, Ingunn Yssen, the International Secretary in the Norwegian Confederation of Trade Unions, has argued in favour of including social clauses in international trade agreements. She stated in the EFTA Bulletin that, "It is therefore important that authorities, when entering into free trade agreements, include social clauses that are based on the core conventions of the International Labour Organization, or that they encourage cooperation between the social partners to develop workers' rights and human rights in parallel with extended trade."[4] She takes as her lead the European Union's PTA with Chile, which includes articles that aim to establish a common consultative committee to promote dialogue and cooperation between the various economic and social organizations in the two parties – including the possibility for wider civil society participation. Whether or not these calls for action gain any traction is doubtful and could anyhow complicate the flexible and apolitical approach characteristic of EFTA PTAs.

Politically, one can argue that the EFTA preferential agreements with the CEECs and the Euro-Med region complement the EU motivation to create a stable and prosperous European post–Cold War order. In a development context, the Norwegians have highlighted the agreement with SACU countries. According to Lars Nordgaard, former Norwegian Chief Negotiator, one of the goals of this agreement was the promotion of fair and equitable trade relations between developed and developing countries. He noted that technical assistance and asymmetrical provisions could help "to facilitate the implementation of the FTA, to enhance trade and investment opportunities, and to support the SACU States' efforts to achieve sustainable economic and social development."[5] However, the political impact of the EFTA states is marginal and does not guide the third-country policy. If anything, the willingness of the EFTA states to grant China market economy status without political conditionality is more characteristic of its pragmatic approach.

Institutionally, EFTA's third-country policy is in effect its sole remaining raison d'être. Indeed, the formation and management of the EEA Agreement and the Secretariat in Brussels have been given the moniker of "EFTA at 3", given that Switzerland is not legally a member. And the management of the intra-EFTA Vaduz Convention is not particularly important given the small size of intra-EFTA trade. Recent developments, such as Swiss displeasure with its overall contribution to the EFTA budget and individual members pursuing bilateral initiatives with larger partners, illustrate the fragility of this institutional relationship.

According to the EFTA Secretariat, concluding second-generation agreements that cover new areas such as services, investment, public procurement and competition is a crucial component of the overall EFTA third-country strategy. Indeed, the scope of EFTA's agreements has generally evolved from first to second generation, evidenced by recent PTAs with Mexico, Chile, Singapore and Korea. This trend needs to be qualified, however, with the caveat that second-generation agreements can be negotiated only if the partner country is willing and able to reciprocate. The EFTA states have been flexible enough in the past to limit their ambitions and adapt to partner country constraints, although they prefer a generally broad and comprehensive scope of issues. But the interests of the EFTA states are not identical when it comes to the scope of its agreements. Individual EFTA states, especially Norway and Switzerland, place a higher priority on different sectors and issues. For example, the Swiss positions on IPR and investment are much more offensive than the Norwegian positions. This is the result of inherent economic priorities, development concerns and the fact that Norway faces constitutional issues regarding investment. Any internal differences to date have been managed successfully, often using creative techniques such as a separate investment agreement between all of the EFTA states and Korea, excluding Norway. In order to better examine what these priorities entail and the outcomes achieved, we are obliged to look at the substance of the agreements.

EFTA's revealed preferences

Industrial goods

According to the EFTA Secretariat, all EFTA preferential trade agreements cover trade in industrial products, including fish, and processed agricultural products. With some minor exceptions, all tariffs on industrial products in the EFTA states are eliminated once an agreement enters into force. Independent research on a select number of agreements reveals this to be the case. The EFTA PTA with Morocco gives Morocco duty-free access to 99.8 per cent of all tariff lines. The Chile agreement provides for 95.2 per cent and easily meets the WTO requirement to cover substantially all trade.

The EFTA states do allow for asymmetrical provisions in the form of extended transition periods. For example, the EFTA–Mexico PTA allows for a transition period of seven years. It is even longer for partners with more acute development needs, such as Morocco and Tunisia.

Agriculture

The EFTA states do not have a common agricultural policy. Trade in basic agricultural products is covered by bilateral arrangements between the individual EFTA states and the respective partner country. According to the EFTA Secretariat, EFTA's agricultural policy can be summed up in three points: EFTA states seek to promote free trade in all processed agricultural products and to maintain duties only on sensitive raw materials incorporated in these products; sensitive products of significant importance generally remain subject to duties; and each PTA should be tailor-made to accommodate the specific trade flows between the EFTA partner and EFTA in agricultural products.

In other words, the EFTA states are protectionist when it comes to their agricultural policies. Independent research reveals that tariff line coverage is limited.

Rules of origin

The rules of origin for industrial goods in EFTA's PTAs are based on the current European model. Indeed, the EFTA states use the Pan-Euro rules of origin model in their preferential trade agreements and have already stated their desire to take an active part in the Euro-Med cumulation zone. For PTAs concluded outside of the Euro-Med zone, the EFTA states have updated the European model by using simplified and less restrictive rules. For example, the EFTA PTA with Mexico allows for some adjustments in the specific rules list to take account of actual trade flows. As a result, there are more liberal rules of origin in sectors where either party is faced with a lack of raw materials or components (such as chemicals, machinery and car parts).

Overall, the EFTA states use restrictive and complex rules of origin in sensitive sectors, particularly in agriculture. They also use restrictive rules for textiles and apparel, similar to the European Union, but flexible measures have been incorporated into some agreements, depending on the trading partner and trade flows. Again, the EFTA–Mexico PTA provides one such example: Mexico allocates quotas to the EFTA states for importation into Mexico of textile and apparel goods under a more liberal regime.

Commercial instruments

In general, the EFTA agreements contain provisions that address commercial instruments, such as anti-dumping, competition, state aid and safeguard measures. However, the EFTA states have yet to apply any commercial instruments to their trade partners and have even agreed on the abolition of anti-dumping provisions – substituting a more stringent competition policy instead – in their agreements with Chile and Korea. The EFTA PTAs also deviate from WTO norms in their stricter timeline for the application of safeguard measures, applying a three-year maximum. Compensation is also to be offered prior to the adoption of any safeguard provisions and various exemptions on the application of safeguard measures on moral and security grounds are foreseen.

Sanitary and phytosanitary measures and technical barriers to trade

The EFTA states are closely linked to the EU SPS and TBT regulatory models. However, SPS and TBT commitments in EFTA's PTAs do not go much beyond reaffirming the parties' rights and obligations under the existing multilateral SPS and TBT agreements in the WTO.

The most comprehensive SPS measures are to be found in the EFTA–Chile PTA, which mentions consultation, cooperation, contact points and the prospect of developing bilateral arrangements, including agreements between their respective regulatory agencies at some future point. Nowhere in any of EFTA's PTAs is there mention of mutual recognition, equivalence or harmonization measures. This might reflect the fact that the EFTA states do not want to forgo any policy flexibility in their protected agricultural sectors.

Regarding TBT commitments, the EFTA PTAs contain three basic types of provision on technical regulations:
- The PTA with Turkey contains an information procedure on draft technical regulations.
- Other PTAs, such as those with Morocco and Tunisia, contain no such information procedure but provide for consultation and cooperation. They also foresee notifications in accordance with the (weaker) WTO Agreement on Technical Barriers to Trade.
- The PTAs with Mexico, Chile and Singapore state that the rights and obligations of the parties are to be governed by the WTO TBT Agreement. They specify areas of cooperation and call on the parties to facilitate the exchange of information. As is the case with the second category of PTAs, a consultation mechanism has been set up, the aim being to work out solutions in conformity with the WTO TBT Agreement.

Government procurement

All of the EFTA states are signatories to the plurilateral WTO Agreement on Government Procurement (GPA). As such, the EFTA states aim to incorporate provisions of the GPA into their preferential trade agreements, or at least induce partners that are not signatories to take on certain provisions of the GPA. In their dealings with fellow GPA members Singapore and Korea, the GPA is incorporated into the agreements. With non-members, such as Chile, the EFTA threshold is identical to its GPA commitments, with the noted exception of the electricity sector. And the EFTA threshold with Mexico is also identical to its GPA commitments, while that of Mexico is identical to its NAFTA commitments. Here EFTA has followed the same approach as the European Union in reconciling the GPA and NAFTA. For developing partners and first-generation agreements such as the EFTA–Morocco PTA, the ambition is limited to language seeking the progressive liberalization of government procurement at some future date.

Services

The EFTA PTAs contain a positive-list approach to services commitments, save for the agreement with Mexico, which has a negative-list approach. GATS-plus provisions differ between agreements, characteristic of EFTA's flexible approach and specific interests vis-à-vis different partners. For example, although most of the second-generation agreements provide for new commitments on rules in financial services and telecommunications, the PTA with Mexico is different in its provision on maritime transport services and a standstill provision on new discriminatory measures. In general, all of EFTA's PTAs contain commitments to eliminate further trade discrimination within given time-frames.

For the EFTA states, services account for approximately 70 per cent of their overall GDP. Trade in services is particularly important because the share of services in total external trade is higher than for any other core entity. This is especially true for the two Nordic countries. According to the United Nations Common Database, trade in services accounted for 36 per cent of overall trade in Iceland, 28 per cent in Norway and 20 per cent in Switzerland in 2003.

According to the Swiss Secretary of State for Economic Affairs, the EFTA motivation to strengthen services commitments through its PTA network stems from frustration with the perceived lack of progress at the multilateral level.

The GATS negotiations were finished in 1994, i.e., more than 10 years ago. Considering the dynamism experienced in trade in services over this last decade, it is fair to assume that the commitments are not up-to-date anymore .... In this situation, bilateral negotiations on services allow parties to move ahead and benefit from an "early harvest" on the offers made in the WTO context.[6]

Investment

The EFTA states were frustrated by the exclusion of investment provisions from the Doha Development Agenda and regarded bilateral agreements as a more conducive format for achieving their investment ambitions. The goal here is twofold: to improve legal security for foreign economic operators and to open new sectors to foreign investment. The EFTA states have WTO-plus investment measures with a number of partners. The PTA with Singapore is among the most progressive in terms of investment provisions, covering for the first time (for EFTA) the right of establishment for nationals of each respective partner. It also foresees the possibility of direct dispute settlement between a party to the agreement and an investor of another party. An evolutionary clause and institutional cooperation mechanisms also encourage parties to take further liberalizing measures once the time is ripe.

Intellectual property rights

The EFTA states include a chapter on the protection of intellectual property in all their PTAs. Indeed, many industries in the EFTA states are based on research and development, such as Swiss pharmaceutical firms, and would benefit from a strong legal framework that would secure a level of protection. According to Ingo Meitinger, Deputy Head of the International Trade Relations Department of the Swiss Federal Institute of Intellectual Property, the idea behind the chapter on IPR in preferential trade agreements is to create a legal environment which is beneficial for all parties.[7] Although the agreements themselves reaffirm the parties' commitments to international agreements[8] such as the Agreement on Trade-Related Aspects of Intellectual Property Rights (TRIPS), specific substantive issues reveal that the EFTA approach is dependent on the partner country in question. For example, provisions for geographical indicators vary widely from agreement to agreement. However, it can be said that EFTA PTAs are TRIPS-plus when it comes to the following IP issues: industrial designs, patents and undisclosed information.

Environment and labour

The EFTA states have to date not incorporated any environmental or labour standards into their preferential trade agreements. Calls for their inclusion have thus far been minimal, but a growing awareness of the importance of EFTA's third-country policy combined with the increased exposure of environmental and labour concerns could galvanize influential voices within the EFTA states to demand their inclusion. However, given EFTA's role as an intergovernmental organization with a limited mandate, a more pragmatic, commercially driven approach is likely to prevail.

Notes

1. ASEAN, Central America, India, China, Japan, Vietnam, Pakistan, Russia, Malaysia, Montenegro and South East Europe.
2. Joseph Deiss, "EFTA Free Trade Agreements and Swiss Foreign Economic Policy", in *EFTA Bulletin: EFTA Free Trade Relations*, July–August 2006, p. 14; available at ⟨http://www.efta.int/content/publications/bulletins/EFTA_Free_Trade_Relations_July-August_2006.pdf⟩ (accessed 18 September 2008).
3. "Icelandic Chamber of Commerce", in *EFTA Bulletin: EFTA Free Trade Relations*, July–August 2006, p. 44.
4. Ingunn Yssen, "Social Clauses in Trade Agreements – EFTA Must Follow up on EU Initiatives", in *EFTA Bulletin: EFTA Free Trade Relations*, July–August 2006, p. 40.
5. Lars Erik Nordgaard, "Trade and Development – The EFTA–SACU Agreement", in *EFTA Bulletin: EFTA Free Trade Relations*, July–August 2006, p. 28.
6. Christian Etter, "Services and Investment", in *EFTA Bulletin: EFTA Free Trade Relations*, July–August 2006, pp. 21–22.
7. Ingo Meitinger, "Intellectual Property Rights", in *EFTA Bulletin: EFTA Free Trade Relations*, July–August 2006, p. 23.
8. In the case of EFTA this means the commitments of the individual countries, because EFTA has no competence in intellectual property.

9

Japan

Japan has been a latecomer to bilateral preferential trade agreements (PTAs), with only six having entered into force (Singapore, Mexico, Malaysia, Chile, Thailand and Indonesia). Three other agreements have been signed (Philippines, Brunei and Association of Southeast Asian Nations). And negotiations are under way with five countries or regions (Gulf Cooperation Council, India, Vietnam, Australia and Switzerland). Negotiations began with Korea in December 2003 but were suspended in November 2004 (see Annex 4 for details).

Japan's relatively recent embrace of PTAs has contributed to the fact that the countries with which it has agreements account for only a small proportion of Japan's trade: 7.1 per cent in 2005. This value would increase to 33.8 per cent if all PTAs in the pipeline or contemplated came to fruition but is still smaller than corresponding figures for the United States (36 per cent) or the European Union (60 per cent) (Urata, 2007).

Japan calls most of its agreements Economic Partnership Agreements (EPAs) to indicate that they go beyond traditional PTAs to include agreements on the free movement of labour, tourism, intellectual property considerations, etc. There seems to be consensus (and admission by the Ministry of Economy, Trade and Industry) that EPAs are in practice similar to what other countries would call PTAs – or, rather, free trade agreements (FTAs).

The rise of bilateralism: Comparing American, European and Asian approaches to preferential trade agreements, Heydon and Woolcock,
United Nations University Press, 2009, ISBN 978-92-808-1162-9

Japan's motivations for negotiating PTAs

As will be developed more fully below, although Japan has particular motivations for negotiating PTAs, the shift from a multilateral-only approach to trade diplomacy can be seen as part of an Asia-wide change of tack. This change has been prompted by a range of factors, including concern about the trade diversion effects of the North American Free Trade Agreement (NAFTA), political incoherence in Southeast Asia following the Asian financial crisis of 1997–1998, the failure of the Seattle and then the Cancun Ministerial Meetings of the World Trade Organization (WTO), and a growing realization of the limited trade liberalization potential of Asia-Pacific Economic Cooperation (APEC) (Garnaut and Vines, 2006).

A fear of being left out

The immediate response of senior Japanese politicians to the conclusion of negotiation of the Korea–US PTA was a vivid illustration of Japan's fear of being left out. Japan's Foreign Minister at the time, Taro Aso, emphasized the importance of resuming free trade talks with Korea; Chief Cabinet Minister Yasuhisa Shiozaki said that "Japan is ready to resume FTA negotiations [with Korea] at any time and will intensify our call to restart the process at an early stage"; and Shinzo Abe, then Japan's Prime Minister, widened the scope of the response by saying that a PTA with the United States was something "Japan needs to consider as a future topic" (*Financial Times*, 4 April 2007).

Underpinning this reaction are data prepared by the Ministry of Economy, Trade and Industry (METI) suggesting that, as a result of closer integration, NAFTA's share of global inflows of foreign direct investment grew from 20 per cent to 35 per cent between 1991 and 1999, and the European Union's share grew from 40 per cent to 50 per cent from 1986 to 2000. METI, saying that "promoting EPAs is the key to energizing economies", records the intra-NAFTA share of US exports as rising from 30 per cent to 40 per cent between 1990 and 1999, and the intra-EU share of EU members' exports as growing from 60 per cent to 80 per cent from 1986 to 2000 (METI, 2005).

Dissatisfaction with progress in the multilateral trading system

Dissatisfaction with the pace of WTO negotiations is widely cited in the academic literature as a motivation for Japan's pursuit of bilateralism and regionalism, and the failure of the Seattle Ministerial in 1999 and of Cancun in 2003 can certainly be seen as triggers for the subsequent spate of

PTA activity. But, in the official documentation of the Japanese government, the link is implicit rather than direct. Thus METI's explanation of the policy goals that EPAs are intended to address includes to "substantially expand and facilitate trade in goods and services" (a key goal of the Doha Development Agenda); "eliminate economic disadvantages caused by absence of EPA/FTA" (a task of ongoing most favoured nation liberalization and rules-strengthening in the WTO); "promote acceptance of specialized and skilled workers" (in part the goal of Mode 4 negotiations in the General Agreement on Trade in Services, GATS) (METI, 2005).

Opportunities for deeper integration

Japan's pursuit of PTAs needs to be seen, at least in part, within the broader context of East Asia – still the main arena for Japan's preferential agreements. Among the motivations for cooperation in Asia was the experience of the Asian financial crisis of 1997–1998 and the lessons drawn from it. The crisis, and the perceived failure of APEC to respond to it, prompted the regional economies to realize the importance of closer economic cooperation among themselves (Kawai, 2004). This extended well beyond trade, and included important financial sector cooperation, including the creation of a regional liquidity support arrangement, establishment of surveillance mechanisms and the development of Asian bond markets. But cooperation through trade was also part of the move to closer integration and helps explain, for example, the Japan–Singapore EPA initiative. Closer integration through preferential trade arrangements was also prompted by the growing increase in intra-Asian trade intensity.[1] In 2001, East Asia's trade intensity index (at 2.22) was higher than that of either NAFTA (2.12) or the European Union (1.67), suggesting a trade environment conducive to preferential deals (see the theoretical discussion in Chapter 11, where Lipsey points out that opportunities for trade creation are enhanced and risks of trade diversion reduced where a PTA groups countries that are already major trading partners). Closer formal integration therefore represented a response to crisis, an institutionalization of the strong trade and economic links already established and an attempt to further intensify those linkages.

The institutionalization of East Asian linkages is acknowledged by the Gaimusho (Ministry of Foreign Affairs) as an important driver of Japan's pursuit of PTAs:

> Economic relations between Japan and East Asian countries in particular have deepened and developed rapidly, and given the necessity for the formation of a legal structure commensurate to these new relations, Japan has moved to promote EPAs. (Ministry of Foreign Affairs, 2006: 172)

The objective of concluding a comprehensive agreement between Japan and ASEAN (the Japan–ASEAN Comprehensive Economic Partnership) is presented, by METI, as an attempt to foster regional integration by building on individual bilateral agreements and, through the Japan–ASEAN Cumulative Rules of Origin, enabling companies located in the Japan–ASEAN region to do business with no tariffs.

Consistent with the (somewhat contrived) distinction drawn by Japan between EPAs and PTAs, Japan's promotion of regional liberalization is thus portrayed as "an attempt to achieve deeper integration with its trading partners on a formal basis, going beyond reductions in border restrictions – pursuing investment liberalization, promoting greater competition in the domestic market, and harmonizing standards and procedures" (Kawai, 2004: 15).

A stimulus to domestic reform

Among the objectives of Economic Partnership Agreements, METI includes the need to "promote Japan's economic and social structural reforms". As one of the strongest advocates of PTA analysis by the Trade Committee of the Organisation for Economic Co-operation and Development (OECD), Japan invokes, among other things, the role of PTAs in helping promote domestic reform. And in some particular areas of reform, such as financial sector liberalization, the role of preferential agreements has been emphasized.

A stimulus to the multilateral trading system

There appears to be no Japanese equivalent to the advocacy by the United States of "competitive liberalization". Nevertheless, the Foreign Ministry states that "Japan is also promoting rule-making appropriate for the diverse range of economic relations that exist among countries through Economic Partnership Agreements as a means to complement the functions of the WTO" (Ministry of Foreign Affairs, 2006: 172). Beyond this, it has been observed that, in negotiating EPAs, Japan's "challenge is to maintain not only consistency with, but also to promote, the WTO liberalization framework" (Kawai, 2004: 15).

A complement to foreign policy objectives

As with all the core entities, foreign policy and broader strategic objectives are a key element of Japan's drive to preferential trade arrangements. Referring to deliberations of the Council of Ministers on the Promotion of Economic Partnership on 21 December 2004, METI (2005) includes the following among the policy objectives of EPAs, under the heading of "Creation of international environment beneficial to our country":

- "Community building and stability and prosperity in East Asia"
- "Strengthen our economic power and [ability to] tackle political and diplomatic challenges"
- "Reinforce Japan's position [in] international society"

METI (2005) also invokes what is perhaps the most pervasive of all the elements of Japan's economic diplomacy – the need to "[p]romote stable import[s] of natural resources and safe food, and diversification of suppliers". The recently concluded PTA between Japan and Indonesia includes an energy security partnership clause that will oblige Indonesia to honour all existing energy-supply contracts with Japan, even if it imposes broad restrictions on oil and gas exports. Indonesia is currently Japan's largest supplier of natural gas, third-largest supplier of coal and sixth-largest supplier of crude oil. In return for Jakarta's undertakings on energy, Tokyo has offered to increase technical assistance in areas such as energy-saving measures and coal-to-liquid technology.

The Gaimusho observes that "in concluding the EPA with Chile it is expected that Japan would secure a base in the South American region".

The dominant and growing role of China is also a key element in Japan's foreign economic diplomacy. In the framework of PTAs, this is seen most clearly in Japan's advocacy of the Comprehensive Economic Partnership in East Asia (CEPEA), a PTA covering ASEAN+6 (Australia, China, India, Japan, Korea and New Zealand). This proposal is widely considered to be a counterproposal to that of China of an East Asia free trade agreement covering ASEAN+3 (China, Japan and Korea). By extending the range of the grouping to include Australia, India and New Zealand, Japan would draw in important food and raw material suppliers, but would also dilute the influence of China, not least through the presence of India. Widening the net even further, Japan has also expressed support for a free trade area of the Asia Pacific, a US proposal that would see APEC converted into a preferential arrangement. Japan is thus drawn in opposing directions: the pursuit of closer Asian integration with neighbours and key trading partners; and the widening of formal economic linkages beyond the East Asian region in order to pursue broader economic, foreign policy and strategic interests.

In the case of the United States, it was concluded that, although foreign policy considerations loom large, concern about improved market access was the most widely held and strongly advanced motivation for the pursuit of PTAs; it was found to be the single most important direct driver of US PTA policy. In the case of Japan, the situation is less clear. As with the United States, Japanese motivations based on the fear of being left out, dissatisfaction with the progress in the WTO and maximizing opportunities for deeper integration all have an important market access dimension. METI (2005) has lauded the Japan–Mexico EPA on the grounds that "Mexico will become increasingly attractive as a base not only for exporting to the North American market but also to Latin America as well (Mexico has FTA agreements with Venezuela, Colombia, Bolivia, Uruguay, etc.)". And the Gaimusho has said of the Japan–Malaysia EPA that it "provides a framework for expansion and liberalization of bilateral trade and investment". A primary aim of the PTA under negotiation with Switzerland will be to increase Japanese exports of electronic goods, while also strengthening the protection of intellectual property rights. However, compared with the United States, Japan has been less successful in implementing PTAs that reflect a high level of ambition, albeit not always realized, to improve market access.

The substance of Japan's PTAs: Japan's revealed preferences

Tariffs

We have seen that tariff liberalization in the Japan–Chile EPA goes further than that in the earlier agreement with Singapore, for example liberalizing 32 per cent more of the total Japanese agricultural schedule and providing significantly more duty-free treatment of industrial lines. Against this, however, it must be acknowledged that Japan–Singapore is particularly restrictive – only India could claim to be more defensive on either agricultural or industrial goods in any of the studied agreements. So, despite the shift following the agreement with Singapore, Japanese agreements as a whole remain relatively defensive. Both of the agreements examined in detail (with Singapore and Chile) exclude over half of Japan's agricultural schedule, and Japan's industrial schedules are more restrictive than those of any of the other core entities. Japan has also made increasing use of longer transition times for sensitive sectors. With the 2005 agreement with Mexico, Japan extended transition times to 11 years; more recent agreements with Malaysia, Chile and Thailand include transitions of 16 years. And Japan–Mexico introduced tariff rate quotas for the first time. It is reported that, in negotiation of the Japan–Switzerland PTA, agricultural products will not be comprehensively covered (*Bridges Weekly Trade News Digest*, 17 May 2007). And Japanese scholars have observed that, given the complexity of tariff provisions in Japan's PTAs, the preferential tariffs in Japan's EPAs may not actually be used, even if they are lower than MFN tariffs (Ando and Kimura, 2007).

Because of Japan's relative defensiveness, Japan's PTA partners are more liberal in agricultural and industrial goods, and have less resort to quotas than Japan. It might thus be argued, in purely mercantilist terms, that Japan through its EPAs is succeeding in gaining market access in its overseas markets without yielding commensurate concessions. But, by offering less, Japan is presumably getting less in return than it might otherwise achieve, and also forgoing the opportunity to promote domestic reform and restructuring.

Rules of origin

Although the Asian rules of origin regime, which is used by Japan, has been characterized by its simplicity, newer agreements tend to adopt a hybrid version of the more restrictive criteria found in the NAFTA and Pan-Europe models. Material from other sources tends to confirm these findings in respect of tariffs and rules of origin.

Completion of the Japan–ASEAN Economic Partnership Agreement was delayed by Japanese reluctance to reduce and then phase out agricultural tariffs and by its insistence on restrictive and often product-specific rules of origin, especially for agricultural products (Sally, 2006). Under the agreement, rice, beef and dairy products will remain protected as sensitive products (*Bridges Weekly Trade News Digest*, 16 April 2008).

The suspension of talks between Japan and Korea is essentially owing to market access factors and the reluctance (of both parties) to eliminate tariffs in sensitive areas, ranging from tobacco to gear boxes.

In the Japan–Thailand agreement, Japan has exempted rice, cassava, beef, dairy, sugar and some other products; rules of origin are very restrictive on agricultural and fisheries products – at Japan's insistence; and Thailand has long transition periods for phasing out tariffs in steel and auto parts, and it has exempted large passenger cars from the agreement.

And in the Japan–Indonesia agreement, sensitive farm products such as rice, wheat and meat have been excluded from the agreement.

Safeguards

Like the other core entities, Japan's PTAs involve a shorter permissible duration for the use of safeguard measures than is found in the WTO, but the length of the permitted period has become progressively longer in Japan's successive agreements with Singapore, Mexico and Malaysia.

Government procurement

Whereas the Japan–Singapore EPA is WTO-plus in having thresholds that are lower than in the plurilateral Agreement on Government Procurement, this is not the case in the more recent Japan–Mexico agreement, where Japan has excluded its Defence Ministry from the central government entities. And in the Japan–Malaysia EPA there are no government procurement provisions.

Services

Japan's PTAs are not strongly GATS-plus. Their treatment of new financial services tends to be more restrictive than in the GATS Understanding. Japan trails both Korea and Singapore in the depth of services liberalization achieved in its PTAs. And, in the Japan–Malaysia EPA, Malaysia's services commitments offer only limited value-added relative to the GATS (Fink and Molinuevo, 2007).

Investment

The investment chapter in the Japan–Singapore EPA is based on NAFTA, but it is weaker than the investment chapter in NAFTA.

Intellectual property rights

Many of the agreements negotiated by Japan do not even include sections dealing with intellectual property rights.

Conclusion

One must conclude either that (1) for Japan, like the United States, improved market access is a key objective but the power of vested interests has so far constrained the realization of the objective to a greater extent than it has in the United States, or that (2) for Japan, the principal motivation for PTAs is the attainment of foreign policy objectives – including security of raw material supplies – through formal arrangements of cooperation rather than the aggressive pursuit of improved market access. Evidence would suggest that the first explanation is the most likely. It has thus been said (Urata, 2007) that Japan's ability to embark on a bold and strategic economic policy is undermined by its own domestic policy-making dynamics. The demonstration of this, it is suggested, is the success of the agricultural and labour lobbies in avoiding substantial liberalization commitments and in compromising the quality of Japanese PTAs. The problem is compounded by coordination arrangements within the Japanese bureaucracy. Whereas an Overseas Economic Cooperation Council has been established to coordinate Official Development Assistance strategies, no such Council has been established to assess trade strategies. There is a Council of Ministers on the Promotion of Economic Partnership Agreements, but it is not active and is not involved in discussion of EPA strategies (Urata, 2007). It has thus been observed that the negotiation of Japan's PTAs is characterized by vertical segmentation along sectoral lines (Mulgan, 2007), in a decentralized fashion without top-down leadership (Kimura, 2007).

A related question arises from the apparent lack of a blueprint for Japan's PTAs. As already noted, there is a mixture of positive and negative listing from one agreement to another. There is not a consistent treatment of domestic tariff schedules in Japan's PTAs. And rules of origin are similarly varied. For example, the Japan–Mexico agreement is one of the strictest overall, with regional value content (RVC) at around 50–60 per cent – equivalent to NAFTA levels – and with specific rules on tobacco requiring a 70 per cent RVC and no possibility for cumulation. The Japan–Malaysia agreement, on the other hand, has rather lenient rules that are less stringent in terms of content requirements. This might reflect a deliberate flexibility on Japan's part, so that agreements can reflect particular circumstances and differing wishes of Japan's partners. It might equally, however, reflect domestic political constraints on the implementation of a consistently ambitious approach to PTAs.

Only with the conclusion of more agreements is the picture likely to become clearer. Two of Japan's pending agreements will warrant particularly close scrutiny: the bilateral PTA with Australia, because of a likely Japanese inclination to carve out agriculture; and the bilateral with India, because of a likely Indian inclination to shield domestic banking, triggered by concerns that its PTA with Singapore has exposed Indian banks to undue control by Singaporean sovereign wealth funds. In short, both of these agreements will be a test of the ability of one partner to advance a key sectoral interest against the wishes of the other to shield precisely that sector.

Note

1. A calculation of intra-regional trade shares with a control for a region's relative size in world trade.

10

Singapore

Singapore has become one of the leading exponents of preferential trade agreements (PTAs) over the recent past. Although a leading member of the Association of Southeast Asian Nations (ASEAN) and a founding member of Asia-Pacific Economic Cooperation (APEC), Singapore pursued an active policy of unilateral and multilateral liberalization until the mid to late 1990s. Most of Singapore's PTAs began to attract the attention of its trading partners around the world with the Singapore–New Zealand Closer Economic Partnership Agreement in 1999. But it is important to bear in mind that Singapore had been an active member of ASEAN from its inception. In 1991, Singapore was one of the main movers behind the aim of creating the ASEAN Free Trade Area (AFTA), with the goal of eliminating tariffs within ASEAN by 2010.[1] AFTA can be seen as motivated by a desire to promote economic integration within the region and as a response to developments elsewhere, such as the deepening of regional integration within Europe, with the European Union's Single Market programme and the beginning of negotiations on the North American Free Trade Agreement (NAFTA). However, AFTA has had rather limited success in fostering trade amongst its members (see Box 1.1).

Singapore's trade policy

Singapore has conducted a policy of unilateral liberalization that has resulted in essentially zero applied tariffs. Much of its trade policy has

The rise of bilateralism: Comparing American, European and Asian approaches to preferential trade agreements, Heydon and Woolcock,
United Nations University Press, 2009, ISBN 978-92-808-1162-9

therefore been concerned with tariff binding and deeper integration or regulatory issues. In this sense it contrasts with many developing countries or emerging markets, for which tariffs are still a major policy issue. Singapore's interest in negotiating deeper integration issues dates back to the mid-1990s when it was instrumental in promoting the ASEAN Framework for Services (signed in 1995), the ASEAN Investment Area agreement, signed in 1995, and the ASEAN Framework Agreement on Mutual Recognition Agreements, signed in 1998. These initiatives sought to promote deeper integration within ASEAN and provided Singapore with experience in negotiating deeper integration agreements more widely.[2]

Singapore's trade policy was therefore already well prepared for negotiations on more comprehensive trade agreements than straightforward tariff liberalization. Indeed, zero applied tariffs in Singapore made such negotiations of little value. This meant Singapore was well placed when the general shift to negotiating deeper PTAs came in the late 1990s and early 2000s.

Singapore's motivations for negotiating PTAs

Strategic considerations

Singapore, like the other core entities, has been motivated by a number of factors to negotiate PTAs. These include strategic reasons, such as the desire to address China's growing presence in the region and to retain US engagement. ASEAN was initially a security arrangement for Southeast Asia in the face of the perceived communist threat from the North. Singapore's PTA policy has continued to be influenced by developments in China. For example, the ASEAN+3 negotiations are seen as a means of placing relations with China on a sound footing. The Japan–Singapore EPA (JSEPA), negotiated between 2000 and 2003, was also in part motivated by a desire to respond to the growing influence of China. The US–Singapore PTA, concluded in 2003, was also partially motivated by a desire to consolidate ties with the United States for political and strategic reasons.

Promoting the hub

Commercial motivations have taken a number of forms. First, Singapore has sought to establish business links with all regions. Singapore has long held a position as a regional hub, but the negotiation of PTAs with all regions appears to be an extension of this strategy, with a view to establishing Singapore as a hub in the wider global economy. This may, for example, explain Singapore's interest in PTAs that include investment and e-commerce. Singapore's agreements with Jordan in 2003, the European Free Trade Association (EFTA) and the Trans-Pacific Strategic Economic Partnership Agreement (TPSEPA, which groups Brunei, Chile, New Zealand and Singapore, and which is also known as P4) were all justified in terms of establishing firmer foundations for trading ties around the world.

External stimulus

Singapore has also been motivated by the actions of other parties. As noted in Chapter 9, the Asian financial crisis of 1997/98 is generally seen as the trigger for the growth of PTAs in the Asian region (Dent, 2003). This led to a recognition of the need for the region to strengthen the institutional basis for trade and cooperation; hence the efforts to strengthen ASEAN and the agreement with Japan. At the same time, the crisis influenced views of the region in the United States and other members of APEC. The United States began to see APEC as ineffective and ASEAN as immobile, as the Asian economies focused on their domestic problems. This helped trigger the more active use of PTAs by the United States and other APEC members (such as New Zealand) as a means of supporting economic integration with these countries. As the United States began to pursue PTAs, this led to emulation by Singapore and other Asian states.

Institutional interests

By the early 2000s Singapore had developed considerable negotiating expertise in PTAs. It was therefore ready to negotiate with the big players – the European Union and the United States. The European Union, which was still maintaining its *de facto* moratorium on new PTA negotiations, did not respond to Singapore's request for an agreement.[3] If one looks at the timing of Singapore's PTA negotiations (see Figure 10.1), it suggests a managed process in which Singapore's negotiating capacity was used in a rational fashion. One must therefore assume that, as in all the core entities, there were institutional interests in negotiating PTAs on the part of Singapore's trade negotiators.

The main features of Singapore's PTAs: Singapore's revealed preferences

General characteristics

There are three general features that characterize Singapore's PTAs. First, there is the apparent willingness to negotiate agreements with a

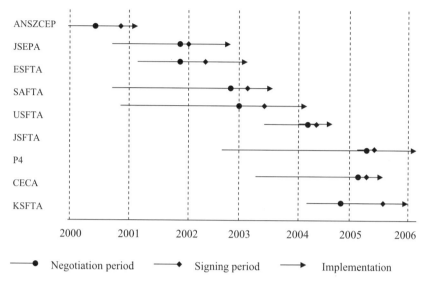

Figure 10.1 Singapore's PTA timetable.
Source: Krirkbhumi Chitranukroh, "The Dynamics of Preferential Trade Agreements and Domestic Institutions – An Alternative Route towards Asian Regionalism: A Case Study of Singapore and Thailand's Preferential Trade Agreements", PhD thesis, London School of Economics, 2008.

wide range of different partners, from Jordan to the United States. As noted above, this is linked to the aim of establishing Singapore as a hub for investment and multinational corporate activity. PTAs that protect investment and intellectual property rights and otherwise facilitate global production and investment will tend to make Singapore an attractive location for multinational companies. Companies with a substantial presence in Singapore will benefit from such agreements, regardless of their origin. Therefore PTAs, combined with Singapore's well-endowed human capital and infrastructure, make for a rational approach to globalization by a small city state.

Second, all Singapore's PTAs, at least since the JSEPA, have involved deeper integration issues. The JSEPA may have excluded agriculture altogether, but it did include services, investment, government procurement and stronger bilateral dispute settlement provisions. The JSEPA was clearly intended to break new ground in the scope of Asian PTAs (Dent, 2003). Singapore's agreement with EFTA was also fairly comprehensive, with a strong focus on services. It was the US–Singapore PTA, however, that set the standard for future agreements. This was comprehensive, with 21 chapters covering the range of topics included in the

NAFTA model. The inclusion of investment, commitments that went beyond the General Agreement on Trade in Services (GATS) and commitments that went beyond the Agreement on Trade-Related Intellectual Property Rights (TRIPs) clearly made this WTO-plus (Koh and Lin, 2004). The Singapore–Jordan PTA appeared to be motivated by a desire to match the US–Jordan agreement, and thus the "gold standard" being sought by the United States in its PTA policy. The TPSEPA (or P4), which covered trade in goods, measures on technical barriers to trade (TBT) and sanitary and phytosanitary (SPS) measures (including detailed provisions on standards, mutual recognition and conformance assessment), services, public procurement, intellectual property rights, competition and dispute settlement, showed that Singapore's desire to include deeper integration issues was not the result of pressure from more developed PTA partners. The TPSEPA/P4 even included environment and labour issues. This desire to negotiate comprehensive PTAs was also reflected in the India–Singapore Comprehensive Economic Cooperation Agreement of 2005, which included provisions on services, investment protection, mutual recognition for TBT and SPS, movement of persons and cooperation in intellectual property rights. Finally, the Korea–Singapore agreement concluded in August 2005 follows a similar pattern.

The third characteristic of Singapore's PTAs is that they are pragmatic, in the sense that they allow their PTA partners wide flexibility in terms of the depth and coverage of the agreements. This is probably a feature of the limited negotiating leverage of Singapore, given its previous unilateral liberalization and small market. The result, however, is that there is no uniformity in the detailed substance of Singapore's PTA partners' commitments. The pragmatic or flexible nature of Singapore's PTA policy is revealed in a number of policy areas.

Tariffs

Singapore generally liberalizes 100 per cent of its tariff lines immediately on the entry into force of a PTA. Only 6 of 10,000 tariff lines have been excluded (these relate to alcoholic drinks). The liberalization is straightforward and simple, achieved often by means of a single sentence. This compares with the very complex schedules of the European Union, EFTA and Japan. When it comes to liberalization by Singapore's PTA partners, however, things look very different. In the PTA with Japan, 81 per cent of all agricultural tariff lines were excluded from any liberalization, with the result that agriculture was largely excluded from the agreement. In the case of the "Comprehensive" Economic Partnership Agreement with India, India committed to liberalize just 25 per cent of all industrial tariff lines after a transition period, and only 12 per cent of agricultural tariff lines. Singapore has also shown flexibility when it comes to the structure of tariff schedules, allowing either positive or negative listing by its PTA partners.

Rules of origin

A similar picture emerges in rules of origin. There are virtually no uniform rules of origin in Singapore's preferential agreements. The PTA with the United States contains the more than 300 pages of NAFTA origin rules designed to address the interests of US sectors such as textiles. The PTA with EFTA uses Pan-Euro rules and that with Korea a complex combination of rules on changes of tariff chapter, changes of tariff heading, exceptions attached to changes of tariff heading and value content. On the other hand, Singapore's agreements with developing countries, such as Jordan, use a simple, liberal 35 per cent value content rule across the board. With such a diversity of rules of origin, Singapore does not exhibit any of the counter-trend observable in Europe towards harmonization. This is clearly one of the down-sides of a flexible approach to PTAs. Singapore's agreements may also be becoming more complex as its Asian PTA partners begin to develop more complex rules of origin.

Commercial instruments

When it comes to commercial instruments, flexibility has had the positive effect of allowing experimentation. Thus anti-dumping rules have been linked to competition in a number of Singapore's PTAs. And the criteria for assessing dumping have been tightened in a fashion that has not been possible at the multilateral level.

TBT and SPS

Singapore has a sophisticated and centralized system for dealing with technical barriers to trade and regulating risk. It is therefore able to negotiate comprehensive agreements covering mutual recognition, standards harmonization and cooperation across a range of standards-making and certification issues. This is reflected in the agreements Singapore has signed with Korea and the P4. Singapore is also a signatory to a range of mutual recognition agreements under the APEC framework and is negotiating mutual recognition agreements with its trading partners in Asia and in the P4. On the other hand, the PTA with the United States, which is otherwise WTO-plus in many respects, has only very modest provisions on TBT and SPS and adopts the preferred approach of the United States, which is for a minimum of institutional structures. There is no Joint Committee but only "coordinators" for TBT measures to deal with market barriers on a pragmatic basis. So, once again, Singapore tailors the content of its PTA to the preferences of its partner.

Government procurement

In government procurement, Singapore is a signatory to the WTO's Agreement on Government Procurement (GPA). In agreements with other signatories to the GPA there is therefore simply a reference to existing obligations. Otherwise, Singapore appears to be only slightly GPA-plus, in that some of the thresholds used to determine coverage are slightly lower than the GPA thresholds. In PTAs with developing partners, Singapore, like Japan, is happy to drop procurement if the partner is not keen to include it.

Services, investment and intellectual property rights

Singapore's commitments on services have been GATS-plus, and there has been a tendency for Singapore to negotiate fairly ambitious provisions on skilled/essential workers. There is also a mutual recognition agreement with Korea for engineers. The flexibility or pragmatism in service negotiations has taken the form of accepting the preferred scheduling approach of Singapore's PTA partners, i.e. either positive or negative listing. In investment, Singapore has in effect adopted the NAFTA approach in its PTAs, provided its partners have been willing to accept this. In other words, the investment provisions are comprehensive, including pre- and post-investment national treatment and investor–state dispute settlement. The Singapore–US agreement constituted the benchmark for provisions on intellectual property rights when it was negotiated, and therefore included a number of TRIPs-plus provisions.

Asymmetric provisions

By virtue of Singapore's flexible approach to PTAs, there is plenty of scope for asymmetric provisions. Singapore has clearly been willing to accept less by way of commitments from some of its developing country partners. The agreement with India, for example, constitutes a highly asymmetric agreement in terms of tariffs, which no doubt reflects the relative size of the markets concerned as much as anything. Singapore also provides technical assistance to its Asian PTA partners that are less developed.

Notes

1. In order to accommodate the Mekong 4 (Cambodia, Laos, Myanmar and Vietnam), the deadline for total tariff elimination was extended to 2015, but remained at 2010 for the more developed ASEAN members including Singapore.
2. Singapore's first experience with such measures probably dates from its involvement in similar work in APEC.
3. The European Commission argued that there was not a "business" case for a PTA with Singapore because the market was largely open anyway.

Part IV
The effects

The Choice

11

Assessing the economic impact of PTAs

Our study of revealed preferences has shown that there is considerable variation in the degree of ambition among preferential trade agreements (PTAs). How far are these differences reflected in the effects of agreements on patterns of trade and investment? And what is the overall impact of PTAs on trade and economic welfare? These questions will be the focus of the present chapter. First, some observations will be drawn on the basis of data obtained in the present study. This will be supplemented by a review of the literature, together with an examination of both ex post and ex ante approaches to measurement and their theoretical underpinnings. Finally, we will consider the effects of PTA formation on the incidence of dispute settlement in the World Trade Organization (WTO).

Preferential agreements are found to have discernible effects on trade and investment, particularly when measured at the micro level of individual commodities or of specific PTA provisions, such as those related to investment. Strong effects on welfare are less apparent, though the modest results may be owing, at least in part, to the negative effects of trade diversion. An important conclusion drawn in this section is that, for the vast majority of countries, concerns about preference erosion are not a valid basis for avoiding commitment to multilateral trade liberalization.

The rise of bilateralism: Comparing American, European and Asian approaches to preferential trade agreements, Heydon and Woolcock,
United Nations University Press, 2009, ISBN 978-92-808-1162-9

Evidence from the study

United States

Notwithstanding the problems of data availability and interpretation, there is evidence of a linkage between trade and investment flows and the *implementation* of US PTAs. On the basis of data over time and of flows expressed in real terms as a percentage of total (global) activity, such an apparent linkage is seen, for example, in the movement of US goods trade with Chile. US exports and imports with Chile grew, respectively, 133 per cent and 135 per cent in the three years following the implementation of the US–Chile agreement in January 2004. As a percentage of US totals, US exports to Chile grew by 63 per cent and imports by 62 per cent (see Figure 11.1).

US services exports to Mexico grew 137 per cent in the 10 years following the implementation of the North American Free Trade Agreement (NAFTA) in 1994. This followed two years of declining exports prior to the PTA. When calculated as a percentage of total US exports, services exports to Mexico increased by 34 per cent during this period. And outflows of US foreign direct investment (FDI) to Mexico have increased 263 per cent since implementation of NAFTA. As a percentage of total

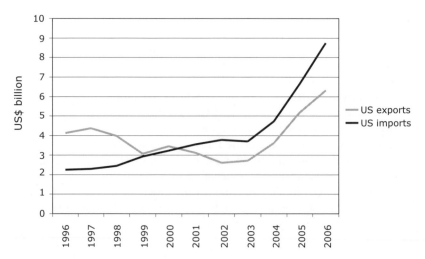

Figure 11.1 Trade in goods between the United States and Chile.
Source: Compiled by the authors from data from the Bureau of Economic Analysis, US Department of Commerce.

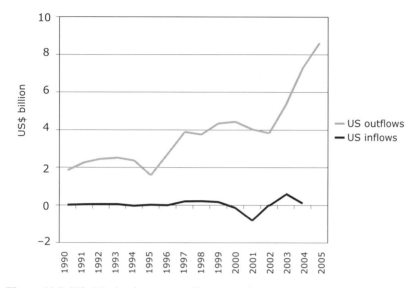

Figure 11.2 US–Mexico investment flows.
Source: Compiled by the authors using data from the Bureau of Economic Analysis, US Department of Commerce.

US outflows, FDI to Mexico has increased by 10 per cent over the past 10 years (see Figure 11.2).

There may also be a linkage between trade and investment activity and the *announcement* of PTA negotiations, though this is much harder to substantiate. Investment activity could increase, on the part of efficiency-seeking investors, in anticipation of improved resource allocation flowing from freer trade. Trade flows themselves might increase as a result of the increased legal certainty of the trading regime that a PTA would bring, and through greater market awareness generated by the announcement of negotiations. Against this, however, some traders might defer action until a more liberal regime is established. Following the announcement of intent to negotiate a PTA with Oman in November 2004, US exports and imports grew, respectively, 142 per cent and 115 per cent in two years. As a percentage of total US trade, exports to Oman grew by 92 per cent and imports by 71 per cent. And there is anecdotal evidence that there were changes taking place in the Korean market in anticipation of the PTA, including price discounting by imported car dealers, in the expectation that the agreement could narrow the price differentials between domestic and foreign cars (Schott, 2007).

European Union

As with the United States, but perhaps less markedly, there is evidence of linkage associated with EU PTA *implementation*. On the basis of data over time and flows expressed in relative terms, this is reflected, for example, in EU goods trade with Mexico; Chilean goods exports to the European Union, following implementation in February 2003; EU services exports to Chile; and EU services exports to Egypt.

There may also be linkage associated with the *announcement* of negotiations; for example, as seen in two-way FDI flows between the European Union and Egypt, but again this is much harder to substantiate.

EFTA

There seem to be few discernible trends in European Free Trade Association (EFTA) trade and investment with individual PTA partners. Moreover, such trade, in total, represents a relatively small percentage of EFTA exports and imports (about 14 per cent of trade in goods outside the European Union). There are nevertheless observations that can be made in respect of EFTA PTAs that may also have wider significance.

Overall, EFTA trade with PTA partners rose 8.1 per cent between 1992 and 2002, compared with only 0.7 per cent with the rest of the world. Within this trade, EFTA imports of goods increased more than EFTA exports, because of the asymmetric liberalization provisions of the agreements. And, even where aggregate trade with a partner did not increase, trade in products that were subject to significant liberalization did increase. For example, whereas Swiss trade with Mexico relative to the rest of the world fell from 2002 to 2005, exports of pharmaceuticals and watches, each subject to tariff dismantling, grew strongly. This observation highlights the importance of product specificity in seeking to identify trends related to PTA activity.

Japan

Unlike US and EU experience, Japan's PTAs appear to have had a negligible effect on flows of trade and investment, the possible exceptions being Japanese exports to Mexico, which rose 53 per cent in real terms between 2004 and 2006, and Singapore's FDI in Japan. Nor is there a discernible pattern in trade and investment in anticipation of PTAs.

The relative newness of Japan's agreements, and associated data limitations, mean, however, that any observations at this stage can only be tentative.

Singapore

There appear to be no discernible trends in Singapore data, though the limited number of agreements and their relative newness make any observation very difficult.

Before looking at more sophisticated approaches to measuring the effects of preferential agreements, it is necessary to consider some of the theoretical underpinnings of such approaches.

Some theory: A review of the literature

The theory of preferential trade agreements dates from Viner (1950), who identified trade-creating and trade-diverting effects resulting from PTA formation. If partner country production displaces higher-cost domestic production, then there is trade creation. If, however, partner country production displaces lower-cost imports from the rest of the world, then there is trade diversion. This analysis falls within the theory of "second-best" welfare economics. As long as some distortions remain within the economy, it is not necessarily true that removing partial distortions (via a PTA) is welfare improving.

Three conditions have been identified under which PTAs are more likely to be welfare-enhancing (Geloso Grosso, 2001).

Meade (1955) showed that, the higher pre-arrangement most favoured nation (MFN) tariffs, the higher the pressure for trade diversion following formation of the PTA. Conversely, when the external barriers of a bilateral or regional arrangement are low, the potential for trade diversion is low because lower external tariffs provide less scope for the displacement of imports from third countries. An important policy implication of this observation is that ongoing reduction of MFN tariffs in the framework of the WTO plays an important role in containing the distorting effects of preferential trade arrangements.[1]

Lipsey (1957) pointed out that opportunities for trade creation are enhanced and risks of trade diversion reduced where a PTA groups countries that are already major trading partners. This is because, before the introduction of preferences, trade flows are consistent with least-cost sourcing, reducing the likelihood that the removal of trade barriers will lead to trade diversion from third-country least-cost suppliers. Summers (1991), using similar reasoning, developed the "natural trading bloc" argument.

Corden (1972), by bringing scale economies into the theory of PTAs, demonstrated that trade preferences and resulting shifts in demand in favour of intra-PTA trade enable firms to achieve greater economies of scale and lower output prices as they capture larger markets for their products, domestically and overseas. Consistent with this observation is the principle that gains from PTAs will be greater to the extent that product coverage is comprehensive, covering substantially all the trade (in terms of Article XXIV of the General Agreement on Tariffs and Trade, GATT).

After this brief introduction, let us delve a little deeper. Much of the economic literature on PTAs or preferential agreements has focused on the effects these have on trade and the trading system. This work covers the static effects, essentially assessments of trade creation and trade diversion based on Vinerian customs union theory. There is also some work on the dynamic/growth effects of regional agreements, based on the effects of PTAs on increased competition, increased economies of scale and total factor productivity. Finally, there are economic models of the systemic effects of PTAs that focus on the effects of sequential tariff reductions. A lot of the empirical work done on preferential trade agreements has focused on the static welfare effects, even though "most economists" view the long-term impact of preferential agreements on the trading system as more important (Krueger, 1999: 114).

The static effects of customs unions and free trade areas

The static effect models are based on the Vinerian trade creation and trade diversion distinction. The characterization of preferential agreements in these models is often very simple, "with most focusing on the removal of tariffs but ignoring [other] issues", even those directly related to border measures, such as rules of origin (World Bank, 2005b, Ch. 3: 6). The "standard discussion of PTAs proceeds as if tariffs were the only barrier" to trade (Winters, 1996). As we will see in more detail below, generally speaking the results from such studies either are ambiguous or show small net trade creation effects. This has been a fairly consistent conclusion throughout the past decade.[2] On the other hand, such static assessments based on general equilibrium models do not really come up with compelling evidence in favour of PTAs.

There are a number of difficulties with these conventional approaches. First of all there is the problem of determining the counterfactual, or what would have happened to trade and investment in the absence of the PTA. What, for example, would the levels of European tariffs have looked like in the absence of the European Union? There is no way of knowing whether protection would have been higher or lower. Another limitation is that the studies concerned do not account for anything but tariff preferences. This may have been a reasonable approximation for the impact of PTAs up to the 1970s for developed countries (although not for the European Union, even then). Tariffs are also still important among developing countries today. But the classic trade creation/ diversion analysis fails to address the impact of deep integration in PTAs and thus the impact of rule-making on trade and investment.

Economists see the gains from deep integration as emanating from the reductions in costs, such as through the creation of a common regulatory norm or standard. In most cases of deep integration, both producers and service providers in the preferential grouping as well as those outside will benefit, but the degree to which each benefits will vary. For example, where common rules/norms replace different national standards, any PTA supplier can cover the wider market without incurring the costs of complying with a series of separate national rules. Non-PTA suppliers will also benefit because they can supply the whole market using one rather than numerous national standards and thus benefit from scale economies. Benefits to non-PTA suppliers will, however, be diminished in cases where PTA cooperation is based on mutual recognition agreements, which inevitably involve some degree of discrimination.

If the regulatory barriers addressed by deep integration entail expenditure of real resources (i.e. in compliance with different regulatory norms or standards) rather than the creation of rents, then reducing the barriers saves resources and can be beneficial even if there is some trade distortion. Although views inevitably differ, one conclusion, based on first principles, is that "discriminatory deep integration seems unlikely to be harmful except in the opportunity cost sense of forgoing the greater gains from non-discriminatory integration" (Winters, 1996: 7). This would be the case provided the level of regulatory harmonization in the PTA is not excessive or unreasonable. If PTA norms or standards were set exceptionally high, the distorting effects would outweigh the benefits from having a single set of norms. The question then arises of what is a reasonable level for any standard.[3] The assumption is still that a proliferation of PTA rules is a second-best option to non-discriminatory removal of regulatory barriers.

Another argument made in the discussion of the impact of PTAs on trade and investment is whether PTAs can provide secure market access and, if so, to what degree. PTA rules may, for example, remove or reduce regulatory discretion in the hands of national regulators or governments that might otherwise be used to discriminate against foreign suppliers. Deeper integration can thus provide greater security of market access. In some cases, it may also remove the scope for the use of instruments of commercial defence, such as anti-dumping and countervailing duties, as is the case in some of the PTAs covered in this study.

By analogy to trade creation and trade diversion, it is possible to argue that, if common rules are significantly more stringent than the rules of the signatories before the preferential agreement was signed, then one might argue that preferential rule-making is restrictive of trade. But if PTA rules are broadly on a par with the previous national rules, then the PTA will tend to facilitate trade and investment, by virtue of the greater ease of access to the whole PTA market. The impact of preferential rule-making in such instances cannot be easily determined except on a case-by-case basis. The impact of the "preference" will, for example, depend, among other things, on the extent to which the PTA rules diverge from any agreed international rules.

To sum up on the literature on the static effects of PTAs, tariff-based models and gravity models, discussed in more detail below, are ambiguous in their results. Working from first principles, there is a broad assumption that deeper integration will be beneficial, even if still second best to multilateral rules. But, with the exception of a few studies of specific policy areas, there has been no real attempt to assess the impact of deep integration in PTAs through detailed studies, probably because of the difficulty of applying quantitative methods to measure the effect of rules.

Dynamic effects

In the 1990s, a number of approaches were developed that incorporated assessments of the dynamic effects of preferential agreements. Baldwin, for example, showed that medium-term bonuses could be gained from PTAs (Baldwin, 1989 and 1996; Baldwin and Venables, 1995). By removing barriers to investment, trade and competition, deeper integration could result in increasing returns on investment, increased investment and thus an increase in the stock of investment, leading to a higher growth trajectory.

Generally speaking, those who have employed elements of "new trade theory" that account for imperfect competition, increasing returns to scale, externalities and other dynamic gains have concluded that preferential agreements can generate big welfare gains compared with models that are based on neoclassical production structures (Krueger, 1999: 120). In particular, North–South agreements that lead to more integrated production and thus the application of more advanced production methods in the southern partner(s) can increase total factor productivity (TFP) through technology transfer. This was found to be the case in NAFTA, which was associated with an advance of between 5 and 7 per cent in TFP in Mexico.

The inclusion of investment in any assessment raises the question of whether preferential agreements result in investment creation or investment diversion. For example, if a PTA includes rules of origin, it may result in the diversion of investment from more competitive suppliers outside the region, or create investment by replacing higher-cost, less efficient investors from a PTA partner. From the motivations of smaller southern partners of the United States or the European Union, it would seem that attracting increased flows of FDI is one of the major reasons for negotiating PTAs.

There is, therefore, a need to consider whether preferential agreements contribute to a more predictable environment for investors, which many investors, especially in smaller markets, see as important. Because the investment climate is largely determined by domestic rules and how they are implemented and enforced, it is important to include investment rules and a range of associated rules and regulations in any assessment of the impact of preferential agreements. Ethier (1998) argues that, rather than focus on Vinerian trade (or investment) creation and diversion, assessment of the impact of PTAs should take account of the realities of the current liberal international order created by the countries of the Organisation for Economic Co-operation and Development (OECD) since 1958. Ethier sees the preferential agreements as having adapted to this predominantly liberal multilateral environment. Smaller countries conclude PTAs with larger markets in order to benefit from a number of externalities, such as locking in domestic reforms and attracting FDI. This type of approach helps explain the otherwise paradoxical situation in which developing countries reject the "Singapore" issues of investment, public procurement and competition in the multilateral Doha Development Agenda, but accept the inclusion of these issues in PTAs under very adverse asymmetric power relationships with the United States or the European Union.

Systemic effects of PTAs: The economic models

Work has also been done on the potential systemic effects of preferential trade agreements. Once again, economic studies of such effects have tended to be based on tariffs by modelling the impact of the progressive extension of customs unions and free trade agreements on optimal tariffs. Krugman (1991), whose initial work provoked a series of other papers, argued that the increasing size of regional trade agreements results in an increase in optimal tariffs. In other words, the ever-growing regional blocs would use their market power to enhance their terms of trade through higher tariffs. Krugman's model suggested that, if PTAs advanced to the extent that there were three regional blocs, this would be the worst case for world welfare. Other writers have sought to develop the Krugman approach with somewhat differing results.[4] Although the model may be elegant, in reality tariffs continue to fall internationally and, as with all applications of optimal tariff arguments, tariff bindings within the WTO and potential retaliation to any increase in tariff levels more or less preclude the actual application of an optimal tariff strategy. From the point of view of the entities covered in this volume, the question is whether growing networks of, largely bilateral, deals are able to shape patterns of trade and investment. Intuitively this seems a more likely threat to the multilateral system than the pursuit of optimal tariffs by large trading blocs. In other words, a selfish hegemon could, through sequential hub-and-spokes negotiations with a string of weaker trading partners, shape the rules for trade and investment in its own interest rather than create public goods.

Special considerations may apply to the systemic effects of customs unions. The literature tends to suggest that customs unions are likely to be more restrictive than free trade areas. This may happen because it is easier for countries joining a customs union (with its common external tariff) to accede to requests from lobby groups to raise protection than to expose domestic interests to increased competition. Bagwell and Staiger (1997) thus contend that customs unions are usually more discriminatory because common external tariffs tend to be higher than the pre-union average and because customs unions have the incentive to use their monopoly power (see also Winters, 1994). Against this, however, is the fact that distortions and restrictions associated with rules of origin are absent from customs unions. In any event, with customs unions becoming a relatively rare feature of trade diplomacy, the practical significance of these observations is limited.

The more elaborate models of "bloc formation" developed on the basis of the original Krugman approach included assessments of the effects of asymmetric bloc size. According to these models, a regional bloc gains when it attracts members from other continents, because the terms-of-trade benefits of boosting demand for the bloc's comparative advantage goods outweigh trade diversion, even if the enlarged bloc does not increase its tariff vis-à-vis the other countries. Frankel, for example, argues that a continent can increase its welfare by integrating when other continents retain MFN (Frankel et al., 1995). Other continents then follow the regional option, with the result that all are worse off in the end. Others have produced similar models in which a PTA grows as smaller countries sign up as an "insurance premium" (i.e. to ensure market access), but they pay a price for this insurance. Once such countries join such blocs, they will be less concerned about multilateralism. Because multilateralism is the best option, such a process has negative systemic effects.

This raises the question of at what point a (tariff) preference becomes a disincentive to negotiate multilaterally. In search of an answer to this question, negotiated tariff models have been developed that seek to find the "discount rate" at which blocs are indifferent between defecting (from MFN and the multilateral system) and cooperation. If this rate could be found, it might be possible to determine at which point preferential agreements result in a reduced willingness to cooperate multilaterally. Bond and Syropoulos (1996) argue that the benefits of defection are greater, the greater the size of the blocs, but so is the welfare loss from retaliation. This model also suggests that the outcomes may vary depending on the speed with which a bloc's trading partners retaliate. If retaliation occurs rapidly, there are few gains from defection but, the longer the period the PTA partners can "get away" with discrimination, the greater the likelihood of defection. If the sanctions against preferential agreements are weak or ambiguous, as can be said to be the case for WTO sanctions against PTAs, there is, according to this model, a greater likelihood of defection.

These models of the systemic effects of PTAs are also based on a number of limiting assumptions. For a start, they assume unitary rational actors (in national governments) that are able to assess the costs and benefits of any policy choices, such as the costs of trade diversion against the gains from preferences. As noted above, even if there were a unitary actor none of the economic models developed to date has been able to come to more than ambiguous answers to such questions. Second, the models are again invariably based on tariffs only and say little if anything about the systemic impact of PTAs involving deeper integration. Those studies that have been done of deeper integration in PTAs suggest that the general assumption that deeper integration will be less distorting than tariff preferences is correct, because preferences are less evident and may indeed be impossible in some cases (Mattoo and Fink, 2002). But there is very limited work on the substantive deeper integration provisions in PTAs. Third, the models largely discount the role of institutions and do not therefore take account of any harmonization or emulation of rules, which the chapters in this book show is clearly happening.

Perhaps the biggest shortcoming of these systemic approaches, however, is that the models are based on an assumption of growing *regional* blocs, whereas what we are seeing, as we stressed earlier, are agreements that are increasingly bilateral and cross-regional. Indeed, the cross-regional proliferation of bilateral PTAs is imposing a hub-and-spokes pattern to trade diplomacy that serves to weaken regional coherence and thus reduce the likelihood that international trade relations will be conducted amongst three large blocs centred on the Americas, Europe and Asia. The hub-and-spokes literature suggests that, because there is often discrimination among the "spoke" countries, such a pattern is likely to involve less trade liberalization than a standard free trade area.

It does so by offering more scope to exclude sensitive sectors from the coverage of each bilateral agreement (Snape et al., 1993; Wonnacott, 1996). In a free trade area, members will have different preferences for product coverage and the scope for exclusions will be less. It may also be easier for hub countries to maintain contingent protection measures against imports (Winters, 1995). Finally, rules of origin are likely to play an important part in a hub-and-spokes arrangement because of the need to ensure that trade flows are not diverted through the hub from one spoke to another (Hoekman and Kostecki, 1995).

Political economy models

It is possible to differentiate between a number of "political economic" models that use rational choice approaches to model the interaction between protectionist and liberal sectors of the economy (Grossman and Helpman, 1994) and wider "political economy" approaches that consider the interplay between broader political and commercial interests at the systemic and domestic levels (Mansfield and Milner, 1999). In the "political economic" models, trade policy and, in particular, decisions on whether to negotiate preferential or multilateral trade agreements are assumed to be determined endogenously by the interplay between different domestic sector interests. Grossman and Helpman provided the basis for a number of studies using such an approach. They argued that PTAs are negotiated when producers believe they will gain from trade diversion. Utility-maximizing governments (i.e. governments seeking re-election) will then support preferential agreements if the benefits of the PTA outweigh the general welfare effects of multilateral trade liberalization. The subsequent use of this model has often assumed that it is "good politics" to negotiate preferential agreements, because producer interests in trade diversion are easier to identify than the consumer losses.

Krishna (1999) then takes this line of argument still further by suggesting that, the greater the trade diversion, the more likely PTAs are to be supported, because protectionist interests will be more effective in their efforts. Some studies then go so far as to argue that bilateral agreements can never increase political support for multilateralism, because the benefits of bilateral agreements for protectionist interests are such that the "reservation utility" of the protectionist sector interests is raised above the multilateral free trade level, with the result that such groups will always block multilateral free trade (Levy, 1997).

Although there is intuitively a clear case that interests benefiting from preferences will resist the erosion of such preferences by multilateral liberalization, the explanatory value of these political economic models is undermined by some of the assumptions on which they are based. For example, many models are based on unrealistic assumptions that the median voter has perfect foresight concerning the impact of the choice between PTAs and multilateral trade. To facilitate the model-building, the models are also still based on tariff protection. Perhaps the most striking thing about these political economic approaches is that, like most of the tariff-based models discussed above, they are developed from first principles with only very generalized references to the nature of PTAs (and the multilateral trading system). As Winters (1996) suggests in his summary of the models, the difficulties with the existing models mean there is a need to consider actual cases. Finally, the political economic approaches fail to take adequate account of path dependency or policy emulation (Bhagwati, 1999). Therefore they offer little policy-relevant guidance on the question of whether PTAs can be seen as building or stumbling blocks for the wider multilateral trade and investment regime.

These shortcomings are addressed in the broader political economy studies of PTAs. Baldwin's domino model of regional enlargement, which draws on European experience, argues that endogenous trade policy models (such as the political economic models discussed above, which are based on competing domestic sector interests) cannot fully explain why governments move to conclude PTAs and, in particular, why policies change over time. He suggests that closer regional integration leads producers in non-member countries to press for accession because they will otherwise find it harder to compete with producers inside the regional market. As the bloc enlarges and more and more markets are included, the costs of non-participation become greater; enlargement then stops when the remaining non-members have high enough (political) objections to accession (Baldwin, 1996). Baldwin's approach therefore takes account of wider systemic factors exogenous to the nation-state and explicitly links regional and other levels of trade policy.

The wider political economy approaches to the analysis of PTAs also seek to include a range of institutional and systemic/international factors as well as societal (i.e. interest group) factors. The domestic societal factors are essentially the same as the sector interests included in the political economic models, but inclusion of institutional elements enables such factors as the relationship between economic (and political) reform and trade agreements to be addressed. In most cases, the debate is rather general and along the lines that preferential agreements can promote democratic reform (as in the case of EU enlargement) and economic liberalism (for example, NAFTA locking in Mexican economic reform). The political economy literature also does not generally address the detail of rule-making in investment, competition, etc.[5]

The political economy literature does, however, consider the wider international political context, such as the role of power, security and international institutions. Echoing our earlier discussion of US PTA motivations in Chapter 6, the rise of PTAs has, for example, been related to the relative decline in US hegemony, with the United States shifting to a more aggressive use of PTAs when it is no longer able to shape the multilateral trade regime as it wishes, with others following suit. Gilpin (1987) argues, on the basis of observation of the United States, that hegemons become more aggressive as they go into relative decline. He therefore explains the growth in preferential agreements as a defence against such aggressive US policies. But he questions whether the United States is really in relative decline and whether regionalism represents a competing force for the United States.[6] This touches on the role of preferential agreements in shaping the international regimes for trade and investment, which the empirical case studies in this volume address.

Political economy models clearly have a role to play, but, again, to the extent that they are based on a *regional* paradigm (as with lessons from EU enlargement), they will have less resonance in a world where cross-regional bilateralism is becoming the norm.

Although the various theoretical approaches described here each have something to contribute in fostering our understanding of the proliferation of bilateral PTAs, none is found to be entirely satisfactory. It is not surprising therefore that attempts at measuring the impact of PTAs – underpinned by these theoretical constructs – also have shortcomings. It is to these attempts at measurement that we now turn.

Measurement techniques and results

Two principal techniques of empirical measurement are available, each with their own strengths and weaknesses.
- *Ex post studies* seek to measure trade creation and diversion by taking actual statistical data of intra-agreement trade flows and controlling for factors influencing trade (such as geographical size and distance). The standard way to control for other effects is via an econometric model, usually a gravity model or a growth regression. The limitations of such approaches are that they are static, cannot capture the interplay of variables, do not establish causality (in the case of regressions), and (Lucas, 1976) are of limited use for policy evaluation because policy changes themselves change the model.
- *Ex ante studies* use computable general equilibrium (CGE) models to allow for the interaction of variables. Such studies take their parameters from econometric analysis, together with estimates that are chosen so that the model fits the data for a chosen base year. The drawback of

such models is that they are not usually fitted to the data as precisely as in econometric models and are not subject to statistical testing.

Geloso Grosso (2001) draws the following conclusions from the literature:

- Overall, the findings of ex post studies produce a fairly mixed picture, indicating that some PTAs boosted intra-bloc trade significantly, whereas others did not. There is some evidence that external trade is smaller than it might otherwise have been in at least some of the groupings, but the picture is mixed enough that it is not possible to conclude whether trade diversion has been a major problem. In addition, these studies do not reach any definitive answer on the welfare impact of PTAs. Most of the studies using growth regressions suggest that PTAs have had little impact on economic growth.

- Broadly, the conclusions from ex ante studies are also that there has been evidence of weak trade diversion, but that the recent wave of preferential trade agreements has been trade creating on a net basis and welfare improving for member countries. However, the variation in simulated economic gains is wide, depending on the model used. In models assuming perfect competition, the combined effect of trade diversion and trade creation typically gives very small welfare gains. However, CGE models of imperfect competition with increasing returns to scale suggest that the pro-competitive effects of PTAs might be more significant for OECD countries than for developing countries. These models increase the estimated gains considerably for the European Union and NAFTA.

More recent quantitative analysis is broadly consistent with these tentative findings. In an econometric model of NAFTA, Waldrich (2003) finds, as does the present study (see above), a clear positive effect of NAFTA on FDI in Mexico. He estimates that, between 1994 and 1998, US and Canadian FDI in Mexico would have been around 42 per cent lower without NAFTA. Moreover, he finds that the positive effect comes almost exclusively from increased investment from the United States and Canada, rather than from other countries wishing to access the NAFTA market. The World Bank (2003), using a gravity model of NAFTA, finds that Mexican exports and imports would have been, respectively, 25–30 per cent and 50 per cent lower without NAFTA. Although most research shows no significant trade diversion, one study (Fukao et al., 2003) finds, at a disaggregated level, trade diversion in the textile and apparel sector. The use of gravity models to assess the impact of preferential agreements includes the effects of tariff and other measures including rules, because they seek to measure outcomes against what would be expected in terms of market size, proximity and a range of other variables such as common language. But the results of gravity models have often proved contradictory, depending on the varying starting assumptions used. In an effort to overcome this problem, the World Bank produced a meta analysis that took the individual observation point estimates of the relevant parameters from different studies. This set of observations was then used to test whether the various coefficients are statistically different from zero. The results of this work are not encouraging, however, as the "overall impact is uncertain" (World Bank, 2005b, Ch. 3: 5).

A recent study using regression analysis takes a somewhat different tack and is directly relevant to the building/stumbling block debate, to which we will turn in the concluding chapter. The study draws on the experience of 10 Latin American countries over the period 1990–2001 to examine the effects of preferential tariff reductions on MFN rates (Estevadeordal et al., 2008). The study finds that, if a country offers free access to another country in a sector where it applies a 15 per cent MFN tariff (the average in the sample of 10 countries), it would tend subsequently to reduce that tariff by over 3 percentage points. A reduction of 1 percentage point in the preferential tariff in a PTA is found to induce a reduction of some 0.2 percentage points in the MFN tariff in the subsequent year (interestingly though, and consistent with earlier discussion, this effect is found not to apply to customs unions). The authors thus find that PTAs are likely to be building blocks to external trade liberalization, in the sense that there is a complementarity effect between preferential and MFN tariffs.

This finding is consistent with the part of the theoretical literature that postulates that a preferential tariff induces trade diversion and that, because this trade diversion is costly, external tariffs decline to shift some imports back to their original source, thus moderating the extent of trade diversion (see, for example, Bagwell and Staiger, 1999; Freund, 2000; Richardson, 1993; and Ornelas, 2005).

The finding, however, is not backed up by all the theoretical literature. Some studies that focus on general equilibrium effects of preferential tariff reduction find a case for raising external tariffs (Cadot et al., 1999, and Panagariya and Findlay, 1996, cited in Estevadeordal et al., 2008). A PTA could indeed generate higher tariffs against outsiders when a key object of the PTA is to promote non-trade objectives related, for example, to labour or environmental standards and where lower external tariffs, and hence lower preferences, would reduce the willingness of partners to comply with these objectives (Limao, 2007). Such a consideration has particular relevance for two of our core entities, the United States and the European Union, for which non-trade objectives are relatively important in their PTAs. It has thus been found that the United States and the European Union liberalized less during the Uruguay

Round in sectors where preferences were granted (Karacaovali and Limao, 2008).

Moreover, even if we accept that, in agreements among developing countries, relatively high MFN tariffs (and consequently high risks of trade diversion) and a weak focus on non-trade concerns may induce post-PTA MFN tariff reductions, the fact remains that such reductions will still be considerably less than those within the PTA. In short, there will still be trade diversion and all the negative consequences associated with it. It is thus hard to endorse the finding that Latin American experience "offers an optimistic view of the ongoing regionalism trend for the efficiency of the world trading system" (Estevadeordal et al., 2008: 37).

Turning to ex ante approaches, in a model of EU–Chile, Francois et al. (2005) estimate a 5 per cent increase in Chile's exports to the European Union as a result of the agreement. This is also consistent with the tentative findings that we have outlined from the present study. An ex ante model of US–Chile by the International Monetary Fund finds that, consistent again with the present study, Chilean exports of processed crops, textiles and clothing would receive a boost, with small welfare gains (Hilaire and Yang, 2003). The modest welfare gains are attributed to trade diversion because machinery and equipment-based manufactures from the United States replace lower-cost imports mainly from the European Union. Another ex ante study of US–Chile, by the US International Trade Commission, finds that the most important benefits are related not to reciprocal tariff elimination but to non-tariff provisions (USITC, 2003). A study for the Swiss government of a possible US–Switzerland PTA (Hufbauer and Baldwin, 2006) found that, in a static CGE framework, trade flows between the two countries would increase by 20 per cent, but that this increase would lead to negligible changes in US and Swiss GDP levels. The study also drew on dynamic analysis, reflecting improved production methods, the exit of less efficient firms and scale and network economies. Under this dynamic analysis, it was found that annual GDP gains to each partner could be of the order of US$1.1 billion, amounting to a permanent gain – level effect – for Switzerland of some 0.5 per cent of GDP. Importantly, in both the static and the dynamic analysis it is assumed that trade coverage of the PTA is comprehensive. The importance of comprehensive coverage is highlighted in one study which finds that, if agriculture is not covered, Chile suffers a welfare loss in US–Chile, the benefit of the Free Trade Agreement between the United States and Central America (US–CAFTA) is significantly reduced and, in US–Australia, a negligible welfare loss for Australia turns into a significant one (Hilaire and Yang, 2003). It follows that estimated welfare effects are likely to differ significantly between parties. It has been found, for example, that, in a PTA between the European Union and the Southern African Development Community, South Africa would gain considerably whereas Botswana and Tanzania could see their welfare reduced (Keck and Piermartini, 2005).

One important issue that has been the subject of recent (ex ante) analysis is that of *preference erosion*. As noted above, lower MFN tariffs will help reduce the risks of trade diversion. But, as the other side of the coin, lower MFN tariffs will also reduce preference margins. Hence the fear that PTAs will create vested interests among preference beneficiaries against multilateral reform. However, although particular sectors may suffer from preference erosion, this does not necessarily mean that there will be economy-wide losses. Indeed, a range of studies find that, for all but a handful of countries, the gains from across-the-board MFN tariff reduction more than offset any losses arising from the erosion of preferences. One particular study (OECD, 2004) postulates a 50 per cent reduction in *ad valorem* tariffs across all regions and examines the net effects on welfare after allowing for the erosion of preferences (not just from PTAs but from preferential arrangements such as the US African Growth and Opportunities Act). The study finds that, although preferential exports decrease as a consequence of erosion, new opportunities from MFN tariff reductions offset the negative effect for all but five countries (Colombia, Madagascar, Mozambique, Tanzania and Uganda). For those particular countries, special efforts and assistance are required to help diversify exports. But for the vast majority of countries the lesson is clear: concerns about preference erosion, including from PTAs, are not a valid basis for avoiding commitment to multilateral trade liberalization.

A note of caution

Before concluding this section, a cautionary note is in order. It is prompted by a particular study (Krueger, 1999), which finds that there had indeed been increased trade between Mexico and its NAFTA partners but that these increases owed more to other factors than NAFTA. Among those factors one can count the devaluation of the *peso* during the Mexican financial crisis, strong growth in the United States and Mexico's reform of investment regulations in 1989. Indeed, even the most sophisticated modelling techniques are hard pressed to isolate totally the effects of a PTA from the other factors that determine flows of trade and investment. One way of addressing this problem is to narrow the focus of analysis. An example of such an approach is described in the following section.

The effects of PTA investment provisions on trade and investment flows

A recent study conducted at the OECD, using a gravity model, reaches conclusions that are broadly consistent with the above findings in respect of ex post models, but with somewhat greater specificity because the study is focused exclusively on the effects of investment provisions in PTAs.[7]

On the one hand, the removal of trade barriers between countries can lower intra-group FDI when investment is mainly market seeking or tariff jumping. On the other hand, efficiency-seeking investment may increase because freer trade of goods and services enables companies with low fixed costs to localize their activity in different countries and then trade intermediate inputs. In this case, investment complements trade.

The approach taken in the OECD study is to: (1) classify provisions in the 24 North–South PTAs selected as containing substantive investment-related rules; (2) create an index of the extensiveness of those provisions; and (3) use the index to perform a quantitative analysis, via a gravity model, of the impact of the investment provisions on patterns of trade and investment.

Compilation of the index is based on six broad categories of provisions:
- the right of establishment and non-discrimination in the pre-establishment phase
- non-discrimination for post-establishment
- investment in services (national treatment and MFN)
- investment regulation and protection
- dispute settlement
- investment promotion and cooperation

The study finds that investment provisions are positively associated with trade and investment flows, and that they matter more for FDI flows than for trade flows. It is estimated that the entry into force of a PTA with substantive investment provisions is associated with a 60 per cent increase in FDI flows between the parties and a 20 per cent increase in exports. The positive (albeit modest) relationship observed between the extensiveness of investment provisions and trade flows is in line with the literature, and indicates that trade and investment are complements rather than substitutes, reflecting more efficiency-seeking than market-seeking FDI.

The results for trade and investment creation and diversion were found to be somewhat mixed. There is evidence of trade creation and diversion for both the reporter and partner countries, but the pattern does not hold completely across the data set. The results for investment are more ambiguous than those for trade, because most of the PTA-specific variables are not "significant". It might be tentatively concluded that the apparently large FDI stimulus, combined with limited evidence of invest-ment diversion, suggests that the higher FDI flows are additional rather than displacing.

The study finds an insignificant result for the variable that represents the existence of a bilateral investment treaty between the country pairs. This prompts the conclusion that either substantive investment provisions in PTAs affect trade and investment more profoundly, or substantive in-vestment provisions and provisions liberalizing other parts of the econ-omy come together to have a more significant impact on trade and investment flows.

In concluding this discussion of attempts to measure the impact of PTAs on trade and investment, two further notes of caution are in order. First, the realization of benefits will depend crucially on the ability of countries, through the flexibility of their businesses, to take advantage of the oppor-tunities presented. Second, the biggest gains from PTAs may come not from their preferential features but rather from the regulatory reform that the agreements may prompt. This, for example, could well be the major source of benefit to Korea from the Korea–US Free Trade Agree-ment (KORUS), given the impediments to growth identified by the OECD.

The impact of PTAs on dispute settlement in the WTO

Given the difficulties of directly measuring the effects of PTAs on pat-terns of trade and investment, an alternative approach is to look at the link between PTA formation and the incidence of WTO dispute settle-ment, i.e. the link between PTAs and the perception of resulting discrim-ination.

Third parties cannot challenge the formation of PTAs, but they can challenge the legality of specific policies associated with them (Mavroidis, 2002). The most direct way to do this is to argue that policies are incon-sistent with Article XXIV of the GATT (or the corresponding Article V of the General Agreement on Trade in Services). Article XXIV permits exceptions to the MFN principle embodied in Article I of the GATT, but in doing so imposes a number of conditions: that duties and other regula-tions shall not on the whole be higher than prior to the formation of the agreement; that formation should occur within a reasonable length of time; and that duties and other regulations are reduced on substantially all the trade between the constituent parties. Thus the formation of the European Economic Community (EEC) in 1957, and the accompanying

Common Agricultural Policy, prompted multiple complaints by third parties that the agreement raised protection on a range of agricultural products (Hudec, 1993). In 1996, India filed a complaint against Turkey for raising its protection against textile imports as a result of forming a customs union with the European Communities.

It is also open to third parties to challenge trade policies that are associated with PTAs though not necessarily in breach of Article XXIV. For example, in 1996, the EEC filed a complaint against Mexico that it applied cif (cost, insurance, freight) valuation on imports from non-NAFTA countries, compared with a lower valuation fob (free on board) criterion for imports originating from NAFTA partners (yielding lower tariffs). In 2002, Korea and other countries took the United States to dispute settlement for exempting NAFTA partners from duties imposed on US imports of steel (WTO, 2002b).

Beyond these scattered examples, Haftel (2004) makes a comprehensive study of the extent to which the formation of three preferential trading arrangements – the European Union, NAFTA and Mercosur (the Common Market of the Southern Cone) – is associated with complaints filed in the GATT/WTO dispute settlement system. The study finds that the number of complaints filed against members of the three PTAs in the year following their formation was over two and a half times greater than before. The study also suggests that deeper integration results in more complaints filed, such that moving from a free trade area to a customs union leads to a doubling of complaints.

There is thus persuasive evidence that the formation of PTAs is associated with increased litigation in the trading system, meaning that there is not only greater strain on the dispute settlement mechanism but also the perception that PTAs lead to increased discrimination in the conduct of international trade.

Notes

1. A recent study finds that the average applied industrial tariff among parties to existing bilateral agreements of Singapore is significantly lower (at 4.8 per cent) than that for US bilaterals (7.5), which in turn is lower than that for EU (9.2) and Japanese (10.0) bilaterals (Messerlin, 2007).
2. See, for example, the findings of the World Bank in its *Global Economic Prospects* (2005b, Ch. 3: 3), which are based on comprehensive work by Burfisher et al. (2003) and Harrison et al. (1994).
3. Other recent studies of the effects of PTAs in services make the same arguments (see Mattoo and Fink, 2002).
4. For a summary of the various approaches, see Winters (1996).
5. The OECD (2000b) has, however, looked at this issue by including an assessment of the impact of regional trade agreements on regulatory reform in a range of countries.

6. The wider political economy approaches therefore address the role of relative power in the negotiation of regional trade agreements. They also address the potential security considerations in the formation of regional blocs. Gowa (1994) argues that security externalities shape countries' trade policies, including their approaches to PTAs. Gilpin (1975) also introduces the idea of benign or malign regionalism. Benign regionalism can be seen as regionalism that promotes stability, multilateral liberalization and peace, whereas malign regionalism would be mercantilist, damage economic welfare and foster inter-state conflict.
7. This section draws on Miroudot and Lesher (2006).

Part V

Conclusion

12

Key findings and looking ahead

This study has identified, with some confidence, a number of broad trends in the evolution of preferential trade agreements (PTAs). With a weakening in the momentum of multilateral trade liberalization, preferential agreements negotiated on a bilateral basis have become the principal arm of trade diplomacy, adding further constraints to multilateral efforts and weakening the fabric of regional cooperation. The study has also identified some recent developments where the outcome is less certain but potentially important. First, the key findings.

Key findings

Trends in the growth and development of preferential trade agreements

As an arm of economic diplomacy, preferential trade agreements have become the centrepiece of most countries' trade policy. Though all countries tend to stress, rightly, the primacy of the multilateral system, the focus of their officials' attention is increasingly devoted to the negotiation of bilateral arrangements with privileged partners.

The annual average number of PTA notifications since the World Trade Organization (WTO) was established has been 20, compared with an annual average of less than 3 during the four and a half decades of the General Agreement on Tariffs and Trade (GATT). There are also a

The rise of bilateralism: Comparing American, European and Asian approaches to preferential trade agreements, Heydon and Woolcock,
United Nations University Press, 2009, ISBN 978-92-808-1162-9

large number of South–South PTAs adopted under the Enabling Clause that are not notified to the WTO. These clearly also add to the complex network of agreements. Within the past five years, the share of world trade accounted for by PTAs has risen from some 40 per cent to over half.

Behind these numbers, some clear trends are apparent.

Preferential agreements are showing an increased degree of sophistication in the range of issues they address. Many of the newer agreements cover trade in services and include provisions dealing with technical barriers to trade (TBTs), sanitary and phytosanitary (SPS) measures and intellectual property rights (IPRs). Most PTAs are also tackling issues that have been withdrawn – as too hard or too distracting – from multilateral negotiation, notably investment, competition policy and government procurement. Though the focus of each of these three issues is on the formulation of agreed rules, they each have important implications for the attainment of effective market access, whether, for example, through commercial presence (General Agreement on Trade in Services, Mode 3) and associated investment in the delivery of services, through access to distribution channels and infrastructure networks facilitated by disciplines on the abuse of dominance, or through freedom to tender for government-sponsored contracts.

Within the latest wave of PTAs, a clear preference for free trade agreements (FTAs), as opposed to customs unions, is apparent. Among projected agreements, 92 per cent are planned as free trade areas, 7 per cent as partial scope agreements and only 1 per cent as customs unions.

There is also a pronounced increase in the number of North–South PTAs, which now represent the main cluster of agreements. In these, reciprocity features as a shaping factor in negotiations, although there are some examples of asymmetric measures benefiting developing country partners. On the one hand, comprehensive coverage goes hand in hand with high expectations with regard to reciprocity (such as the United States' self-proclaimed "gold standard" for PTAs). On the other hand, more flexibility means more partial agreements, as witnessed in the agreements of Singapore, Japan and, to a lesser degree, the European Union and the European Free Trade Association (EFTA).

In parallel with the increase in North–South agreements there is a trend towards more cross-regional PTAs. Whereas only 12 per cent of PTAs notified and in force are cross-regional, the number rises to 43 per cent for agreements signed or under negotiation, and to 52 per cent for those at the proposal stage.

Finally, an increasing number of PTAs are being concluded on a bilateral basis, often with a hub-and-spokes configuration. Bilateral agreements account for 80 per cent of all agreements notified and in force; 94 per cent of those signed or under negotiation; and 100 per cent of those at the proposal stage.

Motivations

Together, these trends point to some broad observations about the underlying motivations for entering PTAs.

The desire for speed and flexibility favours free trade agreements over customs unions, given the complexity of agreeing on, and maintaining, a common external tariff. This has been graphically demonstrated in the course of the Doha Development Agenda (DDA) negotiations, with a call from the least developed countries (LDCs) that special consideration be given to developing countries that are in a customs union with LDCs. Otherwise, if, for example, South Africa were required to lower tariffs markedly, Lesotho, a fellow member of the Southern African Customs Union, would have either to accept similar cuts or to compromise the union's common external tariff.[1] The desire for flexibility will also favour bilateral over plurilateral agreements, given the opportunities to reach agreement on areas of sensitivity. The effective carving out of much agricultural trade from the Japan–Switzerland bilateral accord is evidence of such an accommodation.

There is nevertheless a concern – with some modulation among the key players and with a particular focus on areas of national priority – to conclude agreements that are ambitious both in the scope of issues covered and in the sharing of liberalization commitments among the parties. This is reflected in the emphasis placed, for example, by Japan on provisions dealing with investment, by the United States on conditions relating to labour standards and the environment, or by the European Union on comprehensive approaches to TBT.

In some cases there may be a clash of motivations. This is the case with the European Union's concern, on the one hand, to foster regional cooperation among developing countries by concluding region-to-region agreements and, on the other, to get WTO-plus agreements, which results in the European Union opting for bilateral PTAs with individual countries willing to sign up. The proliferation of bilateral cross-regional agreements may even be weakening regional integration and diluting intra-regional trade patterns. For example, the Economic Partnership Agreements (EPAs) negotiated at the close of 2007 between the European Union and certain African, Caribbean and Pacific (ACP) countries have, perhaps inevitably, failed to act as a catalyst for more regional integration. In West Africa, some countries, such as Ghana and Côte d'Ivoire, signed bilateral pacts ahead of the end-year expiry of EU preferences.[2] Nigeria, however, saw little interest in making "concessions" to retain EU market access because most of its exports are oil and gas. And other nations in the grouping, such as Benin and Mali, are least developed countries that had little to lose because their privileged access to the European Union did not expire at the end of the year.[3] In southern Africa, some members of the Southern African Customs Union, such as Botswana, Lesotho, Namibia and Swaziland, signed interim EPAs whereas South Africa did not. In other words, the European Union has had to choose between concluding the EPAs in order to comply with the end of 2007 expiry of the WTO waiver for preferences and holding fast to a coherent region-to-region policy.

Even though there continue to be multiple drivers behind PTAs, including political and strategic aims, enhanced market access – not always realized – emerges as the overarching motivation. This is explored in more detail below, in looking at individual country positions. Suffice it to say that we may again be seeing a conflict of motivations, in that the political or strategic factors that may single out distant partners may not satisfy the economic criteria identified by Lipsey (see Chapter 11) under which countries that are already major trading partners will maximize opportunities for trade creation and reduce the risks of trade diversion.

Finally, PTAs feed upon one another, in that a desire to neutralize the real or potential trade diversionary effects of other PTAs has given momentum to the current proliferation of agreements.

Of all the broad trends that we have observed, the one that is the most pervasive, and potentially the most important, is the shift towards bilateral agreements cutting across different regions, with a strong hub-and-spokes configuration. The consequent decline in the relative importance of "regionalism" has two major implications: first, in terms of economic efficiency, it heightens the risk of bilateral accommodations to exclude sensitive sectors, notably agriculture and certain services, from liberalization commitments, hence reducing potential welfare gains from PTAs; second, in terms of economic development, it risks weakening regional cooperation among developing countries, so denying them a key step towards fuller integration into the trading system. Beyond these systemic effects, the rise of cross-regional bilateral agreements also has important implications for our understanding of the nature of preferential trading arrangements by reducing the usefulness of those theoretical approaches to PTAs that are founded on an assumption of growing regional blocs. Future analysis may need to be more aligned to a hub-and-spokes pattern of preferential arrangements.

Trends in specific policy areas

Beyond these broad observations, the present study has also identified a number of issue-specific trends.

There is a clear tendency towards the elimination of all industrial *tariffs* within the PTAs, either immediately or after a fairly short transition, by all the "core entities". There remain some exceptions however, and in some cases protection is provided in the form of longer transition periods. And large parts of agriculture are frequently excluded from tariff and other liberalization.

Two rather contradictory trends characterize *rules of origin*. On the one hand, the recent PTAs are consolidating the NAFTA (North American Free Trade Agreement) and Pan-Euro approaches as the two dominant "poles" for framework rules. These constitute complex rules of origin, so increased influence of these two poles means increased complexity in rules of origin. This study confirms that more complicated rules of origin can be used as political economy tools to ease the pressure on sensitive sectors as tariff protection is removed. At the same time, there appears to be a trend towards the use of more complex rules of origin by emerging markets as they negotiate more comprehensive and sophisticated PTAs. Generally speaking, rules of origin are more restrictive the higher the gap between the preferential and most favoured nation (MFN) tariff. On the other hand, there appears to be a trend towards simpler rules of origin for developing country partners in PTAs.[4]

Trade liberalization has historically always been accompanied by some form of "safeguard" measure, broadly defined. The recent PTAs are no exception. Nevertheless, although all the PTAs include provision for *commercial instruments* such as anti-dumping and safeguard measures, as well as various exceptions to non-discrimination in the various rules related to deeper integration, the objective of deeper integration appears to have resulted in some forgoing, or limiting of the scope, of contingency measures.

Recent PTAs conform to the framework of and principles set out in the WTO provisions on *SPS and TBT* but then go beyond these to adopt more detailed procedural and institutional arrangements to implement these principles. The emphasis placed on TBT and SPS varies with the interests of the core entities and the nature of the existing WTO obligations. Thus the United States is concerned to limit the use of precaution but is content with the WTO disciplines. It therefore only has to defend the existing WTO agreement. The European Union, on the other hand, would prefer an interpretation of precaution that is less science focused than the WTO SPS Agreement. To date, the European Union does not seem to have had much success challenging the SPS Agreement in its PTAs. When it comes to TBTs, however, it is the European Union that would like to see more effective rules to discipline the use of national discretion in this field. For the United States, TBT has never been a topic of much importance for trade negotiators. Perhaps as a result of limited US support for strong multilateral discipline in the field of TBTs, the picture that appears to be emerging is one involving a range of options: from mutual recognition, through unspecified promotion of "equivalence", to the promotion of international voluntary standards.

In *government procurement* the PTAs are bringing about a wider application of the Agreement on Government Procurement (GPA) framework to more and more countries as the core entities include GPA-equivalent provisions in most of the PTAs they conclude. All PTAs conform to the (plurilateral) GPA principles, but coverage can be GPA-plus (or minus) depending on reciprocity-based bilateral negotiations and depending on the coverage of sub-national entities.

There is a growing use of a hybrid listing formula in *services* in North–South PTAs; in other words, negative listing combined with positive listing in sectors where there are strong regulatory sensitivities. The PTAs frequently include WTO-plus features such as: more provisions on the competition policy dimension of service delivery, in part perhaps as compensation for the absence of competition policy from the Doha Development Agenda; and the right of non-establishment (i.e. no local presence requirement) to facilitate cross-border trade via e-commerce. There is, however, a possibly reduced focus on regulatory harmonization, because bilateral PTAs often involve countries that are widely separated, both geographically and economically. And sector and modal coverage tends to carve out the same sectors (such as health, education and audio-visual) as in the General Agreement on Trade in Services (GATS). But there has been modest progress in Mode 4 liberalization, because the facilitation of service-provider mobility at the regional or bilateral level is seen to be less threatening than a possible multilateral commitment.

Investment, which has traditionally been covered by bilateral investment treaties (BITs), is increasingly – with a question mark for the European Union – being incorporated into PTAs. All North–South PTAs with investment provisions have been signed within roughly the past 10 years, starting with NAFTA in 1994. With investment now excluded from the Doha Development Agenda, the treatment of investment in PTAs is clearly WTO-plus. This trend might be expected to continue as long as investment remains outside the scope of multilateral negotiations, but, precisely because of this exclusion, public opinion in both developed and developing countries may come to question the inclusion of comprehensive investment provisions in PTAs. The outcome on this is still not clear, but for the moment the support that PTAs can give to the promotion and protection of investment is likely to be the decisive factor.

For *intellectual property*, recent PTAs have gone beyond the Agreement on Trade-Related Aspects of Intellectual Property Rights (TRIPS) in areas ranging from the extension of patent and copyright terms, to the protection of undisclosed information. These TRIPS-plus provisions have been largely limited to the PTAs negotiated by the United States, although the European Union has used PTAs to eliminate the exceptions for geographical indicator protection allowed in TRIPS. EFTA's PTAs extend the protection for industrial designs. For the most part, agreements negotiated by Japan do not address IPR issues in a way that goes beyond TRIPS.

Many PTAs, especially the more recent ones, mention the resolve of parties to promote sustainable development, and most of them specifically refer to the *environment*. Despite the WTO-plus character of environment provisions in many PTAs, recent trends tend to reaffirm the importance of developments in the WTO: the clear tendency for a number of countries to use Article XX of the GATT as a model for their environment-related exceptions clauses; a tendency, in dealing with the relationship with multilateral environmental agreements, to refer to ongoing negotiations in the WTO; and, as with the WTO, a tendency to facilitate increased public engagement in the resolution of environment-related disputes.

Provisions dealing with *labour standards* have been essentially a characteristic of US agreements. As a result of the accord reached between the US Congress and the US administration in May 2007, parties to US PTAs will henceforth be required to enforce worker protection as set out in the International Labour Organization's 1998 Declaration on Fundamental Principles and Rights at Work. Given the risk of protectionist capture, the fact that labour provisions in PTAs are WTO-plus does not mean that they are therefore "better".

The policies of the core entities

The United States

In the course of the George W. Bush administration, a total of some 18 countries or groups of countries participated in PTA negotiations with the United States, covering countries as disparate as Australia, Colombia, Korea, Morocco and Oman. The United States has a wide range of motivations for pursuing these agreements. The relative importance of these motivations has differed, however, from one branch of government to another.

The focus on the *foreign policy impact* of preferential deals has been sharper in the Office of the President than in Congress. In seeking to ensure passage of the preferential arrangement with Colombia, the administration has said that failure to do so would undermine US national security interests. In writing to the Democratic leadership of Congress on completion of negotiations for a bilateral agreement with Korea (KORUS), President Bush said the deal would "further enhance the strong United States–Korea partnership, which has served as a force for stability and prosperity in Asia" (*Financial Times*, 3 April 2007). The United States Trade Representative emphasized the strategic link, saying: "The KORUS FTA will also further deepen our 50-year-old economic and strategic relationship with the Republic of Korea. In addition, as the United States' first FTA negotiation with a North Asian partner, conclusion of this agreement would underscore the U.S. commitment to deepening and strengthening trade ties with the many dynamic and fast-growing countries of Asia" (Office of the United States Trade Representative, 2007). Washington's view that KORUS would assure the United States' continued clout in the area can also be seen as implying a restraint on China as well as on the idea of an East Asian preferential bloc, first espoused by former Malaysian Prime Minister Mahathir and now characterized as ASEAN+3 (Association of Southeast Asian Nations, plus China, Japan and Korea).

On the other hand, concerns about incorporating into PTAs provisions dealing with *public health, the environment and core labour standards* have been more pronounced in Congress than in the administration, as was witnessed in the 10 May 2007 agreement reached between the White House and Capitol Hill.

One underlying objective, however, appears to have been pursued equally by Congress and the administration: the desire to use PTAs as a lever for improved *market access* for the goods and services produced and exported by the United States. The following US motivations all relate, directly or indirectly, to this key objective: a concern not to be left out of preferential arrangements; dissatisfaction with progress in the multilateral trading system and a weakened US commitment to that system, rationalized through the concept of "competitive liberalization"; a desire to take opportunities for deeper integration; and the wish to advance trade-related issues and so avoid perceived unfair competition in international trade.

The United States has therefore placed PTAs at the centre of its trade policy in a fashion that has not been seen since 1947, although this should be seen as a relative shift towards bilateral and regional agreements, which have been in the background of US trade policy for many years and at least since the early 1980s.

The US approach to the content of PTAs is uniform. In other words the United States starts with a standard agenda (based on versions of the NAFTA). In pursuit of its market access aims it also has high expectations in terms of coverage – the "gold standard". As a result, reciprocal market access drives the process and there is little scope for asymmetry of commitments. The US pursuit of reciprocity was very clearly demonstrated in the, now abandoned, negotiations with the members of the Southern African Customs Union (SACU). SACU concerns that it lacked the institutional capacities to meet US expectations were met with the response that ways should be explored to strengthen the trade and investment relationship in the hope that SACU would be able to undertake the obligations of a US-style FTA in the future. On the other hand, this tough approach appears to have been more successful in the pursuit of comprehensive coverage than the more "flexible" approach of the Europeans, Japanese and Singaporeans. The political economy problem of selling comprehensive coverage to the domestic constituencies is addressed by: excluding a few difficult sectors; focusing on a narrow range of selected partners; avoiding MFN commitments and therefore free-riding by third parties; including something on labour and environment; and, of course, securing reciprocity from partners.

The United States has been significantly WTO-plus in a number of priority policy areas. On the central issue of tariffs, the US "gold standard" takes the form of almost 100 per cent elimination of US tariffs. This is certainly the case for industrial products and is very nearly the case for agricultural products, where there remain some tariff quotas. The standard appears to have slipped, however, in the PTAs with Korea and Australia. In return, the United States has expected and got more or less complete elimination of all tariff lines by its PTA partners. The use of the fairly complex NAFTA list of rules of origin does, however, take some of the shine off the standard. This has provided some consolation for hard-pressed sectors such as textiles and clothing, where rules of origin are particularly restrictive and thus limit preference utilization by the United States' PTA partners.

Services, investment and intellectual property are three areas of deeper integration in which the US PTAs are also significantly WTO-plus. US agreements tend to go beyond the GATS in rule-making in both financial services and telecommunication services. The provision in US agreements – pioneered in NAFTA – that prohibits local presence requirements goes beyond the criteria defined in Article XVI (e) of the GATS on market access. In terms of sector coverage, the United States has sought and obtained GATS-plus coverage in its PTAs. Consistent US support for a negative-list approach can be seen as a commitment to greater transparency and hence to ambitious services liberalization.

Against this, however, is the widespread tendency to use negative-list reservations to exclude services measures maintained at the sub-national level. In investment, the "gold standard" equates to the comprehensive investment provisions of the NAFTA that the United States has obtained in almost all its PTAs, including those with developing as well as emerging market countries. The investment provisions in KORUS will ensure that US investors in Korea have the same rights and enjoy an equal footing with Korean investors. The United States has also been the driving force behind TRIPS-plus provisions in intellectual property rights in PTAs, which have, for example, progressively extended the 50-year term of copyright protection required by TRIPS and the minimum term of trademark protection from 7 to 10 years as well as eliminating the "innocent infringement" clause in TRIPS that precludes penalties for "unknown violation".

In the area of government procurement, the United States has, like the other core entities, used PTAs to extend the number of its trading partners that effectively comply with GPA-type rules. In this sense the United States has pushed for WTO-plus provisions. But in some agreements the coverage of US purchasing entities is considerably below what it has agreed to with some of its GPA partners. Here the concern for reciprocity has meant WTO-minus commitments on the part of the United States.

In some areas the US PTAs have remained WTO consistent. This is generally the case for commercial instruments, although the US PTAs have consistently applied time limitations on the use of safeguard action that are tighter than those found in the WTO, with no reapplication possible on the same product. Additionally, the US–Chile PTA provides that, on the termination of a safeguard, the rate of duty shall not be higher than the rate that would have been in effect one year after the initiation of the measure according to the agreed tariff schedule.

In policy areas of lower priority one finds much less drive for progress. This is, for example, the case for TBT and SPS measures, where the United States is content to rely on the existing WTO agreements. For TBT provisions in PTAs, the United States has preferred the use of equivalence over standards harmonization. Within the US PTAs, parties commonly need to give an explanation when not applying the principle of equivalence to the regulations of other parties, hence going beyond WTO rules. Although there is encouragement for mutual recognition of test results, the US PTAs reflect a preference for a light institutional framework using "TBT coordinators" in preference to Joint Committees.

Finally, as a result of the agreement reached on 10 May 2007 between the US administration and the Congress, parties to US PTAs will henceforth be asked to enforce worker protection, as set out in the International Labour Organization's 1998 Declaration on Fundamental

Principles and Rights at Work, and to implement seven multilateral environmental agreements, including the Montreal Protocol on Substances That Deplete the Ozone Layer and the Convention on International Trade in Endangered Species.

US PTA policy therefore aims for a WTO-plus commitment from its PTA partners and generally gets it. As we have noted, this leaves little scope for asymmetry. There is perhaps a slight trend towards an increase in WTO-plus provisions, but the main distinguishing feature of US PTAs is their uniformity.

Whether US agreements represent a "gold standard" is open to debate; comprehensive coverage – a condition for maximizing welfare gains – is often lacking. And – it should never be forgotten – even where coverage is extensive, the consequent improvements in market access are still on a preferential and hence discriminatory basis.

The European Union

In contrast to the US PTA policies, the EU approach to PTAs has been characterized by differentiation and flexibility, and by relatively modest results. The European Union has differentiated between its PTA partners. Near neighbours and potential accession states were expected to sign up to the full *acquis communautaire*. Euro-Med partners, with which PTAs were motivated by a desire to promote economic and thus political stability in an otherwise volatile region on the European Union's doorstep, were offered free trade in industrial products, but with exclusions for sensitive agricultural products. The European Union has also tended to have a stronger institutional framework for its PTAs than the United States and has provided more financial assistance. The PTAs under negotiation with the ACP states are driven by development objectives, and ultimately presume flexibility to accommodate the needs of the countries concerned, while embodying a shift towards greater reciprocity in the undertaking of commitments. This move towards greater reciprocity (as ACP states are required to open their markets to EU exports) has led some to question the development credentials of these agreements. It should be recalled, however, that the EPAs do provide favourable access to the EU market, long transition periods for the ACP states (commonly 17 years, with some products shielded indefinitely), assistance for export-related capacity-building, and an opportunity for developing countries to dismantle some of their own impediments to trade. More serious charges against the EPAs are that, first, as we have observed, they are weakening regional cooperation and coherence among developing countries as some members of regional groupings sign up and others do not, and, second, they are prompting significant trade diversion as ACP states shift their imports from low-cost suppliers in favour of the European Union.[5] A wide variety of European exports, ranging from beef to processed goods such as beverages and clothing, would gain preferential access to ACP markets and displace lower-cost competition from both rich and poor countries. Finally, there are the PTAs with emerging markets (and developed economies such as Korea), including the proposed PTAs with ASEAN and India, which are motivated by commercial interests and a desire to match what the United States or other countries have already achieved through PTAs.

In concrete terms, EU flexibility finds expression in the European Union's coverage of tariffs in PTAs. Compared with the United States, the European Union excludes relatively more agricultural tariff lines, although it approaches 100 per cent coverage of industrial products. Even for agriculture, coverage varies from PTA partner to PTA partner and reflects the potential competition for EU agriculture. As a result it is not possible to identify any trend over time. In services, the European Union uses a positive-list approach that provides the "flexibility" to exclude sensitive sectors for both itself and its trading partners. Thus the greater flexibility of EU PTA policy means there is more scope for asymmetric provisions favouring the European Union's developing country PTA partners. But on some occasions it is the European Union that is "benefiting" from the asymmetry, such as in agricultural tariff elimination in the EU–Chile agreement.

Another characteristic of EU PTA policy is a desire to use existing, agreed international standards. This contrasts with the US antipathy towards agreed international standards as being too rigid and overtly centralizing and regulatory in nature. The European Union's "domestic" experience with non-tariff barriers and the emphasis placed on the need for comprehensive provisions on TBTs mean that the European Union takes efforts in this field, including the promotion of agreed international standards through cooperation in PTAs, more seriously than the United States. The European Union also tends to stress compliance with existing standards of protection for intellectual property rights in its PTA provisions on IPR, rather then pressing for TRIPS-plus provisions. In these respects the European Union's PTA provisions are in line with agreed international norms. But there are important exceptions. In the field of SPS measures, the European Union favours SPS-minus rules in the sense that it wants an interpretation of precaution that allows for social as well as science-based risk assessment and risk management. In the IPR field, the European Union is seeking to use PTAs to promote its case for TRIPs-plus protection for geographical indicators (GIs). In both these areas, domestic policy developments have had a direct bearing on the content of the European Union's PTAs. The aim in agriculture policies to promote higher value-added agricultural products as part of the reform of the Common Agricultural Policy favours protection for GIs. The desire for the use of the precautionary principle in food safety has been brought about by the BSE and other food safety crises.

On the "Singapore" issues (investment, competition, public procurement and trade facilitation), the European Union has also shown "flexibility" in the PTAs it negotiated up to 2007. There is little or nothing on investment in the European Union's PTAs, except for EU–Chile, but even this is well short of the NAFTA model. There are proposals for a minimum platform for investment provisions in EU PTAs, but these stop short of the comprehensive US rules on investment. It seems unlikely that the European Union will resolve all the competence issues that have inhibited the inclusion of comprehensive investment provisions in its PTAs.[6] As a result, the European Union seems likely to pursue a slow, progressive approach to investment in its PTAs. To date, the EU member states have negotiated bilateral investment treaties for investment protection and there have been no EU-level investment protection agreements, for which there is a demand from the European Union's PTA partners.

Competition and procurement have found their way into the European Union's PTAs, but again the European Union is flexible in pressing its aims. Early EU PTAs with developing countries had only one brief article on procurement, as, for example, in the Association Agreements with the Euro-Med partners. These simply set out the aim of liberalizing public procurement. In contrast, the United States applied the full GPA framework in its PTA with Morocco. More recently, the European Union has pressed for a more or less GPA-equivalent framework for procurement in the text of the PTA with the Caribbean Forum of ACP States (CARIFORUM). But flexibility remains in the sense that the CARIFORUM countries are not required to make "liberalization" commitments from the outset (Woolcock, 2008a). There is a similar picture in competition, although here the European Union has got somewhat more in terms of provisions aimed at the progressive adoption of EU norms and rules for the Euro-Med partners and fairly ambitious provisions in the EU–Chile (and EU–South Africa) agreements, which include positive comity in cooperation between competition authorities. The test for the European Union on the Singapore issues will be in its foreshadowed agreements with ASEAN and especially India.

One aspect of the European Union's flexibility is that there has been scope for asymmetric provisions applying to developing country PTA partners. For example, on industrial tariffs the Euro-Med partners have the ability to reintroduce tariffs as part of infant industry strategies. Positive listing for services leaves scope for developing countries to pace liberalization as they wish, and the European Union has accepted general aims in the Singapore topics rather then forcing developing countries to adopt fully fledged agreements. Finally, the European Union has been relatively generous in its trade-related technical assistance measures, which might be seen as a form of asymmetry.

EFTA

EFTA's PTA policy shares many of the features of the EU policy. But there are also some important differences. EFTA's pragmatic approach to PTAs differs from the European Union in that it reflects EFTA's character as a trade-driven association. EU PTA policy is, like that of all the core entities considered, shaped by commercial interests, but EU policy is also shaped by strategic, political and developmental objectives. This appears to be less the case for EFTA, where commercial considerations are the predominant factor. For example, whereas the European Union's agreements with the Euro-Med and ACP states are motivated, in part, by security and development motivations and a desire (not necessarily matched by outcomes) to promote regional integration in the Mediterranean and the various African regions concerned, EFTA's agreements with the Euro-Med states are shaped by a desire to match EU agreements. EFTA policy is shaped neither by a legacy of colonialism nor by the Lomé and Cotonou agreements. As a result, the only agreement EFTA has with sub-Saharan Africa is with SACU, which was primarily motivated by commercial interests. But this is not to say that the EFTA states do not support a wider Mediterranean free trade area and thus the Barcelona Process in order to promote economic and political development in the region. Equally, the EFTA states pursue development objectives in the agreements they sign with other developing countries, such as with SACU.

EFTA's third-country trade policy since 1990 has had three phases. The first phase focused on free trade in industrial goods with the Central and East European countries and was guided by a desire to re-establish pan-European ties. The second phase, from 1995, expanded EFTA's PTA network to the southern and eastern rim of the Mediterranean, as part of the pursuit of a Euro-Med free trade area. In the third phase, EFTA went global.

In the first two phases EFTA shadowed the EU developments. This is illustrated by the agreements with the Central and East European countries after 1991 and by the Euro-Med agreements after 1995. A central motivation here was to ensure that EFTA's interests were not undermined by the EU agreements. In the third phase, EFTA's PTA policy was also shaped by developments elsewhere. Thus PTAs negotiated with Chile and Mexico reflected a desire to match what the European Union and the United States were doing in terms of preferential agreements. But EFTA then moved ahead of the European Union through negotiations with Canada, Singapore, Korea and SACU.

This shift to a more activist policy was motivated by a pragmatic desire to strengthen EFTA's commercial position in sectors in which it has a comparative advantage, such as services, investment and research-intensive activities. EFTA's PTAs reveal fairly strong WTO-plus provisions in services, investment and intellectual property. In services, EFTA has seen PTAs as a means of moving ahead with liberalization, which has remained static since the conclusion of the Uruguay Round. For economies in which services account for 70 per cent of GDP, this is seen as inadequate. In investment, some EFTA PTAs have been more ambitious than the EU PTAs, although not as comprehensive as the NAFTA model used by the United States. Recent PTAs, such as that with Singapore, have included pre-investment national treatment (the right of establishment) and investor–state dispute settlement provisions. Like the European Union, EFTA states retain bilateral investment treaties that cover investment protection. In intellectual property rights, some EFTA states have been rather more offensive than the European Union in seeking to use PTAs as a means of ensuring effective compliance with agreed international standards for the protection of intellectual property rights by their trading partners.

EFTA is also like the European Union (and Japan) in that its trade policy is influenced by a defensive position on agriculture. This has resulted in the effective exclusion of sensitive agricultural products from liberalization in the PTAs. The position varies from EFTA state to EFTA state, with Norway insisting on some of the most protectionist provisions of all the core entities considered.[7] This clearly influences EFTA's ability to get what it wants in other areas of policy in which it has more offensive interests. As for all PTA signatories, potential welfare gains from preferential deals are reduced to the extent that coverage is less than comprehensive.

In the remaining areas of policy, EFTA's revealed preferences broadly line up with those of the European Union. In TBT and SPS, EFTA's approach is more or less the same as that of the European Union. This should come as no surprise because the EFTA states have always participated in European standards-making that has shaped parts of the EU *acquis*. In SPS, the EFTA states experience the same domestic pressures as the European Union for higher food safety standards and better animal rights as an integrated approach to food production and consumption. If anything, the EFTA states appear to be even more cautious than the European Union when including provisions on TBT and especially SPS rules in PTAs. This is probably in part owing to a wish to retain as much discretion as possible in the sensitive area of SPS measures, which may argue against codifying how the WTO principles should be applied in PTAs. In rules of origin, EFTA uses the Pan-Euro model and as a result benefits from diagonal cumulation with the European Union. It therefore uses the same rules list as the European Union in its preferential agreements with third parties. Here EFTA has also been out ahead of the European Union in introducing a simplified system of rules of origin for developing countries, something the European Union is only now considering. EFTA also shares the EU preferences in the areas of public procurement, competition and commercial instruments.

A feature of EFTA's PTAs is that flexibility permits the inclusion of asymmetric provisions. In this respect, EFTA's agreement with SACU is in stark contrast to the (now abandoned) negotiations between SACU and the United States.

Japan

Japan is a relatively recent participant in PTAs, with only six agreements in force, three signed and six under negotiation.

As for the European Union and the United States, foreign policy considerations loom large for Japan as a motivation for (somewhat belatedly) pursuing preferential deals – not least the dominant and growing role of China. This is seen most clearly in Japan's advocacy of the Comprehensive Economic Partnership in East Asia (CEPEA), a PTA covering ASEAN+6 (Australia, China, India, Japan, Korea and New Zealand). This proposal is widely considered to be a counter-proposal to that of China for an East Asia free trade agreement covering ASEAN+3 (China, Japan and Korea). By extending the range of the grouping to include Australia, India and New Zealand, Japan would draw in important food and raw material suppliers, a pervasive concern for Japan, but would also dilute the influence of China, not least through the presence of India. Casting the net even wider, Japan has also expressed support for the free trade area of the Asia Pacific, a US proposal that would convert Asia-Pacific Economic Cooperation (APEC) into a preferential arrangement. Japan is thus drawn in opposing directions: the pursuit of closer Asian integration with neighbours and key trading partners, in part in recognition of regional vulnerability exposed by the 1997–1998 Asian financial crisis; and the widening of formal economic linkages beyond the East Asian region in order to pursue economic, foreign policy and strategic interests at the global level.

We concluded for the United States that, although foreign policy considerations are important, concern about improved market access was the most widely held and strongly advanced motivation for the pursuit of PTAs. Japan's situation is less clear. As with the United States, Japanese motivations based on the fear of being left out, dissatisfaction with the progress in the WTO and maximizing opportunities for deeper integration all have an important market access dimension. The Ministry of Economy, Trade and Industry has vaunted the Japan–Mexico EPA on the grounds that "Mexico will become increasingly attractive as a base not only for exporting to the North American market, but also to Latin America as well" (METI, 2005).[8] And the Ministry of Foreign Affairs has said of the Japan–Malaysia EPA that it "provides a framework for expansion and liberalization of bilateral trade and investment" (2006: 173). A primary aim of the PTA under negotiation with Switzerland is to increase Japanese exports of electronic goods, while also strengthening the protection of intellectual property rights. However, compared with the United States – itself less than perfect – Japan has been less successful in implementing PTAs that reflect a high level of ambition to improve market access. Steadily increased tariff liberalization in Japan's successive PTAs has been accompanied by longer transition periods, the introduction of tariff rate quotas and progressively longer permitted periods for the use of safeguard measures. In the area of services, Japan's PTAs are not particularly GATS-plus.

It might be concluded that for Japan, like the United States, improved market access is a key objective, but that vested interests have so far constrained the realization of the objective to a greater extent than they have in the United States. It has thus been said that Japan's ability to design and implement a strategic vision in economic policy is undermined by its own domestic policy-making dynamics. The agricultural and labour lobbies appear to have been particularly influential in frustrating substantial liberalization commitments and in compromising the quality of Japanese PTAs. The problem is compounded by coordination arrangements – or a lack thereof – within the Japanese bureaucracy.

The apparent lack of a blueprint for Japan's PTAs may stem from the same underlying forces. There is a mixture of positive and negative listing from one agreement to another; there is no consistent treatment of domestic tariff schedules; and rules of origin are similarly varied. This might reflect a deliberate flexibility on Japan's part, so that agreements can respond to particular circumstances and differing wishes of Japan's partners. It might equally, however, reflect domestic political constraints. Only with the conclusion of more agreements is the picture likely to become clearer.

Singapore

Like Japan, Singapore drew lessons from the experience of the Asian financial crisis. Unlike Japan, however, it has a clear strategy for its PTAs.

Singapore is perhaps the leading exponent of an activist and strategic PTA policy. Building on the experience of trade and deeper integration agreements in ASEAN, APEC and the WTO, Singapore has pursued a strategy of using PTAs to consolidate its role as a "hub" in the Asian region. Indeed, one could say that the agreements with countries in many continents appear to have the aim of extending Singapore's role as a focus for investment and trading. With the domestic institutional and human capital resources it has, Singapore appears to be seeking to attract international investors and companies to establish global headquarters in Singapore. By concluding sophisticated agreements covering trade and investment, Singapore can offer access to a range of markets in all continents, not just ASEAN.

This is reflected in the content of Singapore's trade agreements. It offers a high standard in terms of zero tariffs, comprehensive investment provisions, TRIPS-plus provisions on IPR and "European-standard" provisions on TBT, SPS and public procurement. Singapore gets rather less from its PTA partners, however. This is clearly owing to its limited negotiating leverage as a small, liberal trader. In some sectors, such as agriculture, Singapore also has no real offensive interest. One is therefore left with the impression that Singapore adopts a very pragmatic approach to PTAs.

In terms of tariffs, Singapore binds 100 per cent zero tariffs in its PTAs, but has been fairly unsuccessful in getting anywhere near this level of liberalization from its partners. Japan excluded more or less all its agricultural tariff lines from liberalization. India offered only 25 per cent of all tariff lines for full tariff liberalization. This pattern runs through all of Singapore's PTAs.

The effects of PTAs on trade and investment

On the basis of the present study, we find that, not surprisingly, there is a correspondence between the relative ambition of different core entities' PTAs and the effect of these agreements on patterns of trade and investment.

There is thus clear evidence of a linkage between trade and investment flows and the implementation of PTAs to which the United States and, to a lesser extent, the European Union are a party. There may also be a linkage between trade and investment activity and the *announcement* of PTA negotiations, though this is much harder to substantiate.

Unlike the US and EU experience, Japan's PTAs appear to have had a negligible effect on flows of trade and investment. However, the relative newness of Japan's agreements, and associated data limitations, mean

that any observations at this stage can only be tentative. Similar considerations apply in the case of Singapore.

There seem to be few discernible trends in EFTA trade and investment
with individual PTA partners. Moreover, such trade, in total, represents a
relatively small percentage of EFTA exports and imports – about 14 per
cent of trade in goods outside the European Union – since the bulk of
EFTA's external trade is with the European Union. The European
Union's trade relationship with EFTA is covered by the European Economic Area Agreement in the case of Norway, Iceland and Liechtenstein
and by the 1972 Free Trade Agreement in the case of Switzerland.

Nevertheless observations can be made in respect of EFTA PTAs that
also have wider significance. Overall, EFTA trade with PTA partners
rose 8.1 per cent between 1992 and 2002, compared with only 0.7 per
cent with the rest of the world. Within this trade, EFTA imports of goods
increased more than EFTA exports, because of the asymmetric liberalization provisions of the agreements. And, even where aggregate trade
with a partner did not increase, trade in products that were subject to significant liberalization did increase. For example, whereas Swiss trade
with Mexico relative to the rest of the world fell between 2002 and 2005,
exports of pharmaceuticals and watches, each subject to tariff dismantling, grew strongly. This observation highlights the importance of
product specificity in seeking to identify trends related to PTA activity.

Beyond the findings of the present study, what additional information
can we derive from others' attempts at measurement?

Overall, the findings of ex post studies indicate that some PTAs boosted
intra-bloc trade significantly, but others did not. There is some evidence
that external trade is smaller than it might otherwise have been in at least
some of the blocs, but the picture is mixed enough that it is not possible
to conclude whether trade diversion has been a major problem. However, most of the studies using growth regressions suggest that PTAs
have had little impact on economic growth, in part because of the
welfare-reducing effects of trade diversion. Broadly, the conclusions
from ex ante studies are also that there has been evidence of weak trade
diversion, but that the recent wave of preferential agreements has been
trade creating on a net basis and welfare improving for member countries.

Micro analysis of the data tends to produce more conclusive results,
with clearer evidence of trade diversion at a disaggregated level. A study
of the effects of investment provisions in PTAs finds that the entry into
force of a PTA with substantive investment provisions is associated with
a 60 per cent increase in flows of foreign direct investment between the
parties and a 20 per cent increase in trade (Miroudot and Lesher, 2006).

Importantly, given the political focus on the issue of preference erosion, studies of preference erosion as a result of multilateral liberalization tend to find that, although preferential exports decline as a consequence of erosion, new opportunities from MFN tariff liberalization more than offset the negative effects for all but a handful of countries.

Finally, there is persuasive evidence that the formation of PTAs is associated with increased litigation in the trading system, meaning that there is not only greater strain on the WTO's dispute settlement mechanism but also the perception – and frequently the reality – that PTAs lead to increased discrimination in the conduct of international trade.

Looking ahead

In this concluding section we will suggest answers to some of the key questions concerning the likely evolution of preferential trade agreements and the implications for the multilateral trading system.

Will the United States continue to engage in preferential bilateralism?

The shifting priorities of different US administrations, changing political configurations in Congress and the uncertainties surrounding the availability of fast-track negotiating authority all raise questions about the likely direction of US trade policy. However, a number of factors suggest that, although the absence of fast-track authority may slow the pace of negotiation, whatever the domestic political environment – and whatever the fate of multilateral trade negotiations – the United States is likely to continue actively pursuing preferential bilateral trade agreements. Bipartisan support for improved market access through bilateral deals, together with heightened opportunities to address foreign policy, environmental, labour and public health concerns, along with a fear of being left out as other countries sign PTAs, will ensure that the United States continues to seek opportunities for preferential arrangements.

Will the European Union continue to show "flexibility" or will it move to a more uniform, hard cutting edge?

The trend appears to be towards a more aggressive and ambitious PTA strategy on the part of the European Union. In our discussion of individual policy areas, we have seen this in the pursuit of more extensive tariff coverage; in the move away from (potentially distorting) mutual recognition agreements in TBT towards a greater emphasis on compliance with international standards; in attempts to get closer to the goals of the WTO GPA; in moves to advance Mode 4 liberalization in services; and in attempts, via the Lisbon Treaty, to remove competence limitations on greater ambition in the treatment of investment. A more aggressive EU strategy can be expected to continue, at least in some areas, as the European Union seeks to match the sector commitments in services achieved by US PTAs; to extend the number of countries that effectively apply the GPA; to seek more effective enforcement of IPR standards; and to bring greater reciprocity to the EPAs with the ACP states.

Against this, however, a number of impediments to a more ambitious agenda will likely persist: the European Union will be hard pressed to overcome domestic opposition to agricultural liberalization; attitudes towards "precaution" will constrain ambitions in TBT and SPS; and questions of competence will prevent the Commission from matching the ambition of US PTAs in the area of investment. There is also fairly consistent opposition from non-governmental organizations and some parliamentarians in the European Union to the use of economic leverage to get developing countries to adopt comprehensive PTAs that do not reflect development concerns. This can be expected to blunt the cutting edge of EU PTA policy.

The current negotiations with Korea will provide a test for the European Union's determination to establish a new, higher, standard for its PTAs. The EU–Chile agreement was seen as the standard when it was negotiated. The aim with Korea is to bring about a step change to a higher level. Should the European Union succeed in this, the test will then be whether it can negotiate equally ambitious PTAs with India and ASEAN. The European Union is showing some firmness and, perhaps as a measure of its ambition, has said that India, ASEAN and Korea have been chosen as partners precisely because they combine high levels of protection and large market potential (*Bridges Weekly Trade News Digest*, 11(14), 25 April 2007). But the expectation must be that flexibility will again prevail, with the result that the scope of these pending agreements will not match the stated level of ambition.

Will Japan's agreements become more ambitious or will domestic politics continue to constrain them?

As alluded to earlier, in some respects Japan's agreements have become progressively more restrictive. Transition periods for tariff elimination have lengthened (from 11 years in the agreement with Mexico in 2005 to 16 years with Chile in 2007); the Mexico agreement introduced tariff rate quotas for the first time; and the length of the period in which safeguards are permitted has become progressively longer. However, product coverage for tariff reductions has become more comprehensive, notably between the Singapore (2002) and Chile (2007) agreements, and the lengthening of transition periods may need to be seen in that light. In terms of product coverage, there is a clear tendency for Japan's agreements to become more ambitious.

A key factor in confirming this tendency will be agriculture, and here the pending agreement with Australia may provide pointers. There are two elements to this.

First, should it prove possible in the agreement with Australia, and subsequently with other major agricultural exporters, to secure undertakings about security of supply, as it was with Indonesia on energy security, the intellectual underpinnings of support for Japan's farm sector would be greatly weakened. That such a weakening would translate into an improved political climate for agricultural reform in Japan cannot be excluded, but it is by no means sure. Recent developments remind us of the intractable nature of agricultural reform in Japan: the outcome of the July 2007 Upper House elections, which seem to signal a very gradual approach to reform; the fact that preliminary exploration of a possible US–Japan agreement was deferred because of resistance from the Ministry of Agriculture; and the likelihood that agriculture will be effectively excluded from Japan's pending bilateral agreement with Switzerland.

Second, it has been observed (Ando and Kimura, 2007) that agricultural products represent over 20 per cent of Japan's imports from Australia and that if the PTA is to cover "substantially all trade", as required under Article XXIV of the GATT, there will be no escaping some liberalization of Japan's farm sector. Here too, although change cannot be totally discounted, there can be no guarantee of success. Effective implementation of the "substantially all trade" principle has proved notoriously difficult and progress would seem more likely in the framework of a broad-based multilateral agreement than through bilateral accommodations. This leads to our final, and arguably most important, question.

Will the growth of bilateral PTAs help or hinder multilateral trade liberalization?

If we assume that the major players, and many smaller players, will continue to pursue preferential bilateral deals, what will this mean for the multilateral trading system? Because of PTAs' "split personality" – both a subset of liberalization among a selected group of countries and a permitted exception to the MFN principle – they bring both positive and negative elements to the trading system. This is clearly demonstrated in

Table 12.1 Building block or stumbling block?

Building block argument	Stumbling block argument
• PTAs have gone hand-in-hand with globalization and evidence suggests that they have been mostly trade creating.	• PTAs may promote costly trade diversion rather than efficient trade creation, especially when sizeable MFN tariffs remain.
• Expanding the number of PTAs creates stronger exporting interests and shifts the balance in favour of liberalization in trade policy.	• PTAs create vested interests that seek to retain preferences by resisting multilateral liberalization. The alternative of PTAs with exceptions removes the incentive to negotiate multilaterally.
• For both market access and rule-making, PTAs offer a way to make progress more quickly than in the WTO and with more ambition.	• Asymmetric bargaining may be used to force countries to adopt policies that they have opposed in the WTO. And sectors that are hard multilaterally will also be hard in PTAs.
• PTAs "lock in" domestic reform and countries use PTAs to "accede" to the prevailing multilateral liberalization of the countries.	• Competing PTAs (especially different North–South combinations) may lock in incompatible regulatory structures or standards, which may result in inappropriate norms for developing country partners.
• PTAs promote the creation of negotiating and institutional capacity, which can facilitate trade and investment in general, including multilateral trade.	• Proliferating PTAs absorb scarce negotiating resources (especially among poorer WTO members) and "crowd out" policy-makers' attention to multilateral solutions. They also serve to weaken regional cooperation among developing countries.
• Stronger PTA rules ensure more effective implementation and enforcement of principles agreed within the multilateral setting.	• By creating alternative legal frameworks and dispute settlement mechanisms, PTAs may weaken the discipline and efficiency associated with a broadly recognized multilateral framework of rules.

Table 12.1, which sets out these elements in the framework of the familiar building block/stumbling block debate.

Bhagwati (Bhagwati and Panagariya, 1996) identified the need to address what he called the dynamic time path question, but his interest was in whether preferential agreements would grow larger as a result of increased membership of tariff preferences until they became, in effect, a multilateral system. Perhaps of more relevance to the current generation of bilateral agreements is whether the major proponents of PTAs (i.e. the United States and the European Union and others) are acting as "selfish hegemons" in that they use sequential negotiations first with smaller and weaker neighbours in order to set a precedent that other trading partners feel obliged to follow.[9]

Let us take each of these, interrelated, elements in turn.

Trade creation, trade diversion

As we have seen, there is some ambiguity in the various attempts at measuring the trade-creating and trade-diverting effects of PTAs. Although there is clear, and perhaps growing, evidence of trade creation, it cannot be denied that trade diversion occurs, particularly when measured at a disaggregated level, and that the fairly modest welfare gains arising from preferential tariff arrangements arise, in part, because of the effects of such trade distortions.

There is evidence of South–South preferential liberalization leading to lower MFN rates (see the discussion in Chapter 11 based on Estevadeordal and colleagues, 2008), but this may well not apply where the maintenance of preferences is needed to encourage compliance in North–South agreements with non-trade objectives, such as those related to the environment or core labour standards. It has thus been found that the United States and the European Union, for which such objectives are relatively important, liberalized less in the Uruguay Round in sectors where preferences were granted.

Support for trade liberalization

As subsets of liberalization, PTAs can serve to strengthen domestic exporting interests and hence the constituency for market opening. This, however, does not preclude a reduced commitment to multilateral liberalization as parties seek to avoid: (1) the erosion of PTA preferences that lower MFN rates would entail, and (2) the making of liberalization commitments in sensitive sectors – such as agriculture, textiles and clothing, motor vehicles and audio-visual services – that have been effectively carved out from PTA coverage. The DDA negotiations have shown the pervasiveness of concerns about preference erosion despite the fact, as discussed above, that overall gains from broad MFN liberalization will, for all but a handful of countries, more than offset losses from preference erosion.

WTO-plus

The policy issue analysis in this study has shown that PTAs go well beyond the WTO in many respects: by bringing more ambition to negotiating modalities (such as through the use of negative listing in services liberalization); by strengthening disciplines (such as those applying to the use of safeguard action); by widening the scope of trade negotiations, for example through the focus on issues such as investment and competition that have been removed from the multilateral agenda – a tendency that is likely to continue; and by extending the range of countries applying WTO disciplines (such as through the application of the WTO's government procurement principles to countries that are not members of the GPA). Beyond this, it may also be possible that preferential agreements can directly help the multilateral process through synergistic interaction whereby economic diplomacy on different levels interacts in an iterative, two-way process (Woolcock, in Bayne and Woolcock, 2007: 146). There was, for example, some interesting reverse engineering in the way that treatment of financial services in the US–Canada FTA fed into (multilateral) negotiation of the GATS, which in turn influenced the treatment of this sector in NAFTA. And, although mutual recognition agreements among preferential partners can involve discrimination against third parties, it may be possible for deeper integration to be achieved in ways that bring benefits to all countries, for example through the introduction of increased regulatory transparency.

From a stumbling-block perspective, however, it might be argued that PTAs pressure developing countries, as the price for improved market access, to undertake commitments, in areas such as competition policy, that they would be unwilling to undertake in the WTO. This rather begs the question, however, of whether it may not nevertheless be in their self-interest to do so. A more telling qualification to the WTO-plus argument is that sectors that are hard multilaterally, such as agriculture, are likely to be similarly challenging in the framework of PTAs. Indeed, bilateral accommodations, such as that between Japan and Switzerland, may make it easier to exclude sensitive sectors than is the case in a broader multilateral context, where a wider range of interests have to be accommodated. As discussed above, all of the countries studied exclude, to a greater or lesser degree, sensitive agricultural sectors. Deeper integration issues in agriculture are primarily concerned with competition, in other words what kind of national subsidies are permitted. The obvious but important point here is that domestic subsidies cannot be reduced preferentially.[10] There is also a risk that the very fact of having a wider scope in preferential agreements may reduce the incentive to engage multilaterally. Countries that attach high priority to issues that are being addressed bilaterally but are off the multilateral (DDA) agenda, for example Japan and rules on investment, will have a reduced motivation to negotiate multilaterally.

Locking in reform

PTAs may serve to encourage reform, for example in the area of domestic regulation, that might not otherwise happen and to reduce the risk of reform reversal by locking in commitments. This argument is frequently invoked by both developed countries, such as Japan in the pursuit of financial sector reform, and developing countries, in support of South–South cooperation in the framework of preferential arrangements. The counter to this argument is that, in the framework of North–South agreements, developing countries may be obliged to undertake commitments that are incompatible with their regulatory structure and needs. Regulatory harmonization can give rise to such concerns. In practice, however, there is little empirical evidence of the imposition on developing countries of inappropriate regulation. Rather to the contrary, PTAs can be the vehicle for beneficial regulatory reform.

Institution-building

The negotiation of preferential agreements can undoubtedly help build developing country institutional capacity, particularly when, as is often the case, there is accompanying technical assistance. The down-side here comes in the form of the opportunity cost of committing scarce human resources to bilateral negotiations. The resource issues are likely to be real, especially for poorer developing countries.[11] Even developed countries face resource constraints when it comes to negotiating on various levels at the same time.[12] However, there is very little in the way of empirical findings on the question of whether PTA negotiations detract from multilateralism by drawing off scarce resources or "crowding out" policy-makers' attention. Moreover, it is not clear to what extent resource or capacity constraints are a short- or long-term problem. Provisions developed in one PTA or in a multilateral negotiation are frequently used in other negotiations. Very rarely are negotiators working with a blank sheet. This use of precedent, which extends to adopting more or less the same provisions in different agreements, clearly touches on capacity issues. Existing rules may be used because there is no capacity to negotiate new rules, but in most cases existing rules will be used because they offer network efficiencies. Use of existing rules also makes the process of reconciling the proposed rules with domestic interests less burdensome, because the domestic constituencies will have already accepted them once before. If this is the case, then the capacity issues may not be so serious.

Strengthening the multilateral framework of rules

As we have seen, PTA provisions are frequently based on WTO disciplines and wording. This is notably the case, for example, in respect of SPS and TBT. Furthermore, there are provisions in PTAs, especially those that establish framework rules that promote regulatory best practice and transparent procedural measures that implement WTO rules, that complement the WTO system. In many cases PTAs are not significantly WTO-plus and, where they are, they are WTO-plus in terms of the procedures they set out for implementing what are in effect broadly based international rules or norms. Indeed, one can make the case that such a "mirroring" serves to underpin multilateral disciplines. The stumbling-block counter to this argument has three elements. First, PTAs generate a proliferation of rules. The entrenchment, and growing complexity, of three different approaches to rules of origin is a case in point. This is a major qualification to the idea that, as PTAs, with ever-growing membership, spread to cover more and more countries, they will cumulatively generate freer trade. Second, PTAs bring institutional complexity by replicating functions, such as through the spread of different dispute resolution forums. And, third, the atmospherics of multilateral negotiation are not helped by developed country pursuit in PTAs of stronger provisions dealing with labour standards and the environment, each with attendant risks of protectionist capture.

It is not useful, or indeed feasible, to reach an overall conclusion about the way these positive and negative elements balance out though, as we will see shortly, it is possible to reconcile the conundrum – building block *and* stumbling block. What might be noted, however, is that, although the positive contribution of PTAs need not necessarily help the multilateral process in a direct way, the negative aspects are likely to be directly damaging to multilateral efforts.

With the DDA having proved so protracted, some people have suggested that, given the inevitable coexistence between multilateral and bilateral approaches to trade diplomacy, there should be a division of labour, whereby the WTO would focus on rules and the bilateral and regional agreements on market access. Although the protracted nature of the DDA is abundantly clear (see Box 12.1), such an extreme sharing of responsibilities is not a workable solution, for both institutional and substantive reasons.

In institutional terms, the WTO cannot simply vacate the field of market access and leave it to other levels of negotiation. Moreover, as we have seen, there is not a clear-cut distinction between rules issues and market access; more comprehensive rules on investment or competition would greatly improve the prospects of enhanced market access, by, for example, facilitating commercial presence in the delivery of services or access to networks needed for the distribution of both goods and services.

There are two substantive problems with the division of labour argument (WTO for rules, PTAs for market access). The first is that, in

Box 12.1 Another setback for the Doha Development Agenda: The July 2008 Ministerial

The WTO Ministerial Meeting of 21–29 July 2008 succeeded in turning stand-offs ("I will do nothing on agriculture until you do something on non-agricultural market access") into trade-offs. However, the trade-offs tended to be negative ("I will let you exclude X from liberalization if you let me exclude Y") rather than positive ("I will liberalize X if you liberalize Y"). Although this enabled negotiators to keep within the broad modalities (or "headline numbers") offered by the Chairs of the respective negotiating groups, the fine print of exceptions and special treatment seriously diminished the liberalizing potential of the deal in both agriculture and non-agricultural market access (NAMA). In agriculture, this was evident particularly with respect to protection associated with sensitive products, GI price premiums, special products and the special safeguard mechanism, and in NAMA with respect to the flexibilities allowed under different tariff coefficients, weakened commitments to sectoral liberalization, long transitions in textiles and clothing to meet concerns about preference erosion, and special dispensations for members of customs unions.

The result of the mutual lowering of ambition was that, in the end, the potential deal was not worth fighting for. For example, it was pointed out that allowing developed countries to designate 4 per cent of tariff lines in agriculture as "sensitive" would effectively block all of Argentina's exports. Allowing the special safeguard mechanism to be triggered by an import surge of only 10 per cent, as sought by a group of developing countries, would mean that 82 per cent of China's food imports and 64 per cent of India's would be subject to a tariff as high as 30 percentage points above pre-Doha bound rates.

The underlying failure, shared by all, was one of insufficient political will to confront vested interests benefiting from the rents of protection. This was compounded by the seeming inability, or unwillingness, to make the most of potential cross-issue trade-offs. In this respect it was disappointing that more was not made of the positive signals coming out of the talks on trade in services. Contrary to the "complexity" argument advanced to explain lack of progress in the WTO, one could actually argue that the agenda was too narrow, not too broad.

Looking ahead, more will be made of the positive signals coming out of the Ministerial and of the few signs of convergence – such as the US offer to lower the floor to US domestic agricultural support from US$22.5 billion to US$15.0 billion, which United States Trade Representative Susan Schwab said was still on the table (and which, of course, was still double the amount of actual outlays!). Some

Box 12.1 (cont.)

> ministers therefore spoke of a pause rather than a breakdown. It could, however, be a long pause, given the entrenched positions on issues discussed, not to mention the long list of issues hardly broached, such as cotton and bananas, and the largely unexplored area of rules.
>
> USTR Schwab suggested a possible "piecemeal" way forward and identified some "discrete parts of the package" where it might be possible to make progress, namely duty-free quota-free (DFQF) access for LDCs, export competition, trade facilitation and environmental goods and services. However, even here there are unresolved questions, such as what to do about the 3 per cent of tariff lines excluded from DFQF access. And, as Indian Minister Nath rightly pointed out, the DDA is "not a buffet" where you take your favourite item and walk away.
>
> So it is hard to see much happening in the near term. Meanwhile, the onward march of preferential agreements will continue unabated.

practice, areas of market access that are hard multilaterally are also hard at the bilateral or regional level, and are likely to remain so. As we have seen, this is particularly the case with agriculture (Tsai, 2006). Indeed, opportunities for the welfare-reducing carve-out of sensitive, highly protected sectors are greater in bilateral accommodations than in agreements with more players and wider interests.

Second, without ongoing progress to reduce trade barriers on an MFN basis, the distorting effects of preferential arrangements – through trade and investment diversion – would be more acute. It is worth repeating that, even where PTAs are successful in improving market access for the parties involved, there is also a risk – inherent in preferential deals – that third countries will be affected by trade and investment diversion. Such distortion will be reduced, the lower are pre-arrangement MFN tariffs; hence the critical importance of maintaining progress in multilateral tariff liberalization, in parallel with the growth of preferential agreements. In the case of deeper integration issues, such as procurement, services and investment, TBT and SPS, the element of preference in PTAs is less obvious and may be less pronounced. But preferential agreements on rules could become divergent and thus make multilateralization more difficult. At the same time, PTAs are more likely to be shaped by the dominant proponents of such rules and thus less likely to suit smaller WTO members or developing economies if there is no ongoing discussion of what the basic framework rules should be. This leads us to a reconciliation of the conundrum – building block *and* stumbling block.

The resolution of this apparent contradiction is that *PTAs can complement the multilateral trading system, but only if that system is itself robust* – strengthening trade rules and bringing down MFN barriers, so that the distorting effects of PTAs are held in check. Only with a strong multilateral trading system will it be possible to make multi-level diplomacy work, whereby PTAs help implement and possibly extend WTO rule-making in areas such as TBT/SPS or trade remedies in between multilateral rounds of negotiation or in parallel with a continuous work programme at the WTO. If we accept that PTAs and the multilateral trading system will have to coexist, the basis of this coexistence must be the continued strengthening of multilateral rules and disciplines under the WTO.

Beyond this, however, there is also a need for strengthened monitoring and disciplining of PTAs. Progress here has been extremely laborious and preferential agreements have never been subject to rigorous examination in the GATT/WTO.

Existing WTO provisions on PTAs are ineffective and on recent experience, in the WTO's Committee on Regional Trade Agreements (CRTA), there would appear to be little prospect of any major breakthrough on key issues of difference such as what constitutes "substantially all trade". The existing WTO provisions concerned are Article XXIV of the GATT, the Understanding on the Interpretation of Article XXIV agreed in the Uruguay Round, the Enabling Clause provisions, which include exceptions for developing countries from the MFN obligations of the GATT for preferential agreements, and Article V of the GATS. Monitoring the PTAs in terms of their compliance with GATT Article XXIV has been an important aspect of WTO work. The CRTA has been tasked with providing a legal analysis of regional agreements and seeking ways of improving the application of WTO rules.[13]

There are a number of well-known ambiguities in the wording of the GATT rules, which have made any definitive view on the application of the MFN exemption for preferential agreements elusive.

First, there is the problem of defining what is "substantially all trade" under Article XXIV. For example, should this be interpreted in a qualitative fashion or a quantitative fashion? Should "trade" be measured according to actual values of transactions (which would not account for sectors where barriers were prohibitive of any trade) or the coverage of tariff lines (which would not allow for the relative weight of different lines). Discussions in the WTO have still to reach agreement on whether "substantially all trade" means 80 per cent, 90 per cent or 100 per cent of trade and what sort of special treatment there should be for developing countries, both in South–South and in North–South agreements. The level that is set clearly has a bearing on the multilateral discipline of PTAs in that a low threshold would enable the continued exclusion of key parts of agriculture from PTAs without infringing GATT rules.

Similar questions arise with the interpretation of GATS Article V. For example, should "substantially all trade" mean that an FTA in services could exclude a whole sector? The schedules in the GATS already provide only selective coverage of services sectors. How should these exemptions be treated in any assessment of "substantially all trade" in PTAs? How should one define a quantitative measure of "substantially all trade", given that many PTAs that include services/investment have schedules (negative lists) that in effect exclude many activities within services sectors that are nominally covered by the agreements?

More generally, should "substantially all trade" include regulatory barriers to trade and, if so, which types of regulatory barriers? Article XXIV 8 (a) (i) (the "substantially all trade" provision) refers to duties and "other regulatory restrictions to commerce". Should "other regulatory restrictions to commerce" include regulatory barriers to trade and, if so, which?[14]

A second area of ambiguity in the GATT rules concerns the treatment of regulatory barriers to trade within the requirement that the *general incidence of protection* in the form of duties or "other regulation of commerce" should not be greater in an FTA or customs union than was the case for the constituent countries before the agreement was concluded. Although there has been some clarification of the treatment of duties (i.e. tariffs) under this provision in the 1994 Understanding on the Interpretation of Article XXIV, the treatment of "other regulation of commerce" remains very unclear. For example, if country B has lower food or safety standards than its PTA partner A and a PTA agreement results in common standards at the level of country A, does this mean that third-country suppliers will face a higher incidence of "protection" in country B, or does the existence of a single standard for the whole PTA facilitate trade, reduce the costs of compliance for third-country suppliers and thus result in a lower "general incidence of protection"? How should one go about measuring these compensatory effects within the WTO context? Some WTO members view new common rules or standards within a PTA as an increase in the incidence of protection, whereas compliance with a single set of rules is seen by others as reducing the costs for third-country suppliers (see Trachtman, 2003).[15]

Article V of the GATS provides for a similar, but not identical, set of criteria for assessing whether PTA provisions on services are compatible with WTO rules. Article V states that "any agreement... shall not in respect of any Member outside the [PTA] raise the overall level of barriers to trade in services within the respective sectors or sub-sectors compared to the level applicable prior to such an agreement". This has been interpreted as being better for non-members of PTAs than the GATT Article XXIV provision, because it requires no rise in the overall level of barriers on a sector-by-sector basis, rather than the GATT requirement that there should be no increase in the incidence of protection "on the whole". The "on the whole" wording in GATT Article XXIV has been the origin of the debate on whether reductions in protection in one sector can be balanced against increases in others. The GATS also requires that service suppliers with "substantive business operations" in signatories to a PTA prior to the conclusion of a PTA should be treated equivalently to suppliers of services from the signatories of the PTA.[16] But there still remains ambiguity concerning the interpretation of Article V of the GATS. For example, in the debate following the European Commission's proposal for an FTA in services between the United States and the European Union in 1998, it was unclear whether such an agreement would satisfy Article V if it excluded the audio-visual sector. The issue was not resolved because the idea of a transatlantic free trade agreement in services did not have sufficient support.[17]

With no clear criteria on the interpretation of Article XXIV (GATT) and Article V (GATS), the WTO has not been able to make much progress assessing the impact of PTAs, despite the work of the CRTA. The Doha Development Agenda contains the mandate to "clarify and improve disciplines and procedures under the existing WTO provisions applying to regional trade agreements", while taking "into account the developmental aspects of regional trade agreements". Progress in the negotiations has been slow. The United States has maintained that substantially all trade should be near to 100 per cent, whereas the European Union has argued for 90 per cent of trade. This issue has assumed importance for developing countries because of the growth of North–South PTAs. Under the Enabling Clause, South–South PTAs are not under the same obligation to cover substantially all trade. But in North–South agreements the northern parties must comply with this rule. Therefore, in negotiations such as those for the EPAs between the European Union and ACP developing countries, the developing parties have argued for greater flexibility to enable them to retain some protection for key industries (Onguglo and Ito, 2003).

With regard to the treatment of other deeper integration issues, the European Union argues that common rules established within a region facilitate trade, whereas India argues that any new rule constitutes a new barrier to trade. The WTO negotiations have made more progress on transparency provisions relating to PTAs. The issue here has been whether a PTA should be notified to the WTO only when it is formed or whether there should be a regular reporting of PTA activities and implementation and, if so, what the frequency should be of such reporting. In 2006 there was agreement on enhanced transparency for PTAs within the WTO.

As noted in Chapter 1, the WTO has thus recently started producing Factual Presentations of the PTAs notified to the Committee on Regional Trade Agreements. This follows the agreement on a Transparency Mechanism for Regional Trade Agreements (WT/L/671) adopted in December 2006. The Factual Presentations should prove helpful as a source of comparable data.

The effectiveness of the monitoring and disciplinary process through the CRTA is not, of course, totally unconnected to general progress, or lack thereof, under the Doha Development Agenda. Within the broad risk – should the process of multilateral negotiation stall – that the WTO would proceed by litigation (through dispute settlement) rather than by legislation (through liberalization and rules strengthening), there is also the prospect that PTA monitoring could become the purview of dispute settlement. In *Turkey–Textiles*, the Appellate Body effectively confirmed that panels and the Appellate Body have the jurisdiction to examine whether a PTA fulfils Article XXIV conditions (Nottage, 2008).

We are led to conclude therefore that sustained efforts at multilateral trade liberalization and improved monitoring of preferential trade agreements need to be backed by a third, and more fundamental, requirement in the form of a change of mindset among trade officials, and economic policy-makers more broadly, that would view market opening as a tool of growth rather than as a concession paid to others. Only in this way could it become possible to agree that preferences granted to regional and bilateral partners would at some threshold point be multilateralized on an MFN basis. However, with preferential deals driven by political-strategic as well as economic motivations, multilateralizing benefits will never be easy. And so the uneasy coexistence of the preferential and the multilateral is set to continue.

Notes

1. Article 63 of the Maseru Declaration issued at the conclusion of the LDC Trade Ministers' Meeting held in Maseru, Lesotho, 27–29 February 2008.
2. The trigger for the bilateral agreements was the expiry on 31 December 2007 of the Article 1 Doha Waiver, which permitted the European Union to grant tariff preferences to the ACP countries otherwise inconsistent with the most favoured nation (MFN) commitment of Article 1 of the GATT. The European Union was aware that once the waiver expired the tariff preferences granted to the ACP would be subject to challenge

in WTO dispute settlement as inconsistent with Article 1. Rather than seek a further waiver, as many ACP states wanted, the European Union proposed EPAs in the form of FTAs within the meaning of Article XXIV of the GATT. In order to ensure consistency with Article XXIV, however, the EPAs require reciprocal liberalization on substantially all the trade between the parties. The Enabling Clause is another way that a developed country can justify tariff preferences otherwise inconsistent with Article 1 of the GATT. However, the Enabling Clause requires preferences to be granted to all similarly situated developing countries and therefore would not have allowed the European Union to separate the ACP from other developing countries.

3. A question that arises is why some LDCs nevertheless chose to sign EPAs. Perhaps the most plausible reason is that rules of origin under EPAs are less restrictive than those applying under Everything But Arms, the regime through which LDCs get privileged access to the EU market.

4. The benefits of simplified rules of origin, such as the uniform use of value content, across the board should not be exaggerated. The costs involved in effective compliance with value content rules can be as great as the compliance costs for other "more complex" rules, because of the requirement for a detailed audit trail of where value is added.

5. A meeting of the ACP Council of Ministers in Ethiopia in June 2008 expressed concern that the MFN clause in the EPAs, requiring that preferences granted by ACP states be extended to the European Union, would stifle trade among developing countries, discourage new trade agreements and thus inhibit the integration of poorer countries into the global trading system.

6. The Lisbon Treaty envisages foreign direct investment becoming a matter for European Union competence, but it does not clarify whether this implies that both investment liberalization and investment protection would become issues for EU competence. There remained a difference of views among the member states on this, so that, even if the treaty were to be adopted, some member states could be expected to wish to retain the existing BITs covering investment protection (Woolcock, 2008b).

7. The EFTA states negotiate separate bilateral agreements on agriculture.

8. The complex rules of origin that apply in NAFTA may present a barrier to entry into the US market for Japanese investment in Mexico, especially in the sectors such as automobiles and textiles in which NAFTA rules of origin are especially restrictive.

9. Bhagwati's approach views US unilateralism and regional or bilateral agreements in the same context. He discusses whether these policies are "malign" or "benign". Malign policies are seen to be those that use power to extract greater gains from trade than the other party. Benign policies are when trade agreements are concluded voluntarily (Bhagwati, 1990). This theme has been picked up in work on PTAs that seeks to differentiate between benevolent and selfish hegemons in their pursuit of PTAs (Maur, 2005).

10. At least not very simply. It is possible to envisage an approach in which domestic subsidies for products that are of relative importance to preferential partners might be reduced. In practice, this kind of a policy would be complicated, not least because some of these schemes benefit the preferential partners. The EU sugar regime is a case in point. Here the high EU price support scheme also provided a preferential subsidy to ACP sugar producers.

11. Kenya, for example, has to juggle membership of two customs unions (the East Africa Community and the Common Market for Eastern and Southern Africa), the African Growth and Opportunity Act with the United States, an EPA with the European Union, and bilateral agreements with Egypt and Pakistan.

12. Interview evidence from discussions with trade officials in the UK Department of Trade and Industry and the European Commission.

13. In fact the CRTA has three tasks; (i) to provide legal analysis of the PTAs (and their compatibility with the rules); (ii) to make horizontal comparisons (inventories of PTA rules have been produced including, for example, safeguards, anti-dumping, intellectual property rights provisions, provisions on technical barriers to trade, investment rules, competition rules in PTAs); and (iii) to debate the context and economic aspects of PTAs. See Sampson (1996).
14. For more discussion on this point, see Mathis (2006), and, for an in-depth discussion of whether TBT and SPS measures should be included in substantially all trade provisions, see Trachtman (2003).
15. There is an argument that "internal measures" taken within a PTA that are non-discriminatory do not fall under "other regulatory restrictions on commerce". On the other hand, agreements between WTO members that adopt higher standards than existing international standards can be seen to be at odds with the MFN obligations in the GATT and specific agreements, such as Article 2.1 of the TBT Agreement.
16. On the other hand, the Committee on Trade in Services, to which notifications of PTAs covering services have to be made, has discretion to waive an examination of the compliance with Article V (an option that does not exist with Art. XXIV), which could mean less effective scrutiny of services provisions in PTAs.
17. This is an illustration of the limits to formal bilateral transatlantic agreements, which have been proposed on a number of occasions but always rejected on the grounds that anything formal would undermine the multilateral rules in the WTO. In the particular case of the free trade agreement in services, there was also opposition from France and other EU member states to the substance of the proposed agreement.

Annexes

Annex 1

The United States of America's preferential trade agreements: Summary of agreements and negotiations as at July 2008

Overview

1. The United States has successfully negotiated and implemented seven free trade agreements (FTAs) since the United States–Israel FTA of 1985. Six of the seven agreements were negotiated and implemented under the Bush administration between 2001 and 2006.
2. Free trade agreements have been implemented with Australia, Bahrain, Chile, Israel, Jordan, Morocco and Singapore.
3. FTAs have been signed, but not yet ratified and/or implemented, with the CAFTA–DR countries, Colombia, Oman, Peru and Korea. Negotiations have been concluded with Panama, but an agreement has not yet been signed.
4. According to the Office of the United States Trade Representative (USTR), FTA negotiations are either ongoing or intended to begin with Ecuador, Malaysia, Thailand and the United Arab Emirates.
5. The United States has also negotiated 40 bilateral investment treaties (BITs) and 24 Trade and Investment Framework Agreements (TIFAs), agreements it considers steps toward future FTAs.

Agreements implemented (7)

1. Australia
Implemented 1 January 2005.

2. Bahrain
Implemented 1 August 2006.
3. Chile
Implemented 1 January 2004.
4. Israel
Implemented 1 September 1985.
5. Jordan
Implemented 7 December 2001.
6. Morocco
Implemented 1 January 2006.
7. Singapore
Implemented 1 January 2004.

Agreements signed and/or agreed upon in principle (5)

1. CAFTA–DR
The United States, Costa Rica, El Salvador, Guatemala, Honduras, Nicaragua and the Dominican Republic agreed in principle to the Central America–Dominican Republic Free Trade Agreement (CAFTA–DR) in August 2004. The treaty has been entered into force by:
United States: 2 August 2005
El Salvador: 1 March 206
Guatemala: 1 July 2006
Honduras: 1 April 2006
Nicaragua: 1 April 2006
Dominican Republic: 1 March 2007
Costa Rica has not ratified CAFTA–DR. The International Affairs Committee of the Costa Rican Congress approved CAFTA–DR on 12 December 2006; and the text was approved by referendum in October 2007.
2. Colombia
Negotiations for a bilateral FTA were launched on 18 May 2004 as part of the negotiations for a US–Andean Free Trade Agreement. It was signed by Deputy US Trade Representative John Veroneau and Colombian Minister of Trade, Industry and Tourism Jorge Humberto Botero on 22 November 2006. The accord reached between the Congress and the administration on 10 May 2007 was expected to help facilitate congressional approval. However, leading congressional Democrats, including House Speaker Nancy Pelosi (California) and Ways and Means Committee Chair Charles Rangel (New York), have said they would oppose the FTA until there is concrete evidence of reduced violence against trade unionists. On 10 April 2008, House Democrats voted to eliminate the

requirement to approve or reject the FTA within 90 days, thus postponing action indefinitely. The fate of the agreement is likely to be linked to action to expand the provisions of Trade Adjustment Assistance.

3. Oman
Signed by President Bush on 26 September 2006 and approved by Congress and Senate in June and July 2007. The agreement has not yet been implemented.

4. Peru
Negotiations for a bilateral FTA were launched on 18 May 2004 as part of the negotiations for a US–Andean Free Trade Agreement. It was signed by US Trade Representative Rob Portman and Peruvian Minister of Foreign Trade and Tourism Alfredo Ferrero Diez Canseco on 12 April 2006. The agreement has not yet been ratified. The accord reached on 10 May 2007 between the Congress and the administration was expected to facilitate congressional approval. Leading Democrats declared the FTA as being worthy of support but required a change in Peruvian labour law prior to giving approval. The House passed the implementing bill for the agreement on 8 November 2007.

5. Korea
Negotiations were completed at the end of April 2007 and the text finalized on 30 June. However, leading Democrats, including House Speaker Pelosi and Ways and Means Chair Rangel, have said they will oppose the FTA because of the imbalance in US–Korea trade in automobiles. As with the Colombia FTA, action is likely to be linked to expansion of Trade Adjustment Assistance.

Agreements with negotiations concluded but no final agreement (1)

1. Panama
Negotiations were completed on 19 December 2006, with the understanding that the FTA is subject to further discussions regarding labour. Democrat leaders have declared the FTA as being worthy of support but require a change in Panamanian law prior to giving approval.

Agreements in negotiation (4)

1. Ecuador
Negotiations for a bilateral FTA were launched on 18 May 2004 as part of the negotiations for a US–Andean Free Trade Agreement.

2. Malaysia
US Trade Representative Rob Portman announced the intention to negotiate a free trade agreement with Malaysia on 8 March 2006. The administration said in March 2008 that it aims to conclude negotiations in 2008. US sticking points are access to Malaysia's financial services market and government procurement.

3. Thailand
President Bush first announced his intent to enter FTA negotiations in October 2003. Progress was made through six rounds of negotiations in 2004 and 2005, but was on hold after the 2006 military coup. Talks resumed in March 2008. A particular US concern relates to protection for intellectual property rights following Thailand's issuance of compulsory licences for drugs to treat HIV-AIDS and heart disease.

4. United Arab Emirates
On 15 November 2004 the USTR announced its intent to negotiate an FTA. Negotiations have been ongoing since March 2005.

Potential negotiations

1. Negotiations could be forthcoming with many countries that have signed either a bilateral investment treaty (BIT) or a Trade and Investment Framework Agreement (TIFA) with the United States. All potential FTA partners must have signed a TIFA with the United States.
2. FTA negotiations are most likely to occur with countries that are potential members of the Free Trade Area of the Americas, countries that are part of the Association of Southeast Asian Nations (ASEAN), and Middle Eastern countries affected by the Middle East Free Trade Initiative.
3. The list of countries that have signed either BITs or TIFAs include: Afghanistan, Albania, Algeria, Argentina, Armenia, the members of ASEAN, Azerbaijan, Bangladesh, Bolivia, Bulgaria, Cambodia, Cameroon, the members of the Common Market for Eastern and Southern Africa, Democratic Republic of the Congo (Kinshasa), Republic of the Congo (Brazzaville), Croatia, Czech Republic, Egypt, Estonia, Georgia, Ghana, Grenada, Jamaica, Kazakhstan, Kuwait, Kyrgyzstan, Latvia, Lithuania, Mauritius, Moldova, Mongolia, Mozambique, New Zealand, Nigeria, Pakistan, Poland, Qatar, Romania, Saudi Arabia, Senegal, Slovakia, Sri Lanka, South Africa, Tajikistan, Trinidad & Tobago, Tunisia, Turkey, Turkmenistan, Ukraine, Uzbekistan, the West African Economic and Monetary Union, Yemen.

Annex 2

The European Union's preferential trade agreements: Summary of agreements and negotiations as at July 2008

Customs unions entered into force (2)

1. Andorra
1 July 1991.
2. Turkey
31 December 1995.

FTAs entered into force (20)

1. Bulgaria
Europe Agreement: 31 December 1994.
2. Romania
Europe Agreement: 1 May 1993.
3. Faroe Islands (Denmark)
Free Trade Agreement: 1 January 1997.
4. Switzerland
Free Trade Agreement: 1 January 1973.
5. Macedonia
Stabilisation and Association Agreement: 1 May 2004.
6. Croatia
Stabilisation and Association Agreement: 1 February 2005.
7. Chile
Association Agreement and Additional Protocol: 1 February 2003.

8. Mexico
Economic Partnership, Political Coordination and Cooperation Agreement: 1 July 2000.
9. South Africa
Trade, Development and Cooperation Agreement: 1 January 2000.
10. Certain Overseas Countries and Territories (OCT/PTOM II)
Association Agreement: 1 January 1971.
11. Algeria
Association Agreement (EU–Mediterranean Agreement): 1 September 2005.
12. Egypt
Association Agreement (EU–Mediterranean Agreement): 31 December 2003.
13. Israel
Association Agreement (EU–Mediterranean Agreement): 1 June 2000.
14. Jordan
Association Agreement (EU–Mediterranean Agreement): 1 May 2002.
15. Lebanon
Interim Agreement (EU–Mediterranean Agreement): 1 March 2002.
16. Morocco
Association Agreement (EU–Mediterranean Agreement): 1 March 2000.
17. Palestinian Authority
Association Agreement (Interim EU–Mediterranean Agreement): 1 July 1997.
18. Syria
Cooperation Agreement (EU–Mediterranean Agreement): 1 July 1977 (negotiations for Association Agreement concluded in 2004, but agreement not yet signed).
19. Tunisia
Association Agreement (EU–Mediterranean Agreement): 1 March 1998.
20. ACP countries
Partnership Agreement (Cotonou Agreement): 1 March 2000.

FTAs signed and/or agreed upon in principle (1)

1. Albania
Negotiating directives for a Stabilisation and Association Agreement were adopted by the Council on 21–23 October 2002. Negotiations formally opened on 31 January 2003. The Stabilisation and Association Agreement with Albania and the Interim Agreement (IA) with Albania were signed in Luxemburg on 12 June 2006. The date of entry into force of the IA is not defined yet.

FTAs in negotiation phase (13)

1. ACP countries
Draft directive adopted by the Commission on April 2002; Council Decision on 17 June 2002.

Negotiation of Economic Partnership Agreements: 1st phase "all ACP" launched on 27 September 2002; 2nd phase "regional negotiations" began in October 2003. Interim EPAs were concluded with a range of ACP states in December 2007, but by no means all. Some EPAs were with regions, such as the Caribbean Forum of ACP States (CARIFORUM), the only region to conclude negotiations on a comprehensive EPA before the December 2007 deadline set by the European Commission in view of the European Union's WTO obligations, and some interim EPAs were concluded with individual countries. Negotiations are ongoing on comprehensive EPAs.

2. Euro-Mediterranean free trade area
At a bilateral level, every Mediterranean country involved in the Euro-Med Partnership, except Syria, has concluded and currently implements Association Agreements with the European Union. Collectively, the Association Agreements replace the previous generation of cooperation agreements signed in the 1970s and constitute the foundation for the FTA.

At the Fifth Euro-Mediterranean Ministerial Trade Conference held on 24 March 2006 in Marrakech, Euro-Med ministers confirmed the ongoing negotiations with a view to conclusion in 2010.

3. Mercosur
Negotiating directives for an Association Agreement: 13 September 1999. Negotiations are ongoing but progress is slow owing to the Doha Development Agenda.

4. Gulf Cooperation Council (GCC)
Revised and updated negotiating directives for an FTA from July 2001. Negotiations are ongoing.

5. Bosnia and Herzegovina
Negotiating directives on a Stabilisation and Association Agreement were adopted on 21 November 2005. Negotiations are ongoing.

6. Iran
Negotiating directives: June 2002. Negotiations are ongoing.

7. Iraq
Negotiating directives: March 2006. Launch: 20 November 2006.

8. Kazakhstan
Recommendation from the Commission to the Council to authorize the Commission to open negotiations for a new Enhanced Agreement negotiation mandate was adopted by the Council on 13 November 2006. Negotiations are ongoing.

9. Montenegro

Negotiating directives on a Stabilisation and Association Agreement were adopted on 3 October 2005 for negotiations with the State Union of Serbia and Montenegro. Following Montenegrin independence in May 2006, new negotiating directives were adopted on 24 July 2006. Negotiations are ongoing.

10. Serbia

Negotiating directives on a Stabilisation and Association Agreement (SAA) were adopted on 3 October 2005 for negotiations with the State Union of Serbia and Montenegro. Following Montenegrin independence in May 2006, revised negotiating directives were adopted on 24 July 2006. Negotiations were put on hold on 3 May 2006 owing to Serbia's lack of cooperation with the International Criminal Tribunal for the former Yugoslavia. In November 2007, the SAA was initialled as a means of promoting political and economic reform in Serbia.

11. South Korea

A negotiating mandate was adopted in April 2007. By February 2008, agreement had been reached on the treatment of anti-dumping, dispute settlement, intellectual property rights (IPRs) and subsidies. But a number of contentious issues had been shelved pending agreement in other areas. Particular difficulties relate to autos trade (where the European Union is seeking the same treatment as is afforded the United States in Korea–United States, as well as Korea's acceptance of international standards as being equivalent to domestic standards) and rules of origin (where Korean manufacturers, which outsource much of their production offshore, seek a relaxation of RoOs requiring 60 per cent of finished items to be produced in Korea).

12. India

During the EU–India summit on 7 September 2005, the European Union and India adopted a Joint Action Plan to further increase bilateral trade and economic cooperation. The European Commission commissioned consultant reports on the feasibility of an EU–India FTA. A negotiating mandate was adopted in April 2007.

In March 2008, India announced that it was not aiming to complete negotiations in 2008. Problem areas for the European Union have been identified as services, IPRs and government procurement. The European Union has a negative list (where there will be no tariff changes) of 416 items, half of which are in chemicals, pharmaceuticals or plastics.

13. ASEAN

Negotiations began on 4 May 2008. Coverage will include investment, Mode 4 of services delivery and IPRs.

FTAs in exploration phase (7)

1. Andean Community (CAN)

At the summit between the European Union and Latin America and the Caribbean (EU–LAC) in May 2002 the door for future negotiations of an EU–CAN FTA was opened. As long as Venezuela is legally a CAN member, it is likely to veto any negotiation with the European Union. Once Venezuela formally leaves the group, the issue is likely to be revived. (Negotiations have now started.)

2. Central American Free Trade Agreement (CAFTA)

At the 4th EU–LAC summit in May 2006, the decision on the launch of negotiations of an EU–CAFTA FTA was taken. The European Commission is currently working on a draft mandate to put to the Council. (Negotiations have now started.)

3. Canada

Recommendation from the Commission to the Council to authorize the Commission to negotiate a bilateral Trade and Investment Enhancement Agreement with Canada (15 June 2004). Under discussion in Council.

4. China

A negotiating mandate to launch negotiations on a new Partnership and Cooperation Agreement with China, including aspects of trade and investment, was approved by the Council in December 2005. Negotiations were formally launched at the EU–China summit in September 2006, but no meeting is scheduled yet. Negotiation modalities are still to be agreed.

5. Russia

Recommendation from the Commission to the Council to authorize the Commission to open negotiations for a new Enhanced Agreement. Negotiation mandate adopted by the Council on 13 November 2006.

6. Ukraine

Recommendation from the Commission to the Council to authorize the Commission to open negotiations for a new Enhanced Agreement. Recommendation not yet adopted.

7. Moldova

Partnership and Cooperation Agreement (PCA) between Moldova and the European Union was signed in 1994 and entered into force in July 1998.

Article 4 of the PCA states that the parties shall examine jointly whether circumstances allow the start of negotiations on the establishment of an FTA. There has been no recent progress.

Annex 3

EFTA's preferential trade agreements and Joint Declarations on Co-operation: Summary of agreements and negotiations as at July 2008

Overview

- The states of the European Free Trade Association (EFTA) claim to have the world's largest free trade network, covering 51 countries and territories, and reaching a population of 900 million people on 4 continents.
- EFTA and the European Economic Community (EEC) were the first two successful examples of regional trade agreements as foreseen by Article XXIV of the General Agreement on Tariffs and Trade (GATT). In addition to the bilateral agreements signed with the EEC in the mid-1970s, the EFTA countries, as a group, signed their first FTA with Spain in 1979.
- Since 1990, EFTA's third-country policy has gone through three distinct phases:
  1. 1990–1995: basic FTAs signed with the transition economies of Central and Eastern Europe.
  2. 1995–2000: basic FTAs signed with countries on the southern and eastern rim of the Mediterranean. As with the first phase, the second phase was a response to EU initiatives for regional integration. This policy was known as *parallelism* and it was meant to avoid any discrimination for EFTA's economic operators vis-à-vis the European Union.
  3. 2000–present: transcontinental agreements that are also broader in scope in that they cover new areas such as services, investment, public procurement and competition.

- In addition to free trade agreements, the EFTA states have also signed a number of Joint Declarations on Co-operation. These are framework agreements signalling both sides' desire to pursue an FTA at some point in the future. The Joint Declarations institutionalize the relationship because the parties meet in a Joint Committee, usually every two years, to review their cooperation on trade and related matters and to discuss any other issues of mutual interest.
- The EFTA states are increasingly using feasibility studies as a first method to explore the possibility of furthering trade relations. For instance, the groundwork for the EFTA–Republic of Korea FTA was established by a feasibility study.
- The EFTA FTAs have thus far been limited to relatively small or medium-sized economies. But the coherence of EFTA as one negotiating partner will be increasingly challenged as the pressure to conclude FTAs with more significant economies mounts. For example, Iceland is negotiating an FTA with China outside of the EFTA framework. Switzerland is also conducting negotiations with Japan without its EFTA partners.

Agreements finalized (19)

1. EFTA 4 (Vaduz Convention)
Entered into force on 1 June 2002.
2. EU 25
The European Economic Area (Iceland, Norway and Liechtenstein): entered into force on 1 May 1994.
Bilateral agreements (Switzerland): entered into force on 21 June 1999.
3. Bulgaria
Entered into force on 1 July 1993.
4. Croatia
Entered into force on 1 April 2002.
5. Faeroe Islands
Bilateral agreements with all EFTA states. Iceland signed a comprehensive trade agreement, creating a common market, with the Faeroes in 2007.
6. Macedonia
Entered into force on 1 May 2002.
7. Romania
Entered into force on 1 May 1993.
8. Turkey
Entered into force on 1 April 1992.

9. Morocco
Entered into force on 1 December 1999.
10. Tunisia
Entered into force on 1 June 2005 for Switzerland and Liechtenstein, 1 August 2005 for Norway and 1 March 2006 for Iceland.
11. Southern African Customs Union (Botswana, Lesotho, Namibia, South Africa, Swaziland)
Signed 26 June 2006; awaiting ratification.
12. Israel
Entered into force on 1 January 1993.
13. Republic of Korea
Entered into force on 1 September 2006.
14. Lebanon
Signed in June 2004; entered into force on 1 January 2007.
15. Palestinian Authority
Entered into force on 1 July 1999.
16. Singapore
Entered into force on 1 January 2003.
17. Chile
Entered into force on 1 December 2004.
18. Mexico
Entered into force on 1 July 2001.
19. Egypt
Negotiations concluded on 31 October 2006; awaiting signature and ratification.

Ongoing FTA negotiations (4)

1. Gulf Cooperation Council (Bahrain, Kuwait, Oman, Qatar, Saudi Arabia, UAE)
The second round of negotiations took place in Riyadh, 13–15 November 2006.
2. Canada
After being stalled for the better part of a decade, owing to differences relating to shipbuilding, FTA negotiations between the EFTA states and Canada were concluded in January 2008. EFTA states have reached bilateral agreements with Canada on the reduction of agricultural tariffs.
3. Thailand
The second round of negotiations between the EFTA states and Thailand took place 16–20 January 2006. A third round was scheduled to take place in April 2006 but was postponed owing to the political situation in Thailand.

4. China

Iceland and China have finalized a feasibility study and have begun FTA negotiations. The Chinese seem to be unwilling to expand this process to the other EFTA states. It is likely that Switzerland's tough stance during China's WTO accession affected this decision.

Ongoing FTA feasibility studies (4)

1. Indonesia
A joint feasibility study between the EFTA states and Indonesia was launched in December 2005.

2. Japan
Bilateral negotiations between Switzerland and Japan began on 15 May 2007. The other EFTA states continue, with "tacit" Swiss approval, to push the Japanese for an EFTA approach. The Japanese have been reluctant to approach Norway and Iceland because of their strong offensive interests in fisheries.

3. India
EFTA ministers signed a Record of Understanding with India's Minister for Commerce and Industry, Mr Kamal Nath, in November 2006. The deal establishes a Joint Study Group to examine the feasibility of negotiating a possible comprehensive Economic Agreement between India and the EFTA states.

4. Malaysia
Feasibility stage.

Joint Declarations on Co-operation

1. Albania
Signed on 10 December 1992.

2. Serbia
Signed on 12 December 2000. There is some confusion following the break-up of Serbia and Montenegro, but it seems that the Joint Declaration on Co-operation applies only to Serbia, as Serbia is legally obligated to take over all agreements formerly signed by Serbia and Montenegro. The EFTA states are following Serbia's developments with the European Union and are unwilling to move towards FTA negotiations at this time. Serbia, however, has made repeated requests to move forward.

3. Ukraine
Signed on 19 June 2000. The EFTA states, especially Norway and Iceland, are eager to move the process forward towards FTA negotiations

but will not do so until Ukraine accedes to the WTO. There is, however, a consensus developing within the EFTA circle to start preliminary, informal "negotiations". This is also influenced by developments in the Ukraine–EU relationship.

4. GCC

Signed on 23 May 2000. Negotiations were launched on 21 June 2006 (see above).

5. Algeria

Signed on 12 December 2002. At the third Joint Committee meeting on 8 November 2005, both sides affirmed their desire to begin FTA negotiations in 2006. Informal negotiations have taken place on the margins of technical assistance workshops. Both sides need to finalize the Agreement to take advantage of the Euro-Med cumulation agreement (2010).

6. Egypt

Signed on 8 December 1995. FTA negotiations were finalized on 31 October 2006. Fish and agriculture had been the main stumbling blocks before the impasse was broken at the political level.

7. Colombia

Signed on 18 May 2006. The first Joint Committee meeting took place in Bogotá on 6 October 2006.

8. Peru

Signed on 24 April 2006. The first Joint Committee meeting took place in Lima on 3 October 2006.

9. Mercosur (Argentina, Brazil, Paraguay, Uruguay)

Signed on 12 December 2000. There have been two Joint Committee meetings, the last in November 2004. There are both substance and political issues that would make future negotiations unlikely in the near future. The EFTA states will, however, keep a close eye on EU–Mercosur developments and, most likely, base future actions on any breakthroughs between the two sides.

Possible future FTAs

Countries for which the EFTA states have indicated an interest, or have been approached, in furthering trade relations:

United States (Switzerland undertook a bilateral study but, reportedly, decided against an FTA because of agricultural concerns)

Vietnam

Central America

Russia (the EFTA states have signed a Memorandum of Understanding and would like to begin FTA negotiations as soon as Russia accedes to the WTO)

Montenegro
Bosnia Herzegovina
Iran
Libya
Syria

Annex 4

Japan's preferential trade agreements as at July 2008

Overview

Japan is a latecomer to bilateral preferential trade agreements, with only six having entered into force (Singapore, Mexico, Malaysia, Chile, Thailand and Indonesia), three agreements signed (ASEAN, Philippines, Brunei), and six agreements under negotiation (Korea, Gulf Cooperation Council, India, Vietnam, Australia and Switzerland).

Japan calls most of its agreements Economic Partnership Agreements (EPAs) to indicate that they go beyond traditional PTAs to include agreements on the free movement of labour, tourism, intellectual property considerations, etc. There seems to be consensus (and admission by the Ministry of Economy, Trade and Industry) that EPAs are in practice similar to what other countries would call FTAs.

Agreements entered into force (6)

1. Singapore
Entered into force on 30 November 2002.
2. Mexico
Entered into force on 1 April 2005.
3. Malaysia
Entered into force on 13 July 2006.

4. Chile
Entered into force in September 2007.
5. Thailand
Entered into force in November 2007.
6. Indonesia
Entered into force in July 2008.

PTAs/EPAs signed (3)

1. Philippines
Signed by Prime Minister Koizumi and President Arroyo on 8 September 2006; ratified by Japan on 6 December 2006.
2. Brunei
Signed in June 2007.
3. ASEAN–Japan Comprehensive Economic Partnership
Signing completed with the formal assent of Malaysia on 14 April 2008. The agreement, which awaits domestic legislative approval, will become active on a country-by-country basis. Rice, beef and dairy will remain protected, as "sensitive" sectors.

PTAs/EPAs in the negotiation phase (6)

1. South Korea
Negotiation of the free trade agreement was launched in December 2003; six rounds of negotiations were conducted, the last of which was held in November 2004. Negotiations then stalled owing to worsened political relations and disagreements over agricultural issues, and have not resumed.
2. Gulf Cooperation Council
The first round of negotiations was held in September 2006.
3. India
Negotiations began in January 2007. The stated aim was to conclude negotiations in two years. The coverage of the agreement will include services, trade facilitation and investment.
4. Vietnam
A first round of formal EPA negotiations was held in January 2007.
5. Australia
Negotiations began in April 2007.
6. Switzerland
Negotiations began in May 2007. It has been reported (*Bridges Weekly Trade News Digest*, 16 May 2007) that agricultural sectors are not on the bargaining table.

Possible future PTAS (14)

Countries for which Japan has indicated that "private sector studies are ongoing ... or their governments/business community have indicated interest in EPA with Japan" include:
United States
Canada
Mercosur
Brazil
Argentina
Iceland
Norway
Israel
Morocco
Egypt
South Africa
China
Taiwan
Mongolia

Annex 5

Singapore's preferential trade agreements as at July 2008

Overview

- Singapore's drive in pursuing preferential trade agreements started in the mid-1990s (the ASEAN Declaration was signed in 1967 but its Common Effective Preferential Tariff came into effect in 1993). Its PTA efforts gained momentum in the late 1990s.
- Singapore's policy of comprehensive PTAs is underpinned by the Ministry of Trade and Industry's goals for Singapore's network of PTAs as going beyond trade and business expansion and addressing support for its business community in moving up the value-added ladder and knowledge chain.
- Singapore has two sets of PTAs: the first group are those addressed as a part of the Association of Southeast Asian Nations (though often with a strong bilateral dimension); the second group are those concluded on a bilateral basis by Singapore alone.

Agreements entered into force (13)

1. ASEAN

The Association of Southeast Asian Nations has two tiers of nations. The "ASEAN 6" (Brunei, Indonesia, Malaysia, Philippines, Singapore and Thailand) are the original members of the ASEAN Free Trade Area (AFTA). The Common Effective Preferential Tariff (CEPT) Scheme for the AFTA came into effect in 1993. In the CEPT, the ASEAN 6 agreed to reduce their tariffs to 0–5 per cent over 15 years, but this schedule was accelerated and this threshold was achieved in 2002.

The second tier comprises the new ASEAN countries that joined between 1995 and 1999 (Cambodia, Lao PDR, Myanmar and Vietnam). The "Mekong 4" have more flexible liberalization commitments.

2. ASEAN–China

The ASEAN–China Trade in Goods Agreement entered into force on 20 July 2005 (initially between China, Brunei, Indonesia, Malaysia, Myanmar, Thailand and Singapore). This was followed by an agreement, signed in January 2007 for implementation in July 2007, for the liberalization of trade in services. The aim is for the FTA to be fully operational by 2015 (five years earlier for the six more advanced ASEAN members).

3. ASEAN–Korea

Entered into force in July 2006, except for Thailand, which continues to negotiate owing to concerns in agriculture.

4. Singapore–Australia

Entered into force on 28 July 2003.

5. Singapore–EFTA

Entered into force on 1 January 2003.

6. Singapore–Hashemite Kingdom of Jordan

Entered into force on 22 August 2005.

7. Singapore–India

The Comprehensive Economic Cooperation Agreement (CECA) entered into force on 1 August 2005. Until this comprehensive agreement was signed, most Indian FTAs tended to concentrate only on goods. The CECA is the first Indian agreement that includes goods, services, provisions on investment protection and a double taxation treaty.

8. Singapore–Japan

Entered into force on 30 November 2002. This agreement is currently being reviewed in order to expand the product coverage, improve the rules of origin and enhance the financial services commitments.

9. Singapore–Korea

Entered into force on 2 March 2006.

10. Singapore–New Zealand

Entered into force on 1 January 2001.

11. Singapore–Panama

Entered into force on 24 July 2006.

12. Trans-Pacific Strategic Economic Partnership Agreement

An FTA between Brunei, New Zealand, Chile and Singapore. The agreement was signed by Chile, New Zealand and Singapore on 18 July 2005, while Brunei signed on 2 August 2005. The Agreement entered into force between New Zealand and Singapore on 28 May 2006, on 12 July 2006 for Brunei and on 8 November 2006 for Chile.

13. Singapore–United States

Entered into force on 1 January 2004. It was the first free trade agreement signed by Washington with an Asian state.

Negotiations concluded (2)

1. ASEAN–Japan Comprehensive Economic Partnership (see Annex 4)

2. Singapore–Qatar

On 10 June 2005 Singapore's Minister for Trade and Industry and Qatar's Minister of Economy and Commerce signed a declaration stating that the negotiations had been substantially concluded.

Agreements under negotiation (11)

1. ASEAN–Australia/New Zealand

The seventh round of negotiations was held in September 2006.

2. ASEAN–India

In November 2006, ASEAN doubled the number of products on its negative list (items exempted from phased tariff cuts), rendering uncertain the outcome of these long-pending negotiations.

3. Singapore–Canada

During the 2006 Ministerial Meeting of the Asia-Pacific Economic Cooperation Council, the Ministers of International Trade of Canada and Singapore agreed to resume formal negotiations, which had stalled in late 2003.

4. Singapore–China

Negotiations were launched on 25 August 2006. The first round of negotiations was held on 26 October 2006 in Beijing.

5. Singapore–Egypt

On 13 November 2006, Singapore and Egypt signed a Declaration of Intent to start negotiations on the Egypt–Singapore Comprehensive Economic Cooperation Agreement, envisaged as a high-standard and comprehensive agreement that will include the establishment of a free trade area between the two countries.

6. Singapore–Mexico

Negotiations for the Mexico–Singapore FTA started in July 2000. Six rounds of trade talks have taken place to date.

7. Singapore–Pakistan

The third round of negotiations was completed in May 2006.

8. Singapore–Peru
The third round of negotiations was concluded on 29 September 2006.
9. Singapore–State of Kuwait
The second round of negotiations was held 11–13 April 2005 in Kuwait.
10. Singapore–Gulf Cooperation Council
During the Prime Minister of Singapore's official visit to Saudi Arabia from 24 to 27 November 2006, the two countries agreed to hold the first round of negotiations in early 2007.
11. Singapore–United Arab Emirates
On 11 March 2005, Singapore and the United Arab Emirates signed an Economic, Trade and Technical Cooperation Agreement, which included the declaration that this agreement would lead to the launch of negotiations of a bilateral trade agreement.

Exploration phase (4)

1. Singapore–Southern African Customs Union (South Africa, Botswana, Lesotho, Namibia and Swaziland)
In April 2005, Singapore and the Southern African Customs Union announced that they would begin talks on a free trade agreement.
2. Singapore–Saudi Arabia
In early 2005 Singapore and Saudi Arabia announced that they were exploring the possibility of signing an FTA along with an Investment Guarantee Agreement (including some of the typical provisions normally included in bilateral investment treaties).
3. Singapore–Bahrain
Preliminary discussions on this FTA were held on the sidelines of the Prime Minister of Singapore's official visit to Bahrain in February 2004.
4. Singapore–Sri Lanka
Exploratory talks began in October 2003 for a Comprehensive Economic Partnership Agreement.

Possible future FTAs (4)

1. Singapore–European Union
In May 2006, Lim Hng Kiang, Singapore's Trade and Industry Minister, urged the European Union, as Singapore's second-largest trading partner, to negotiate a free trade agreement.
2. Singapore–Uzbekistan
On 2 November 2006, Singapore and Uzbekistan signed an Economic Cooperation Agreement, a declaration to strengthen and develop trade and investment cooperation between the two countries.

3. Singapore–Slovak Republic

An Investment Guarantee Agreement (including typical BIT provisions) was signed on 13 October 2006.

4. Singapore–Iran

In July 2004 Singapore and Iran committed to explore a free trade agreement as part of a wider network to deepen bilateral economic ties. This was followed by a visit by then Prime Minister of Singapore, Goh Chok Tong, to Iran. However, the trend towards growing international pressure to curb Iran's nuclear programme and the sanctions mandated by the UN Security Council constitute major setbacks to progress in this FTA.

References

Ando, M. and F. Kimura (2007), "Japanese FTA/EPA Strategies and Agricultural Protection", Keio University Market Quality Research Project, Discussion Paper DP2006-24, Tokyo, January.

Bagwell, K. and R. W. Staiger (1997), "Multilateral Tariff Cooperation during the Formation of Customs Unions", *Journal of International Economics*, 42: 91–112.

—— (1999), "Regionalism and Multilateral Tariff Cooperation", in J. Piggot and A. Woodland (eds), *International Trade Policy and the Pacific Rim*. New York: St Martin's Press.

Baldwin, R. E. (1989), "The Growth Effects of 1992", *Economic Policy*, 9: 247–281.

—— (1996), "Growth and European Integration: Towards an Empirical Assessment", CEPR Discussion Paper Series No. 1393.

—— (2008), "Sequencing and Depth of Regional Economic Integration: Lessons for the Americas from Europe", *World Economy*, 31(1): 5–30.

Baldwin, R. E. and A. Venables (1995), "Regional Economic Integration", in G. M. Grossman and K. Rogoff (eds), *Handbook of International Economics*, Vol. III. Amsterdam: Elsevier.

Bayne, N. and S. Woolcock (2007), *The New Economic Diplomacy: Decision-Making and Negotiation in International Economic Relations*, 2nd edn. London: Ashgate.

Bergsten, F. (2005), "A New Foreign Economic Policy for the United States", in *The United States and the World Economy*. Washington DC: Peterson Institute for International Economics.

Bhagwati, J. (1990), "Departures from Multilateralism: Regionalism and Aggressive Unilateralism", *The Economic Journal*, 100: 1304–1317.

———— (1999), "Regionalism and Multilateralism: An Overview", in J. Bhagwati, K. Pravin and A. Panagariya, *Trading Blocs: Alternative Approaches to Analyzing Preferential Trade Agreements*. Cambridge, MA: MIT Press.

———— (2003), "Testimony", Subcommittee on Domestic and International Monetary Policy, Trade and Technology, US House of Representatives, Committee on Financial Services, 1 April, ⟨http://financialservices.house.gov/media/pdf/040103jb.pdf⟩ (accessed 24 September 2008).

Bhagwati, J. and A. Panagariya (1996), "Preferential Trading Areas and Multilateralism: Strangers, Friends or Foes?", in J. Bhagwati and A. Panagariya (eds), *The Economics of Preferential Trading Areas*. Washington, DC: AEI Press.

Bond, E. and C. Syropoulos (1996), "Trading Blocs and Sustainability of Interregional Cooperation", in M. Canzoneri, W. Ethier and V. Grilli (eds), *The New Transatlantic Economy*. Cambridge: Cambridge University Press.

Bridges Weekly Trade News Digest (various dates). Geneva: International Centre for Trade and Sustainable Development.

Burfisher, M., S. Robinson and K. Thierfelder (2003), "Regionalism: Old and New, Theory and Practice", paper presented at the International Conference on "Agricultural Policy Reform and the WTO: Where Are We Heading?", Capri, Italy, 23–26 June.

Cadot, O. (2004), "Rules of Origin in North–South Preferential Trading Arrangements – With an Application to NAFTA", Research Unit Working Papers, Laboratoire d'Economie Appliquée, INRA.

Cadot, O., J. de Melo and M. Olarreaga (1999), "Regional Integration and Lobbying for Tariffs against Non-Members", *International Economic Review*, 40: 635–657.

Chaitoo, R. (2008), "Services and Investment in the Cariforum–EC Economic Partnership Agreement", ComSec/CALC Workshop, St Lucia, 27–28 May.

Commonwealth Secretariat (2008), "EPAs: The Way Forward for the ACP", High Level Technical Meeting, South Africa, April, ⟨http://www.thecommonwealth.org/files/177585/FileName/SERVICES%20SESSION%20docrevised2.pdf⟩ (accessed 15 September 2008).

Corden, M. W. (1972), "Economies of Scale and Customs Union Theory", *Journal of Political Economy*, 80: 456–475.

Dent, C. (2003), "Networking the Region? The Emergence and Impact of Asian-Pacific Bilateral Free Trade Agreement Projects", *The Pacific Review*, 16(1): 1–28.

Drysdale, P. (2005), "Regional Cooperation in East Asia and FTA Strategies", *Pacific Economic Papers*, 344.

Estevadeordal, A. and K. Suominen (2003), "Rules of Origin in the World Trading System", paper prepared for the seminar on "Regional Trade Agreements and the WTO", World Trade Organization, Washington DC, 14 November.

Estevadeordal, A., C. Freund and E. Ornelas (2008), "Does Regionalism Affect Trade Liberalization Towards Non-Members?", CEP Discussion Paper No. 868, Centre for Economic Performance, London School of Economics and Political Science, May.

Ethier, W. (1998), "Controversy: Regionalism versus Multilateralism: The New Regionalism", *Economic Journal* 108 (July): 1149–1161.

European Commission (2005), *The Rules of Origin in Preferential Trade Arrangements: Orientations for the Future*, COM(2005) 100 final, Brussels, 16 March.
——— (2006), Communication from the Commission to the Council, the European Parliament, the European Economic and Social Committee and the Committee of the Regions, *Global Europe: Competing in the World. A Contribution to the EU's Growth and Jobs Strategy*, COM(2006) 567 final, 4 October 2006, ⟨http://trade.ec.europa.eu/doclib/docs/2006/october/tradoc_130370.pdf⟩ (accessed 16 October 2008).

Evenett, S. and B. Hoekman (2005), "International Cooperation and Reform of Public Procurement Policies", Policy Research Working Paper 3720, World Bank, Washington, DC, September.

Evenett, S. and M. Meier (2007), "An Interim Assessment of the U.S. Trade Policy of 'Competitive Liberalization'", University of St. Gallen Economics Discussion Paper No. 2007-18, February.

Fink, C. and M. Molinuevo (2007), "East Asian Free Trade Agreements in Services: Roaring Tigers or Timid Pandas?", draft.

Fiorentino, R., L. Verdeja and C. Toqueboeuf (2007), "The Changing Landscape of Regional Trade Agreements: 2006 Update", WTO Discussion Paper No. 12, World Trade Organization, Geneva.

Fliess, B. and I. Lejarraga (2005), "Non-tariff Barriers of Concern to Developing Countries", in *Looking beyond Tariffs: The Role of Non-Tariff Barriers in World Trade*. Paris: Organisation for Economic Co-operation and Development.

Francois, J., M. McQueen and G. Wignaraja (2005), "EU–Developing Country FTAs: Overview and Analysis", paper prepared for the United Nations Task Force on the Millennium Development Goals.

Frankel, J. A., E. Stein and S. J. Wei (1995), "Trading Blocs: The Natural, the Unnatural and the Super-natural", *Journal of Development Economics*, 47: 61–95.

Freund, C. (2000), "Multilateralism and the Endogenous Formation of Free Trade Agreements", *Journal of International Economics*, 115: 1317–1341.

Fukao, K., T. Okubo and R. Stern (2003), "An Econometric Analysis of Trade Diversion under NAFTA", *North American Journal of Economics and Finance*, 14.

GAO [General Accounting Office] (2004), *International Trade: Intensifying Free Trade Negotiating Agenda Calls for Better Allocation of Staff and Resources*. Washington, DC: United States General Accounting Office.

Garay, L. J. and P. De Lombaerde (2004), "Preferential Rules of Origin: Models and Levels of Rulemaking", paper prepared for UNU-CRIS/LSE Workshop on "The Interaction between Levels of Rulemaking in International Trade and Investment", Brussels, 17 December.

Garnaut, R. and D. Vines (2006), "Sorting out the Spaghetti: On Reducing the Damage from the Proliferation of Discriminatory Free Trade Areas", Australian National University, Canberra.

Geloso Grosso, M. (2001), *Regional Integration: Observed Trade and Other Economic Effects*, TD/TC/WP(2001)19/FINAL. Paris: Organisation for Economic Co-operation and Development.

Gilpin, R. (1975), *U.S. Power and the Multinational Corporation: The Political Economy of Foreign Direct Investment*. New York: Basic Books.
—— (1987), *The Political Economy of International Relations*. Princeton, NJ: Princeton University Press.
Gowa, J. (1994), *Allies, Adversaries, and International Trade*. Princeton, NJ: Princeton University Press.
Grossman, G. and E. Helpman (1994), "The Politics of Free Trade Arrangements", *American Economic Review*, 84(4): 833–850.
Haftel, Y. Z. (2004), "From the Outside Looking in: The Effect of Trading Blocs on Trade Disputes in the GATT/WTO", *International Studies Quarterly*, 48: 121–142.
Harrison, G., T. Rutherford and D. Tarr (1994), "Product Standards, Imperfect Competition and the Completion of the Market in the EC", Policy Research Working Paper No. 1293, World Bank, Washington, DC.
Heydon, K. (2008), "Asymmetric Integration: The Role of Regionalism", in G. P. Sampson and W. B. Chambers (eds), *Developing Countries and the WTO: Policy Approaches*. Tokyo: United Nations University Press.
Hilaire, A. and Y. Yang (2003), "The United States and the New Regionalism/Bilateralism", IMF Working Paper, WP/03/206, International Monetary Fund, Washington, DC.
Hoekman, B. M. and M. Kostecki (1995), *The Political Economy of the World Trading System*. Oxford: Oxford University Press.
Houde, M.-F., S. Miroudot and A. Kolse-Patil (2007), *The Interaction between Investment and Services Chapters in Selected Regional Trade Agreements*, COM/DAF/INV/TD(2006)40 FINAL. Paris: Organisation for Economic Co-operation and Development.
Hudec, R. E. (1993), *Enforcing International Trade Law: The Evolution of the Modern GATT Legal System*. Salem, MA: Butterworth Legal Publishers.
Hufbauer, G. and R. Baldwin (2006), *The Shape of a Swiss–US Free Trade Agreement*. Washington, DC: Peterson Institute for International Economics.
Hufbauer, G. and S. Rahardja (2007), *Toward a US–Indonesia Free Trade Agreement*. Washington, DC: Peterson Institute for International Economics.
Hufbauer, G. and J. Schott (2005), *NAFTA Revisited: Achievements and Challenges*. Washington, DC: Peterson Institute for International Economics.
Karacaovali, B. and N. Limao (2008), "The Clash of Liberalizations: Preferential vs. Multilateral Trade Liberalization in the European Union", *Journal of International Economics*, 74: 299–327.
Kawai, M. (2004), "Regional Economic Cooperation in East Asia", paper prepared for OECD workshop on "The Impact and Coherence of OECD Country Policies on Asian Developing Economies", Organisation for Economic Co-operation and Development, Paris, 19–20 April.
Keck, A. and R. Piermartini (2005), "The Economic Impact of EPAs in SADC Countries", WTO Staff Working Paper ERSD-2005-04, World Trade Organization, Geneva.
Kimura, F. (2007), "Japan's Free Trade Agreements and Agricultural Protection", unpublished presentation at a symposium of the Australian National

University on "Australia and Free Trade Agreements", Australian National University, Canberra, 1–2 November.

Koh, T. and C. Lin, eds (2004), *The United States Singapore Free Trade Agreement: Highlights and Insights*. Singapore: Institute of Policy Studies.

Krishna, P. (1999), "Regionalism and Multilateralism: A Political Economy Approach", in J. Bhagwati, P. Krishna and A. Panagariya (eds), *Trading Blocs: Alternative Approaches to Analysing Preferential Trade Agreements*. Cambridge, MA: MIT Press.

Krueger, A. (1999), "Trade Creation and Trade Diversion under NAFTA", NBER Working Paper No. 7429, National Bureau of Economic Research, December.

Krugman, P. (1991), "Is Bilateralism Bad?", in E. Helpman and A. Razin (eds), *International Trade and Trade Policy*. Cambridge, MA: MIT Press, pp. 9–23.

Lesser, C. (2007), "Do Bilateral and Regional Approaches for Reducing Technical Barriers to Trade Converge towards the Multilateral Trading System?", OECD Trade Policy Working Paper No. 58, TAD/TC/WP(2007)12/FINAL, Organisation for Economic Co-operation and Development, Trade and Agriculture Directorate, Paris.

Levy, P. (1997), "A Political Economic Analysis of Free Trade Agreements", *American Economic Review*, 87(4): 506–519.

Limao, N. (2007), "Are Preferential Trade Agreements with Non-Trade Objectives a Stumbling Block for Multilateral Liberalization?", *Review of Economic Studies*, 74: 821–855.

Lipsey, R. G. (1957), "The Theory of Customs Unions: Trade Diversion and Welfare", *Economica*, 24(93): 40–46.

Lucas, R. E. (1976), "Econometric Policy Evaluation: A Critique", in K. Brunner and A. H. Meltzer (eds), *The Philips Curve and Labor Markets*. Amsterdam: North-Holland.

Mansfield, E. and H. Milner (1999), "The New Wave of Regionalism", *International Organization*, 53(3): 589–627.

Mathis, J. H. (2006), "Regional Trade Agreements and Domestic Regulation: What Need for Other Restrictive Regulations of Commerce?", in L. Bartels and F. Orfino (eds), *Regional Trade Agreements and the WTO Legal System*. Oxford: Oxford University Press, pp. 79–108.

Mattoo, A. and C. Fink (2002), *Regional Agreements and Trade in Services: Policy Issues*. Washington, DC: World Bank.

Maur, J.-C. (2005), "Exporting Europe's Trade Policy", *World Economy*, 6: 1565–1590.

Mavroidis, P. C. (2002), "Judicial Supremacy, Judicial Restraint, and the Issue of Consistency of Preferential Trade Agreements with the WTO", in D. L. M. Kennedy and J. D. Southwick (eds), *The Political Economy of International Trade Law: Essays in Honor of Robert E. Hudec*. New York: Cambridge University Press, pp. 583–601.

Meade, J. (1955), *The Theory of Customs Unions*. Amsterdam: North-Holland.

Messerlin, P. (2007), *Assessing the EC Trade Policy in Goods*. Brussels: European Centre for International Political Economy.

METI (2005), *Japan's Policy on FTAs/EPAs*. Tokyo: Ministry of Economy, Trade and Industry, March.

Ministry of Foreign Affairs (2006), *Diplomatic Bluebook 2006*. Tokyo: Ministry of Foreign Affairs.

Miroudot, S. and M. Lesher (2006), *Analysis of the Impact of Investment Provisions in Regional Trade Agreements*. OECD Trade Policy Working Paper No. 36, Paris, July.

Mulgan, A. G. (2007), "Japan's FTA Policies and the Problem of Agricultural Trade Liberalisation", paper presented at ANU Symposium on "Australia and Free Trade Agreements", Australian National University, Canberra, 1–2 November.

Nottage, H. (2008), "Trade and Development", in D. Bethlehem et al. (eds), *Oxford Handbook of International Trade Law*. Oxford: Oxford University Press.

OECD (1997), *Regulatory Impact Analysis: Best Practices in OECD Countries*. Paris: Organisation for Economic Co-operation and Development.

——— (2000a), *International Trade and Core Labour Standards*. Paris: Organisation for Economic Co-operation and Development.

——— (2000b), "Trade and Regulatory Reform: Insights from OECD Country Reviews and Other Analysis", paper for the Working Party of the Trade Committee, 7–8 December, TD/TC/WP(2000)21/Final, Organisation for Economic Co-operation and Development, 3 November.

——— (2003), *Regionalism and the Multilateral Trading System*. Paris: Organisation for Economic Co-operation and Development.

——— (2004), "Trade Preference Erosion: Potential Economic Impacts", TD/TC/WP(2004)30/FINAL. Organisation for Economic Co-operation and Development, Paris.

——— (2005), "Standards and Conformity Assessment: Minimising Barriers and Maximising Benefits", Summary Report of Workshop, 21–22 November, Berlin.

Office of the United States Trade Representative (2007), *The 2007 Trade Policy Agenda and 2006 Annual Report of the President of the United States on the Trade Agreements Program*, March, p. 3, at ⟨http://www.ustr.gov/assets/Document_Library/Reports_Publications/2007/2007_Trade_Policy_Agenda/asset_upload_file278_10622.pdf⟩ (accessed 10 September 2008).

Onguglo, B. and T. Ito (2003), "How to Make EPAs WTO Compatible: Reforming the Rules on Regional Trade Agreements", Discussion Paper No. 40, European Centre for Development Policy Management, Maastricht.

Ornelas, E. (2005), "Trade Creating Free Trade Areas and the Undermining of Multilateralism", *European Economic Review*, 49: 1717–1735.

Panagariya, A. and R. Findlay (1996), "A Political-Economy Analysis of Free Trade Areas and Customs Unions", in R. Feenstra, G. Grossman and D. Irwin (eds), *The Political Economy of Trade Reform: Essays in Honor of J. Bhagwati*. Cambridge MA: MIT Press.

Park, W. and D. Lippoldt (2003), "The Impact of Trade-Related Intellectual Property Rights on Trade and Foreign Direct Investment in Developing Countries", Paper 294, *OECD Papers*, 3(11), Paris.

Piermartini R. and M. Budetta (2006), "A Mapping of Regional Rules on Technical Barriers to Trade", preliminary draft for the Inter-American Development Bank and World Bank Meeting in Washington, DC, 26–27 July.

Pugatch, M. P. (2006), "The International Regulation of IPRs in a TRIPS and TRIPS-plus World", in S. Woolcock (ed.), *Trade and Investment Rule-making: The Role of Regional and Bilateral Agreements*. Tokyo: United Nations University Press.

Reiter, J. (2003), "The EU–Mexico Free Trade Agreement: Assessing the EU Approach to Regulatory Issues", in G. Sampson and S. Woolcock (eds), *Regionalism, Multilateralism and Economic Integration: The Recent Experience*. Tokyo: United Nations University Press.

———— (2006), "International Investment Rules", in S. Woolcock (ed.), *Trade and Investment Rule-making: The Role of Regional and Bilateral Agreements*. Tokyo: United Nations University Press.

Richardson, M. (1993), "Endogenous Protection and Trade Diversion", *Journal of International Economics*, 57: 309–324.

Robertson, D. (2008), "Proliferation of PTAs in East Asia: Political and Economic Risks", paper prepared for conference on "Globalisation and the Mekong Economies", ANU College of Asia and the Pacific, Canberra, April.

Roffe, P. (2004), "Bilateral Agreements and a TRIPS-plus World: The Chile–US Free Trade Agreement", TRIPS Issues Paper 4, Quaker International Affairs Programme, Ottawa.

Sally, R. (2006), "FTAs and the Prospects for Regional Integration in Asia", ECIPE Working Paper No. 1/2006, European Centre for International Political Economy, Brussels.

Sally, R. and R. Sen (2005), "Whither Trade Policies in Southeast Asia?", *ASEAN Economic Bulletin*, 22(1).

Sampson, G. P. (1996), "Compatibility of Regional and Multilateral Trading Agreements Reforming the WTO Process", *American Economic Review*, 86(2): 88–92.

Sauvé, P. (2003), "Services", in *Regionalism and the Multilateral Trading System*. Paris: Organisation for Economic Co-operation and Development.

Schott, J. J. (2007), "The Korea–US Free Trade Agreement: A Summary Assessment", Peterson Institute for International Economics Policy Brief, Washington, DC.

Scollay, R. (2001), "New Regional Trading Arrangements in the Asia-Pacific?", in *Policy Analyses in International Economics*. Washington, DC: Peterson Institute for International Economics.

Snape, R., J. Adams and D. Morgan (1993), *Regional Trading Arrangements: Implications and Options for Australia*. Canberra: Australian Government Publishing Service.

Solano, O. and A. Sennekamp (2006), "Competition Provisions in Regional Trade Agreements", OECD Trade Policy Working Paper No. 31, Organisation for Economic Co-operation and Development, Paris.

Stokes, B. (2007), "Beyond Labor Rights", *National Journal*, 26 May.

Summers, L. H. (1991), "Regionalism and the World Trading System", in *Policy Implications of Trade and Currency Zones*, proceedings of a symposium sponsored by the Federal Reserve Bank of Kansas City, Jackson Hole, Wyoming, 22–24 August.

Tebar Less, C. and J. Kim (2006), *Regional Trade Agreements and Environment*, COM/ENV/TD(2005)24 FINAL. Paris: Organisation for Economic Co-operation and Development.

Tinbergen, J. (1956), *Economic Policy: Principles and Design*. Amsterdam: North-Holland.

Trachtman, J. P. (2003), "Toward Open Regionalism? Standardization and Regional Integration under Article XXIV of GATT", *Journal of International Economic Law*, 6(2): 459–492.

Tsai, C. (2006), "Rule-making in Agricultural Trade", in S. Woolcock (ed.), *Trade and Investment Rule-making: The Role of Regional and Bilateral Agreements*. Tokyo: United Nations University Press.

Urata, S. (2007), "Japan's New Foreign Economic Policy: A More Strategic and Activist Model?", East Asian Bureau of Economic Research, *Newsletter*, June, Canberra.

USITC [United States International Trade Commission] (2003), "US–Chile Free Trade Agreement: Potential Economy-wide and Selected Sectoral Effects, Investigation No. TA-2104-5", June, Washington, DC.

Viner, J. (1950), *The Customs Union Issue*. New York: Carnegie Endowment for International Peace.

Vivas-Eugui, D. and C. Spennemann (2006), paper presented at UNCTAD/ICTSD Project on Intellectual Property and Sustainable Development, Costa Rica, 10–12 May.

Waldrich, A. (2003), "The New Regionalism and Foreign Direct Investment: The Case of Mexico", *Journal of International Trade and Development*, 12: 151–184.

Winters, L. A. (1994), "The EC and World Protectionism: Dimensions of the Political Economy", Discussion Paper No. 897, Centre for Economic Policy Research, London.

——— (1995), *Foundations of an Open Economy: Trade Laws and Institutions for Eastern Europe*. London: Centre for Economic Policy Research.

——— (1996), "Multilateralism or Regionalism?", Policy Research Working Paper 1687, World Bank, Washington, DC.

Wonnacott, R. J. (1996), "Trade and Investment in a 'Hub-and-Spoke' System", *The World Economy*, 19(3).

Woolcock, S. (2003), "Conclusions", in G. Sampson and S. Woolcock (eds), *Regionalism, Multilateralism and Economic Integration: The Recent Experience*. Tokyo: United Nations University Press.

——— ed. (2006), *Trade and Investment Rule-making: The Role of Regional and Bilateral Agreements*. Tokyo: United Nations University Press.

——— (2008a), "Public Procurement and the Economic Partnership Agreements: Assessing the Potential Impact on ACP Procurement Policies", Commonwealth Secretariat and London School of Economics, London, May.

——— (2008b), "The Potential Impact of the Lisbon Treaty on European Union External Trade Policy", *Policy Analysis*, Issue 8, Swedish Institute of European Policy, Stockholm, June.

World Bank (2003), *Lessons from NAFTA for Latin America and the Caribbean Countries: A Summary of Research Findings*. Washington, DC: World Bank.

—— (2005a), *The World Development Report*. Washington, DC: World Bank.

—— (2005b), *Global Economic Prospects: Trade, Regionalism and Development*. Washington, DC: World Bank.

WTO (2002a), *Coverage, Liberalization Process and Transitional Provisions in Regional Trade Agreements*. Background Survey by the Secretariat, WT/REG/W/46, 5 April. Geneva: World Trade Organization.

—— (2002b), *Overview of the State of Play of WTO Disputes*. Geneva: World Trade Organization.

—— (2006), "Transparency Mechanism for Regional Trade Agreements: Decision of 14 December 2006", WT/L/671, 18 December. Geneva: World Trade Organization.

Zoellick, R. (2001a), Statement of Robert B. Zoellick US Trade Representative-designate before the Committee on Finance of the US Senate, 30 January.

—— (2001b), "The United States, Europe, and the World Trading System", speech to the Kangaroo Group, Strasbourg, France, 15 May.

Index

environment, enhanced environmental performance, 134

environment, general requirements, 132–33

environment, public participation, 134

fear of being left out, 146

foreign policy impact, 238

foreign policy objectives, complement to, 151–53

"gold standard" PTAs, 6, 13, 21, 33, 64, 102, 153, 156–58, 200, 232, 239–41

government procurement, 155

HS 8 tariff lines for imports, 22t2.1

Indonesia PTA, 152

integration, opportunities for deeper, 147–48

intellectual property rights, 126–28, 156

investment, 109–11, 110t4.3, 156

IPRs, border measures, 128

IPRs, civil proceedings, 127–28

IPRs, copyrights, 126

IPRs, criminal proceedings, 128

IPRs, data exclusivity, 127

IPRs, geographical indicators, 127

IPRs, patents, 127

IPRs, related rights, 126

IPRs, trademarks, 127

Israel PTA, 21, 22t2.1, 109, 269–70

Japan PTA, 252

Jordan PTA, 38t2.7, 39, 94, 109, 111, 135, 151, 158, 200, 269–70

labour standards, 137–38, 238

Malaysia PTA, 12Box 1.1, 163, 269, 272

market access, 238

market access and PTAs, 153–56

Mexico PTA, 22t2.1, 77, 85, 119, 154–55, 208–9, 209f11.2

Morocco PTA, 22t2.1, 23, 38t2.7, 39, 44, 49, 51, 54, 59, 64, 65t3.2, 77, 82, 84–85, 109, 111, 119, 126, 132–34, 145, 154–55, 237, 269–70

multilateral trading system, stimulus to, 150–51

multilateral trading systems, dissatisfaction with, 146–47

NAFTA and services, 93–94

New Zealand PTA, 59

Oman PTA, 49, 77, 82, 84–85, 109, 126, 132, 145, 151, 153, 209, 237, 269, 271

Panama PTA, 149, 269, 271

Peru PTA, 49, 51, 77, 82, 84–85, 126, 132, 134, 147, 149, 151, 163, 269, 271

policies of, 237–41

preferential bilateralism, 250

PTAs, motivations for pursuing, 145–46

PTAs, summary, 269–72

public health, 238

public procurement, 77–82

rules of origin, 154

safeguards, 154

sanitary and phytosanitary measures, 63–64, 65t3.2, 155

services, 155

services, conclusions, 102–3, 105

services, sectoral focus, 94–95

services, world trade in, 92t4.1

Singapore PTA, 12Box 1.1, 22t2.1, 32t2.5, 42, 49, 59, 62–63, 77, 95, 104, 110t4.3, 111, 117–18, 126, 128, 132, 148, 156, 163, 199, 199f10.1, 201–2, 269–70, 289

South Korea (KORUS) PTA, 23, 33, 82, 105, 145–46, 152, 156, 159, 163, 166, 188, 209, 226, 237–40, 269, 271

Southern African Customs Union (SACU), 157, 239

Switzerland PTA, 223

tariff preferences, 20–24, 21f2.1, 22t2.1

tariffs, 153–54

technical barriers to trade (TBT), 54, 59–60, 155

Thailand PTA, 12Box 1.1, 163, 269, 272

Trade Adjustment bill, 160

trade and environmental rules, clarifying, 133

Trade and Investment Framework Agreement (TIFA), 272

trade-related issues, advancing, 148–50

United Arab Emirates PTA, 269, 272

Uruguay Round, 12Box1.1, 17, 30, 48, 56, 71, 76, 88, 147, 150, 245, 254, 260

US. *See* United States (US)

USITC. *See* United States International Trade Commission (USITC)

USTR. *See* United States Trade Representative (USTR)

Uzbekistan PTA, 290

value content [for rules of origin] (VC), 25t2.6, 36–37, 38t2.7, 39–44, 169, 201, 264n4